P9-CDV-940

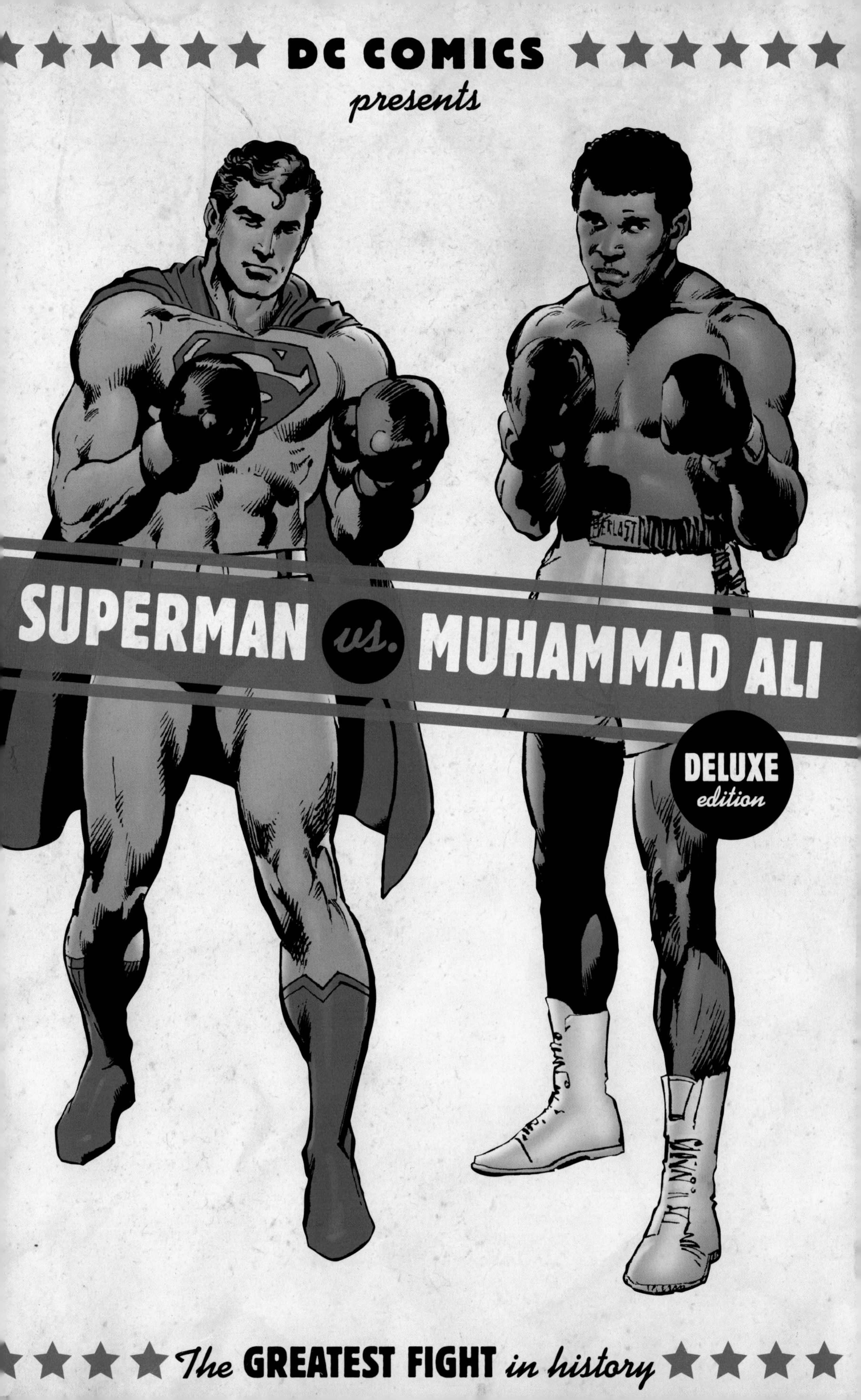
DC COMICS
presents
SUPERMAN vs. MUHAMMAD ALI
DELUXE edition
The GREATEST FIGHT in history

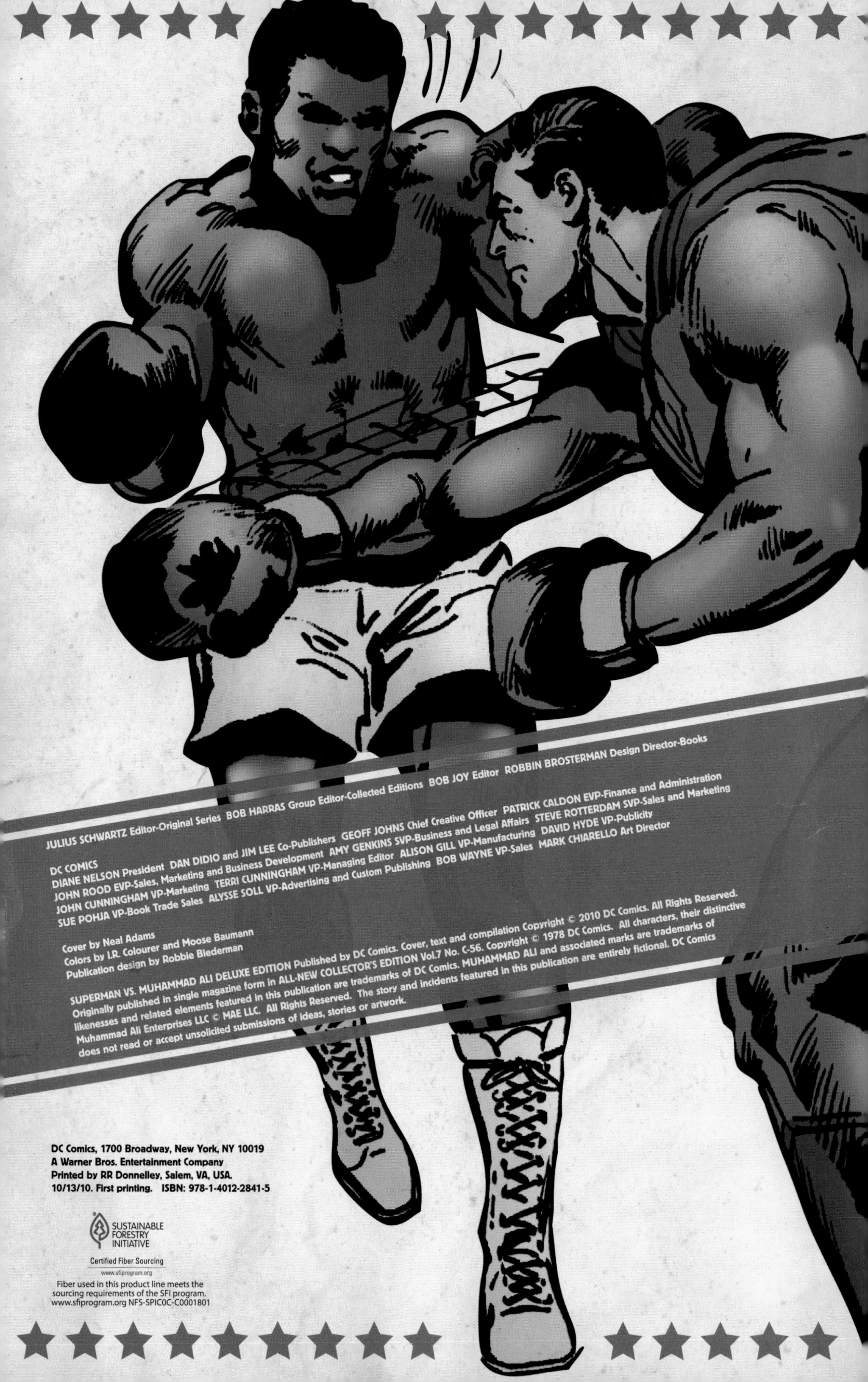

JULIUS SCHWARTZ Editor-Original Series BOB HARRAS Group Editor-Collected Editions BOB JOY Editor ROBBIN BROSTERMAN Design Director-Books

DC COMICS
DIANE NELSON President DAN DIDIO and JIM LEE Co-Publishers GEOFF JOHNS Chief Creative Officer PATRICK CALDON EVP-Finance and Administration
JOHN ROOD EVP-Sales, Marketing and Business Development AMY GENKINS SVP-Business and Legal Affairs STEVE ROTTERDAM SVP-Sales and Marketing
JOHN CUNNINGHAM VP-Marketing TERRI CUNNINGHAM VP-Managing Editor ALISON GILL VP-Manufacturing DAVID HYDE VP-Publicity
SUE POHJA VP-Book Trade Sales ALYSSE SOLL VP-Advertising and Custom Publishing BOB WAYNE VP-Sales MARK CHIARELLO Art Director

Cover by Neal Adams
Colors by I.R. Colourer and Moose Baumann
Publication design by Robbie Biederman

SUPERMAN VS. MUHAMMAD ALI DELUXE EDITION Published by DC Comics. Cover, text and compilation Copyright © 2010 DC Comics. All Rights Reserved.
Originally published in single magazine form in ALL-NEW COLLECTOR'S EDITION Vol.7 No. C-56. Copyright © 1978 DC Comics. All characters, their distinctive
likenesses and related elements featured in this publication are trademarks of DC Comics. MUHAMMAD ALI and associated marks are trademarks of
Muhammad Ali Enterprises LLC © MAE LLC. All Rights Reserved. The story and incidents featured in this publication are entirely fictional. DC Comics
does not read or accept unsolicited submissions of ideas, stories or artwork.

DC Comics, 1700 Broadway, New York, NY 10019
A Warner Bros. Entertainment Company
Printed by RR Donnelley, Salem, VA, USA.
10/13/10. First printing. ISBN: 978-1-4012-2841-5

SUSTAINABLE
FORESTRY
INITIATIVE

Certified Fiber Sourcing
www.sfiprogram.org

Fiber used in this product line meets the
sourcing requirements of the SFI program.
www.sfiprogram.org NFS-SPIC0C-C0001801

SUPERMAN
vs.
MUHAMMAD ALI

DELUXE *edition*

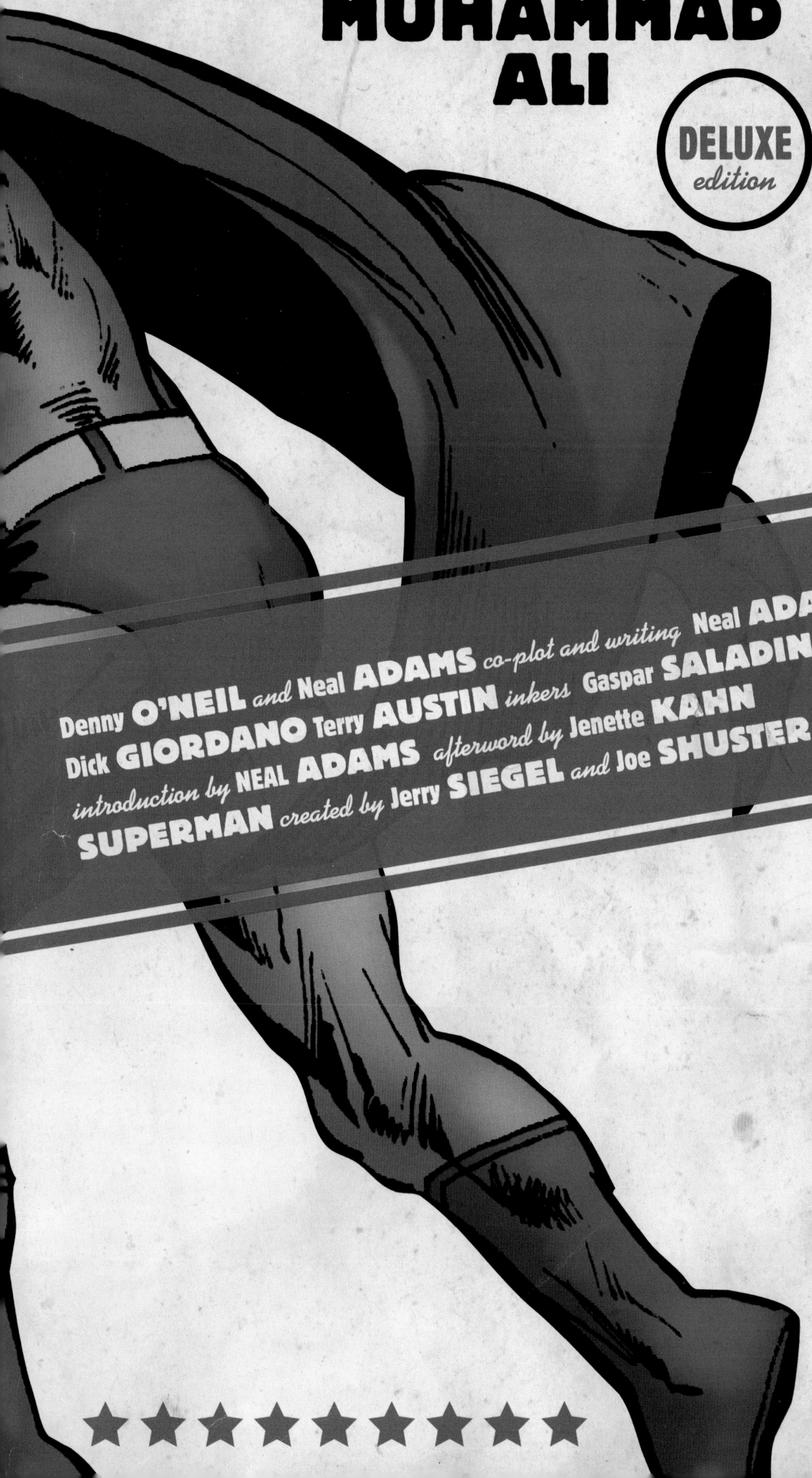

Denny **O'NEIL** *and* Neal **ADAMS** *co-plot and writing* Neal **ADAMS** *art*
Dick **GIORDANO** Terry **AUSTIN** *inkers* Gaspar **SALADINO** *letterer*
introduction by NEAL **ADAMS** *afterword by* Jenette **KAHN**
SUPERMAN *created by* Jerry **SIEGEL** *and* Joe **SHUSTER**

introduction

I defy anyone to have predicted this project: that we would match up Superman and Muhammad Ali in a boxing match in outer space. In fact, when I heard about it, I couldn't believe it. I am told it was the brainchild of Julius Schwartz, assisted by none other than Jenette Kahn, the publisher at that time. In fact, in order to do the comic book, because of the politics in those days, Denny O'Neil, the original writer, and myself, had to be approved by the Honorable Elijah Muhammad. Well, of course, we must've been approved, and the project proceeded apace, even though Denny had to pull out early on. My early doubts disappeared. I know as the creator of this book, I shouldn't be saying this, so I'll modify it… just a little: I think this is one of the best graphic novels/comic books ever done. And I truly believe I helped Muhammad Ali make his statement for the world by doing this book. I certainly got a chance to make my statement. The world has changed since we first did this book, and it's changed for the better. I have never stopped being a fan of Ali, and of course, I never stopped being a fan of Superman. So if there's somebody out there who thinks he can wipe this grin off my face as this book is being reprinted, it ain't gonna happen.

I hope that Ali and his family are happy with the work that we've done here. I know that my recently deceased partner, Dick Giordano, was happy to be working on this project, and those backgrounds there are the first major work of Terry Austin, who blushed every time he showed me his work on these pages. Comic books are a great business to be in, and I would like to think that as an industry, we might take a great deal of pride in this comic book. I certainly take that pride. Please enjoy the following pages.

Neal ADAMS

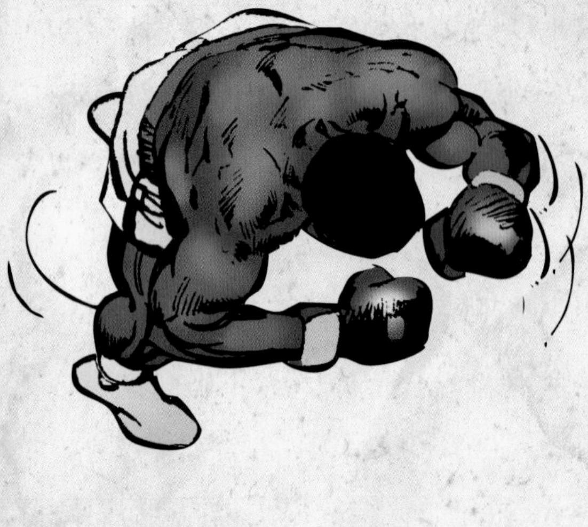

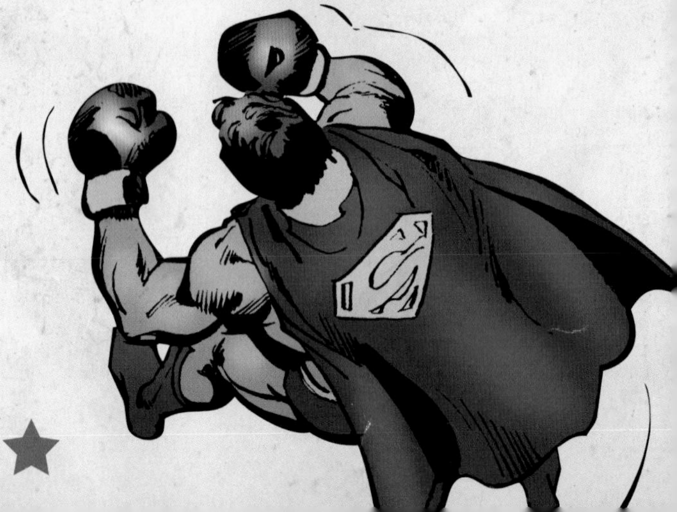

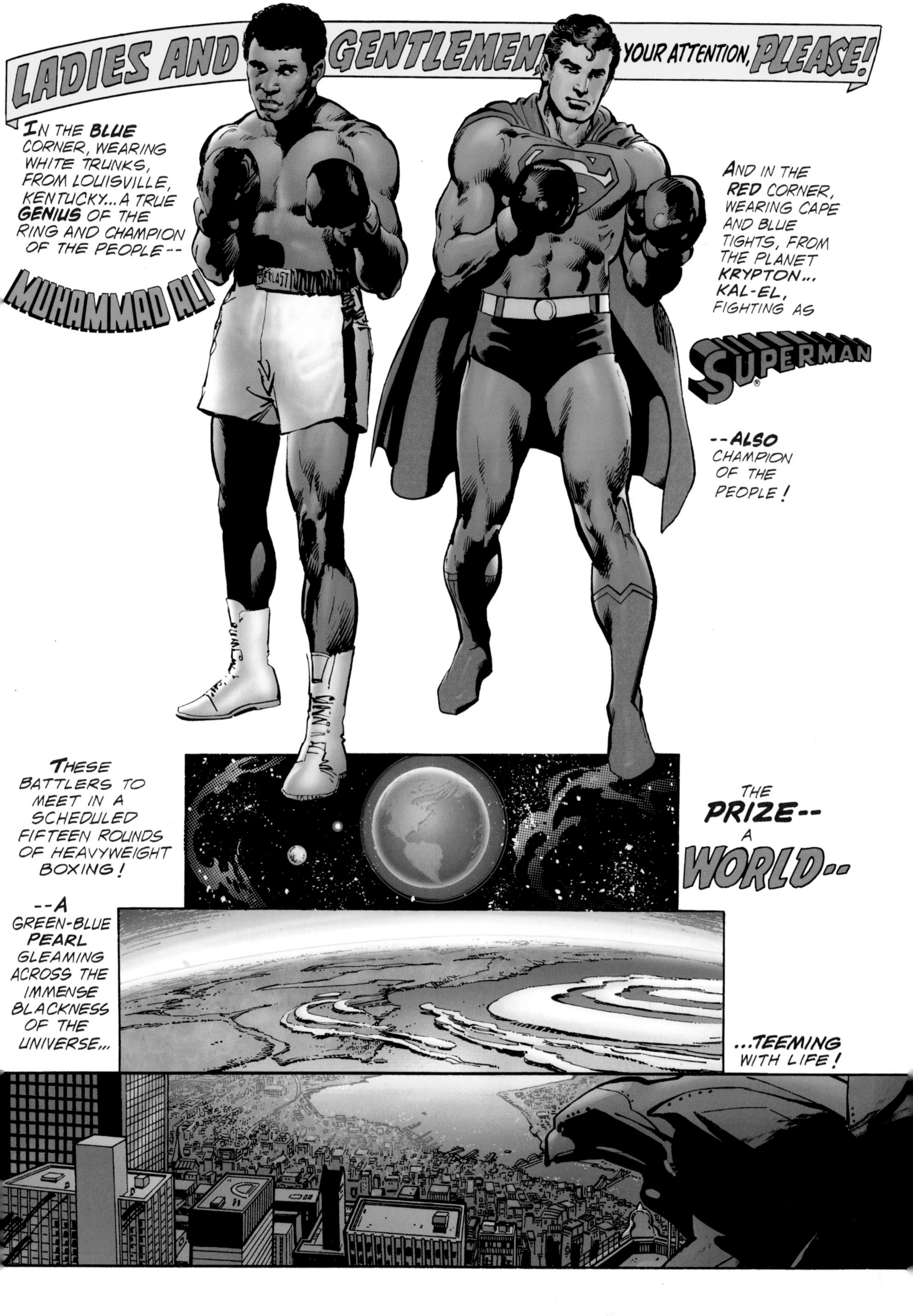
LADIES AND GENTLEMEN, YOUR ATTENTION, PLEASE!
IN THE BLUE CORNER, WEARING WHITE TRUNKS, FROM LOUISVILLE, KENTUCKY... A TRUE GENIUS OF THE RING AND CHAMPION OF THE PEOPLE--
MUHAMMAD ALI
AND IN THE RED CORNER, WEARING CAPE AND BLUE TIGHTS, FROM THE PLANET KRYPTON... KAL-EL, FIGHTING AS
SUPERMAN
--ALSO CHAMPION OF THE PEOPLE!
THESE BATTLERS TO MEET IN A SCHEDULED FIFTEEN ROUNDS OF HEAVYWEIGHT BOXING!
THE PRIZE-- A WORLD--
--A GREEN-BLUE PEARL GLEAMING ACROSS THE IMMENSE BLACKNESS OF THE UNIVERSE...
...TEEMING WITH LIFE!

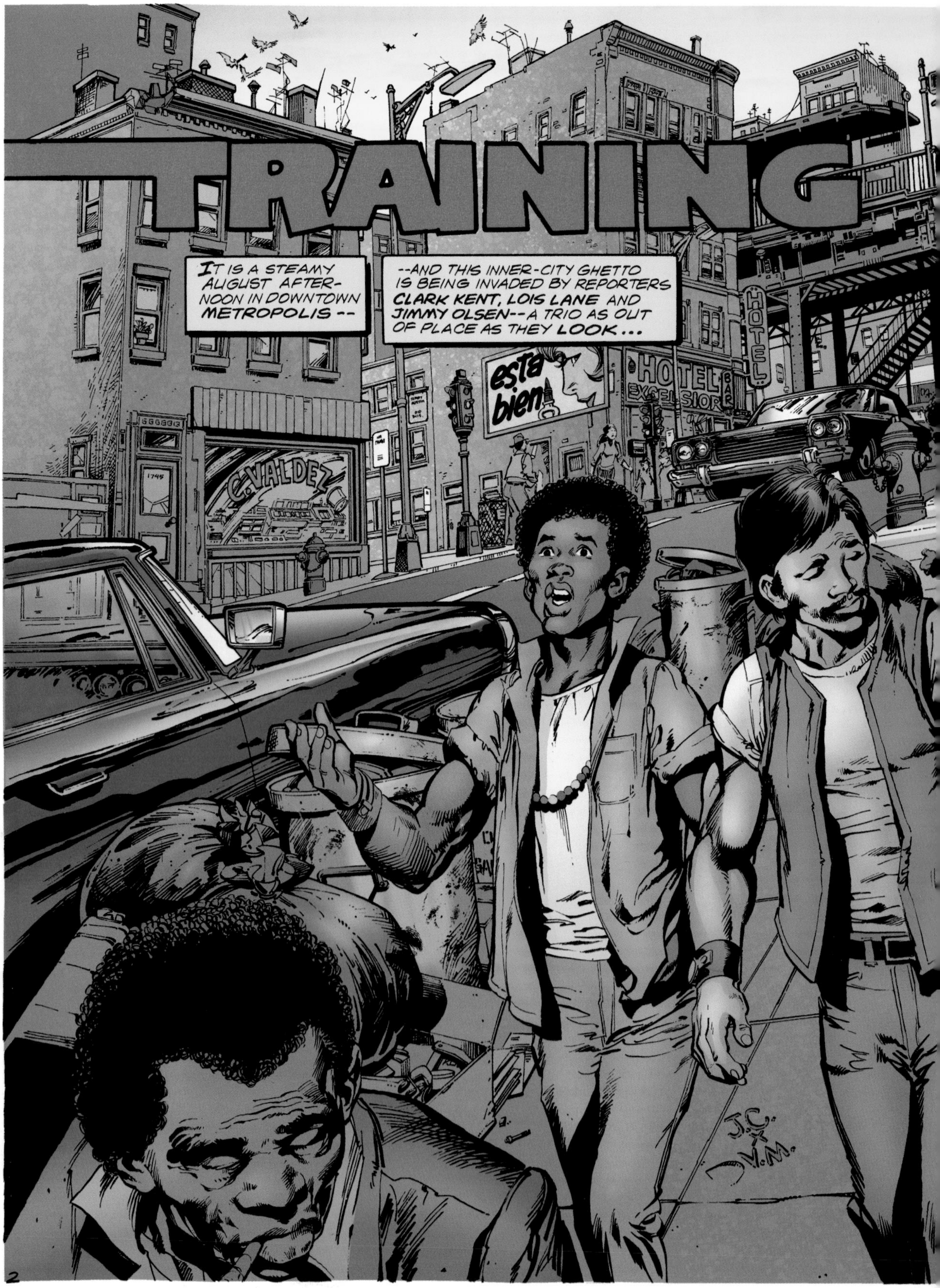
TRAINING
IT IS A STEAMY AUGUST AFTERNOON IN DOWNTOWN METROPOLIS --
--AND THIS INNER-CITY GHETTO IS BEING INVADED BY REPORTERS CLARK KENT, LOIS LANE AND JIMMY OLSEN--A TRIO AS OUT OF PLACE AS THEY LOOK...
C. VALDEZ
esta bien
HOTEL EXCELSIOR
BAR
HOTEL
J.C. X J.M.M.

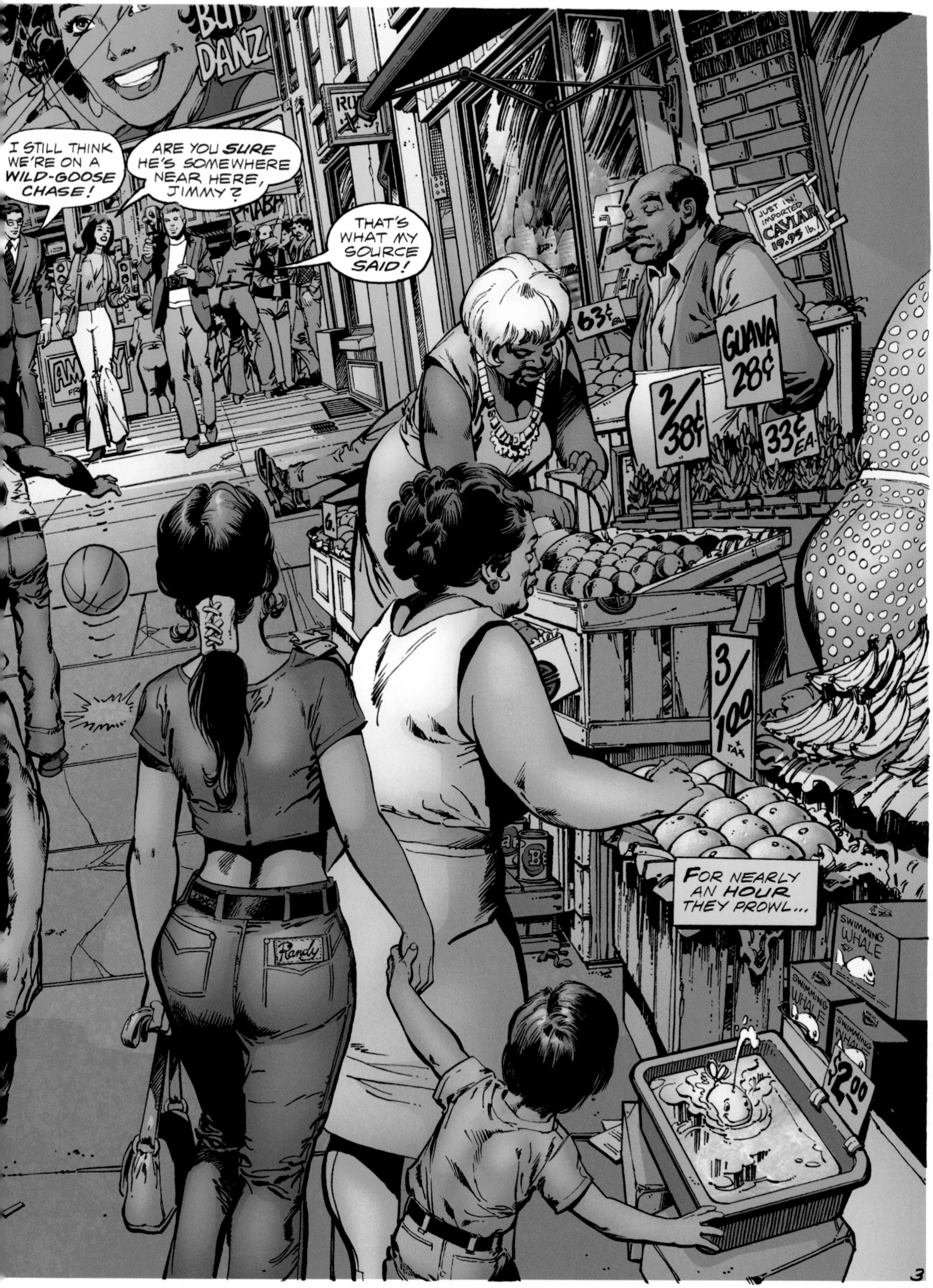
I STILL THINK WE'RE ON A WILD-GOOSE CHASE!
ARE YOU SURE HE'S SOMEWHERE NEAR HERE, JIMMY?
THAT'S WHAT MY SOURCE SAID!
JUST IN! IMPORTED CAVIAR 19.95 lb.
63¢ EA.
GUAVA 28¢
2/38¢
33¢ EA.
3/1.00 +TAX
FOR NEARLY AN HOUR THEY PROWL...
SWIMMING WHALE
$2.00
Randy

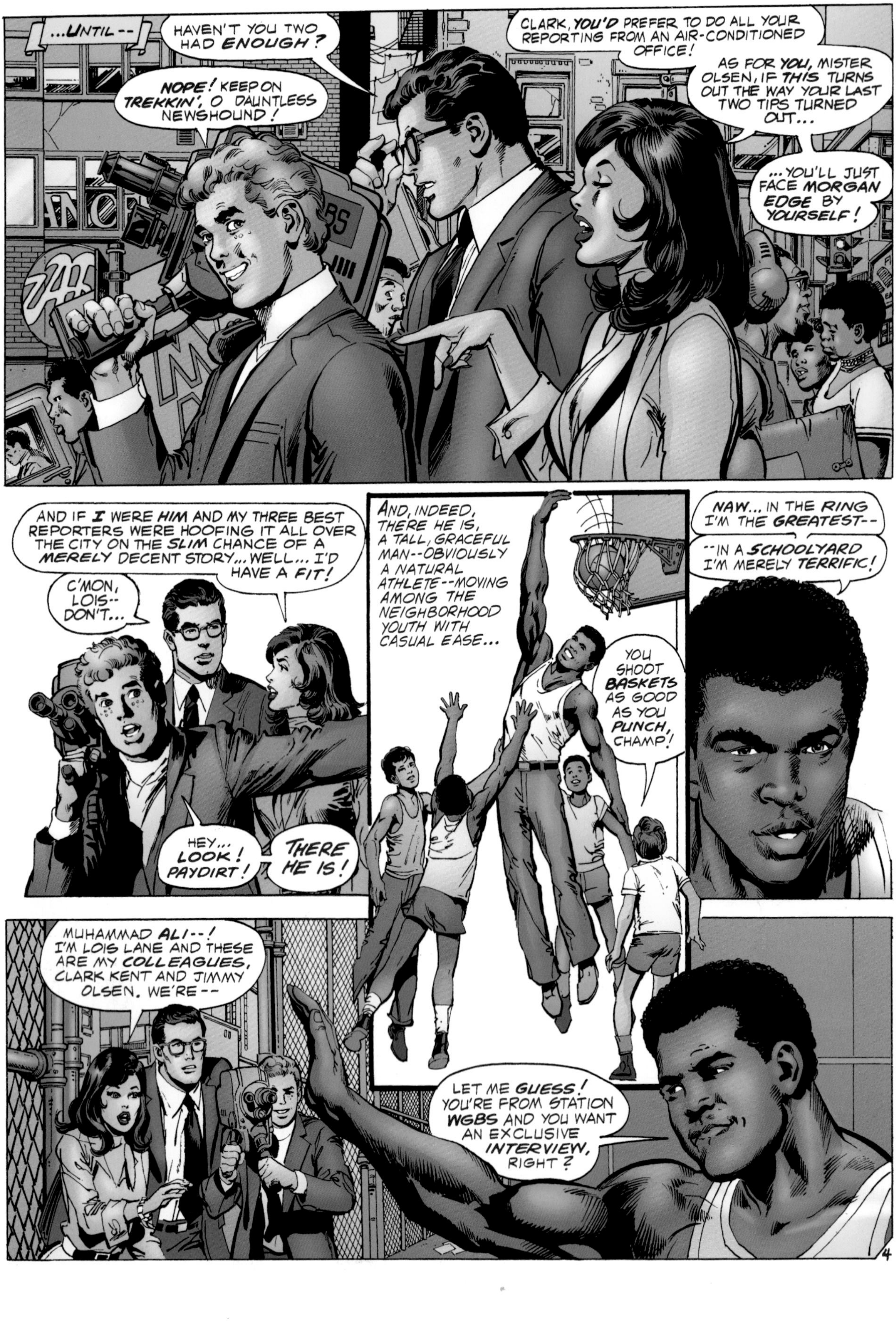
...UNTIL--
HAVEN'T YOU TWO HAD ENOUGH?
NOPE! KEEP ON TREKKIN', O DAUNTLESS NEWSHOUND!
CLARK, YOU'D PREFER TO DO ALL YOUR REPORTING FROM AN AIR-CONDITIONED OFFICE!
AS FOR YOU, MISTER OLSEN, IF THIS TURNS OUT THE WAY YOUR LAST TWO TIPS TURNED OUT...
...YOU'LL JUST FACE MORGAN EDGE BY YOURSELF!
AND IF I WERE HIM AND MY THREE BEST REPORTERS WERE HOOFING IT ALL OVER THE CITY ON THE SLIM CHANCE OF A MERELY DECENT STORY...WELL... I'D HAVE A FIT!
C'MON, LOIS-- DON'T...
HEY... LOOK! PAYDIRT!
THERE HE IS!
AND, INDEED, THERE HE IS, A TALL, GRACEFUL MAN--OBVIOUSLY A NATURAL ATHLETE--MOVING AMONG THE NEIGHBORHOOD YOUTH WITH CASUAL EASE...
YOU SHOOT BASKETS AS GOOD AS YOU PUNCH, CHAMP!
NAW... IN THE RING I'M THE GREATEST--
--IN A SCHOOLYARD I'M MERELY TERRIFIC!
MUHAMMAD ALI--! I'M LOIS LANE AND THESE ARE MY COLLEAGUES, CLARK KENT AND JIMMY OLSEN. WE'RE--
LET ME GUESS! YOU'RE FROM STATION WGBS AND YOU WANT AN EXCLUSIVE INTERVIEW, RIGHT?
4

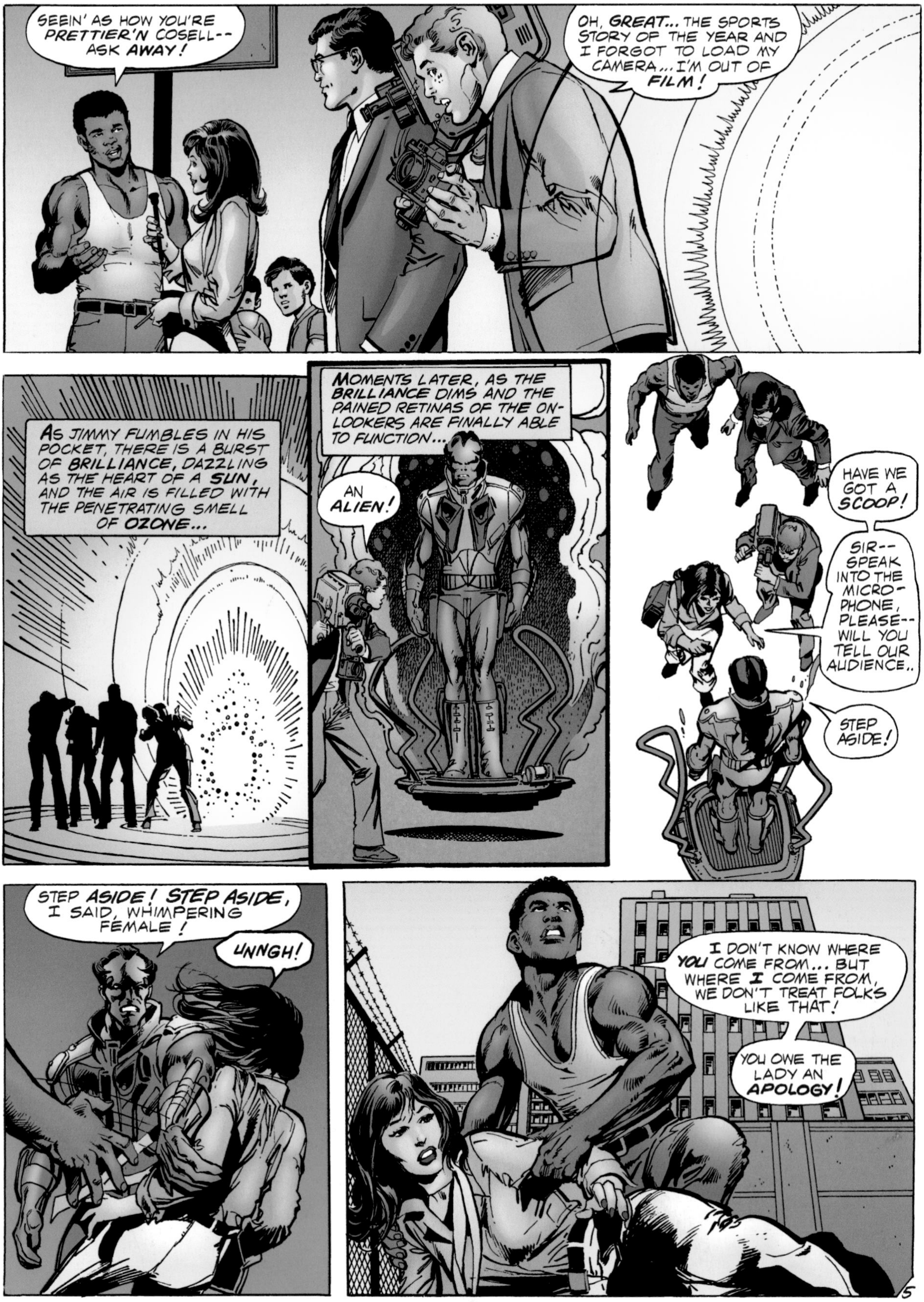

SEEIN' AS HOW YOU'RE PRETTIER'N COSELL-- ASK AWAY!
OH, GREAT... THE SPORTS STORY OF THE YEAR AND I FORGOT TO LOAD MY CAMERA... I'M OUT OF FILM!
AS JIMMY FUMBLES IN HIS POCKET, THERE IS A BURST OF BRILLIANCE, DAZZLING AS THE HEART OF A SUN, AND THE AIR IS FILLED WITH THE PENETRATING SMELL OF OZONE...
MOMENTS LATER, AS THE BRILLIANCE DIMS AND THE PAINED RETINAS OF THE ON-LOOKERS ARE FINALLY ABLE TO FUNCTION...
AN ALIEN!
HAVE WE GOT A SCOOP!
SIR-- SPEAK INTO THE MICRO-PHONE, PLEASE-- WILL YOU TELL OUR AUDIENCE..
STEP ASIDE!
STEP ASIDE! STEP ASIDE, I SAID, WHIMPERING FEMALE!
UNNGH!
I DON'T KNOW WHERE YOU COME FROM... BUT WHERE I COME FROM, WE DON'T TREAT FOLKS LIKE THAT!
YOU OWE THE LADY AN APOLOGY!

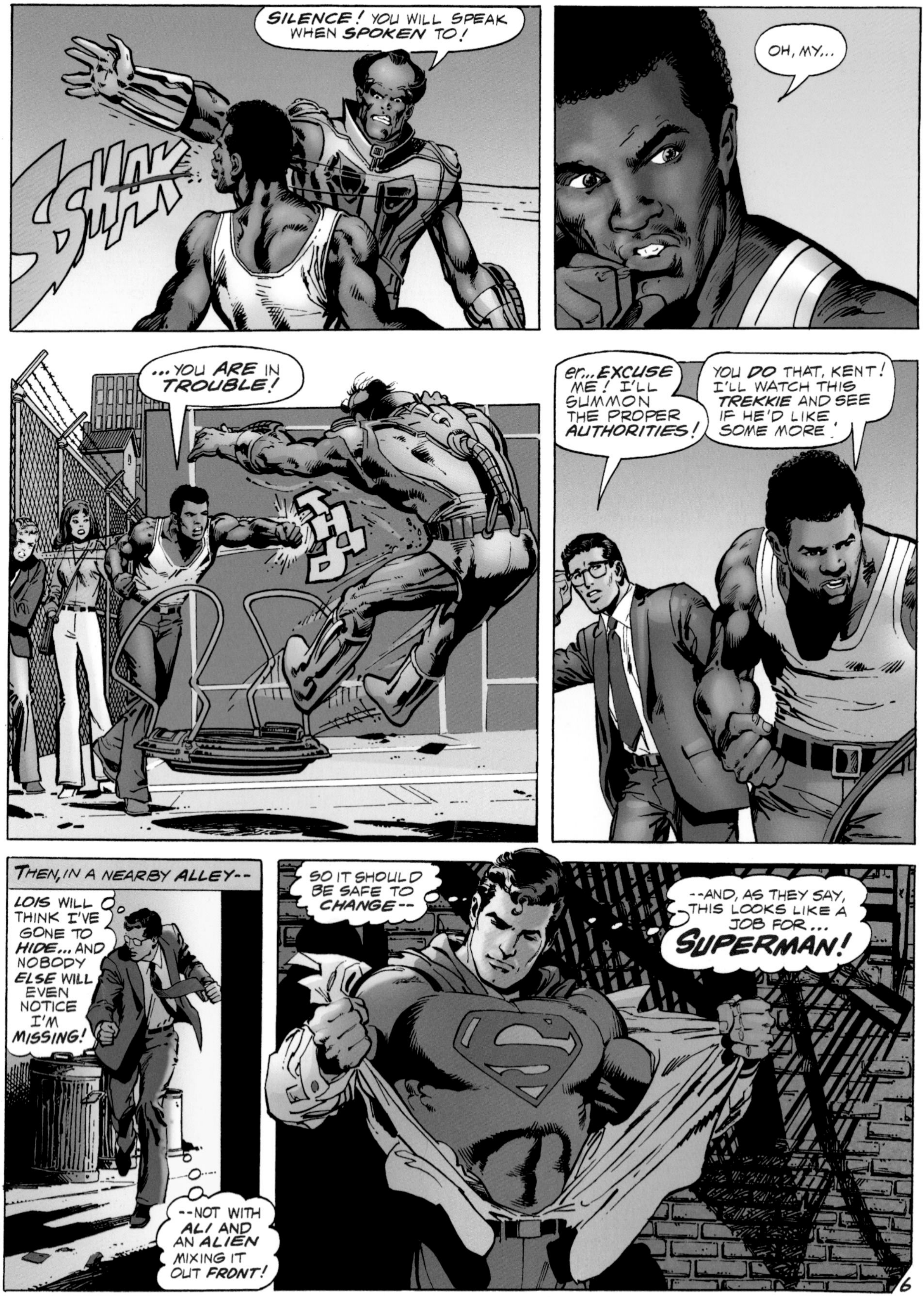
SILENCE! YOU WILL SPEAK WHEN SPOKEN TO!
S-SHAK
OH, MY...
...YOU ARE IN TROUBLE!
er...EXCUSE ME! I'LL SUMMON THE PROPER AUTHORITIES!
YOU DO THAT, KENT! I'LL WATCH THIS TREKKIE AND SEE IF HE'D LIKE SOME MORE!
THEN, IN A NEARBY ALLEY--
LOIS WILL THINK I'VE GONE TO HIDE...AND NOBODY ELSE WILL EVEN NOTICE I'M MISSING!
--NOT WITH ALI AND AN ALIEN MIXING IT OUT FRONT!
SO IT SHOULD BE SAFE TO CHANGE--
--AND, AS THEY SAY, THIS LOOKS LIKE A JOB FOR... SUPERMAN!

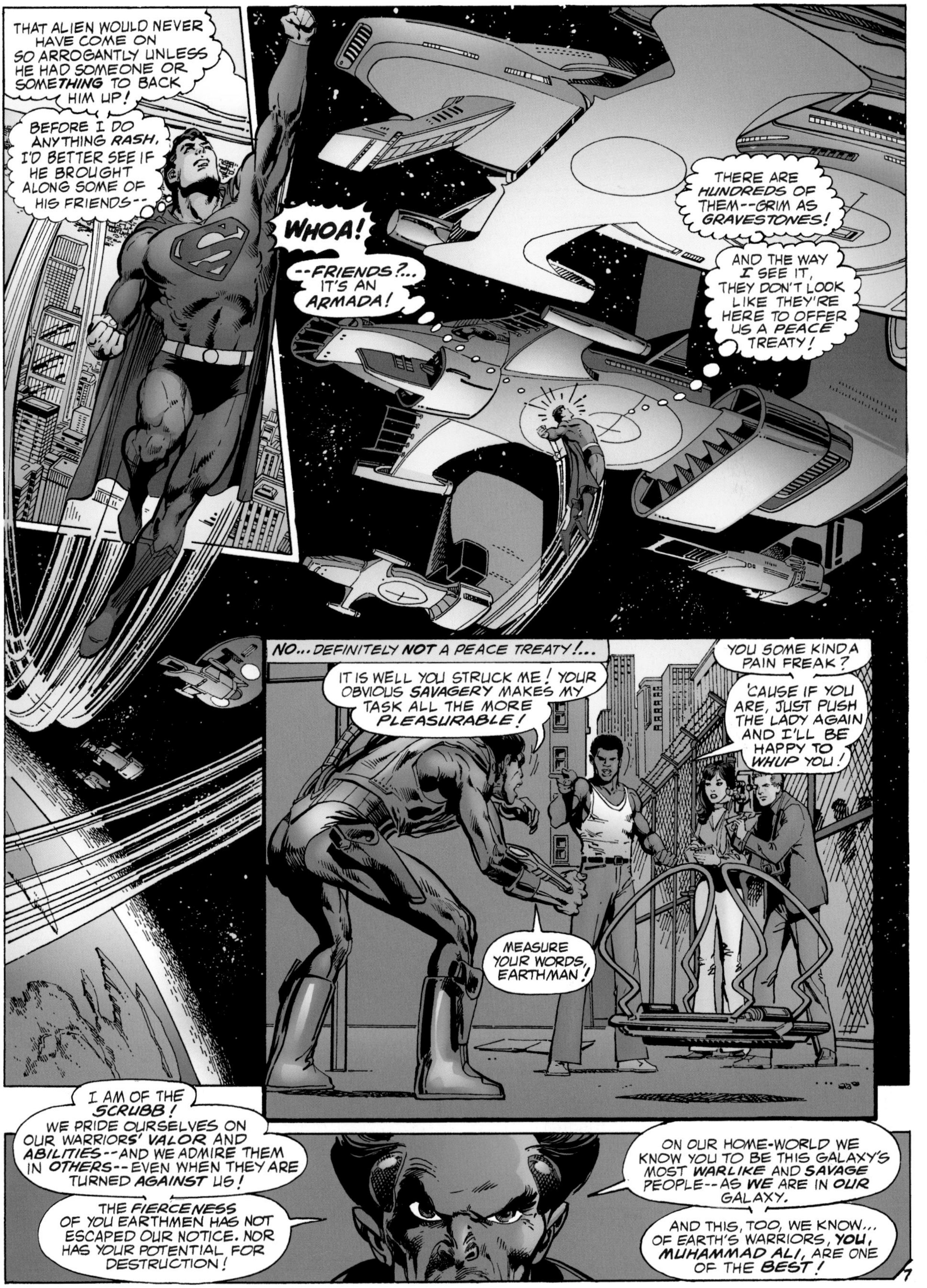

THAT ALIEN WOULD NEVER HAVE COME ON SO ARROGANTLY UNLESS HE HAD SOMEONE OR SOMETHING TO BACK HIM UP!
BEFORE I DO ANYTHING RASH, I'D BETTER SEE IF HE BROUGHT ALONG SOME OF HIS FRIENDS--
WHOA!
--FRIENDS?... IT'S AN ARMADA!
THERE ARE HUNDREDS OF THEM--GRIM AS GRAVESTONES!
AND THE WAY I SEE IT, THEY DON'T LOOK LIKE THEY'RE HERE TO OFFER US A PEACE TREATY!
NO... DEFINITELY NOT A PEACE TREATY!...
IT IS WELL YOU STRUCK ME! YOUR OBVIOUS SAVAGERY MAKES MY TASK ALL THE MORE PLEASURABLE!
YOU SOME KINDA PAIN FREAK?
'CAUSE IF YOU ARE, JUST PUSH THE LADY AGAIN AND I'LL BE HAPPY TO WHUP YOU!
MEASURE YOUR WORDS, EARTHMAN!
I AM OF THE SCRUBB! WE PRIDE OURSELVES ON OUR WARRIORS' VALOR AND ABILITIES--AND WE ADMIRE THEM IN OTHERS--EVEN WHEN THEY ARE TURNED AGAINST US!
THE FIERCENESS OF YOU EARTHMEN HAS NOT ESCAPED OUR NOTICE. NOR HAS YOUR POTENTIAL FOR DESTRUCTION!
ON OUR HOME-WORLD WE KNOW YOU TO BE THIS GALAXY'S MOST WARLIKE AND SAVAGE PEOPLE--AS WE ARE IN OUR GALAXY.
AND THIS, TOO, WE KNOW... OF EARTH'S WARRIORS, YOU, MUHAMMAD ALI, ARE ONE OF THE BEST!

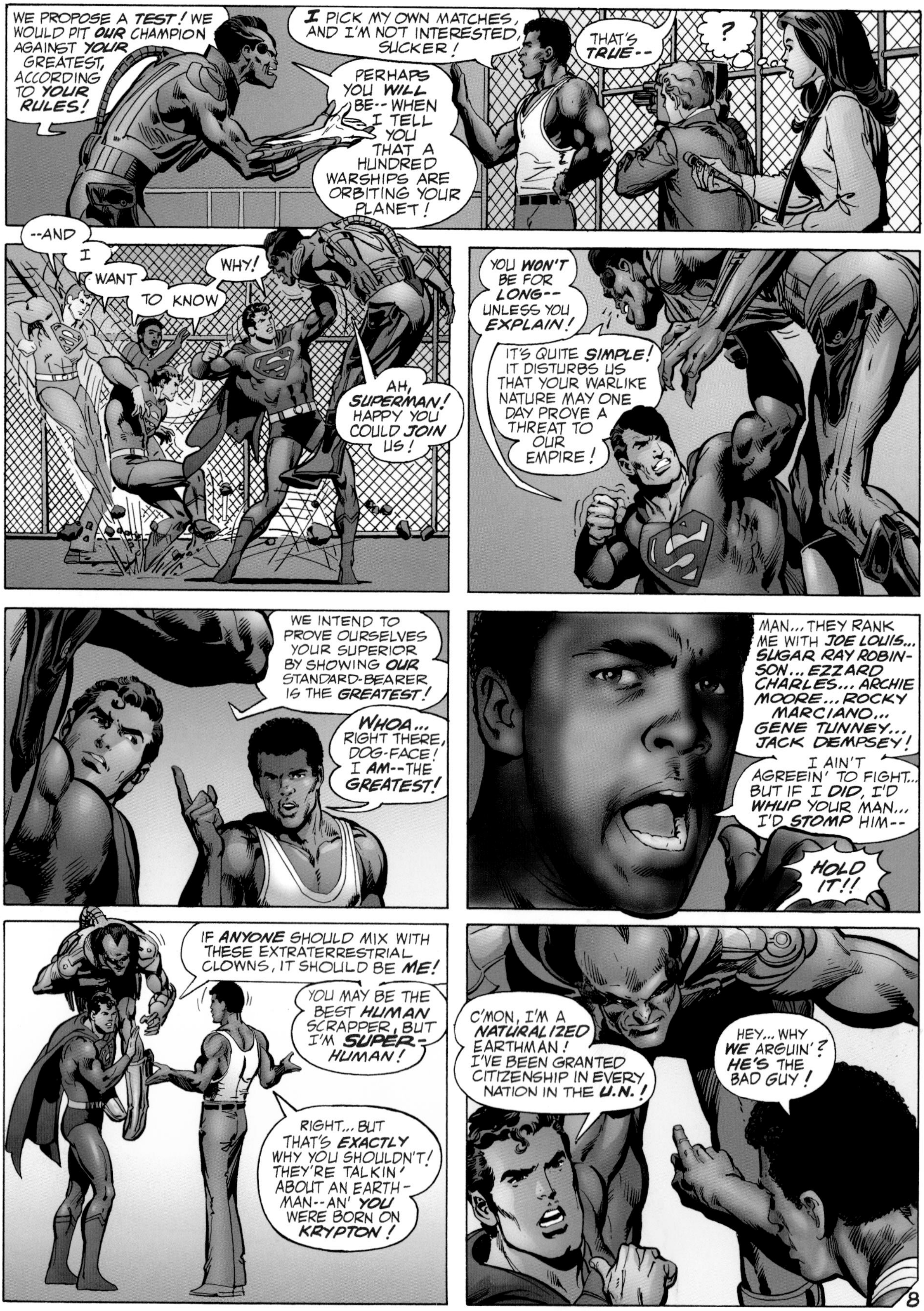
WE PROPOSE A TEST! WE WOULD PIT OUR CHAMPION AGAINST YOUR GREATEST, ACCORDING TO YOUR RULES!
I PICK MY OWN MATCHES, AND I'M NOT INTERESTED, SUCKER!
PERHAPS YOU WILL BE--WHEN I TELL YOU THAT A HUNDRED WARSHIPS ARE ORBITING YOUR PLANET!
THAT'S TRUE--
?
--AND I WANT TO KNOW WHY!
AH, SUPERMAN! HAPPY YOU COULD JOIN US!
YOU WON'T BE FOR LONG-- UNLESS YOU EXPLAIN!
IT'S QUITE SIMPLE! IT DISTURBS US THAT YOUR WARLIKE NATURE MAY ONE DAY PROVE A THREAT TO OUR EMPIRE!
WE INTEND TO PROVE OURSELVES YOUR SUPERIOR BY SHOWING OUR STANDARD-BEARER IS THE GREATEST!
WHOA... RIGHT THERE, DOG-FACE! I AM--THE GREATEST!
MAN... THEY RANK ME WITH JOE LOUIS... SUGAR RAY ROBINSON... EZZARD CHARLES... ARCHIE MOORE... ROCKY MARCIANO... GENE TUNNEY... JACK DEMPSEY!
I AIN'T AGREEIN' TO FIGHT... BUT IF I DID, I'D WHUP YOUR MAN... I'D STOMP HIM--
HOLD IT!!
IF ANYONE SHOULD MIX WITH THESE EXTRATERRESTRIAL CLOWNS, IT SHOULD BE ME!
YOU MAY BE THE BEST HUMAN SCRAPPER, BUT I'M SUPER-HUMAN!
RIGHT... BUT THAT'S EXACTLY WHY YOU SHOULDN'T! THEY'RE TALKIN' ABOUT AN EARTH-MAN--AN' YOU WERE BORN ON KRYPTON!
C'MON, I'M A NATURALIZED EARTHMAN! I'VE BEEN GRANTED CITIZENSHIP IN EVERY NATION IN THE U.N.!
HEY... WHY WE ARGUIN'? HE'S THE BAD GUY!
8

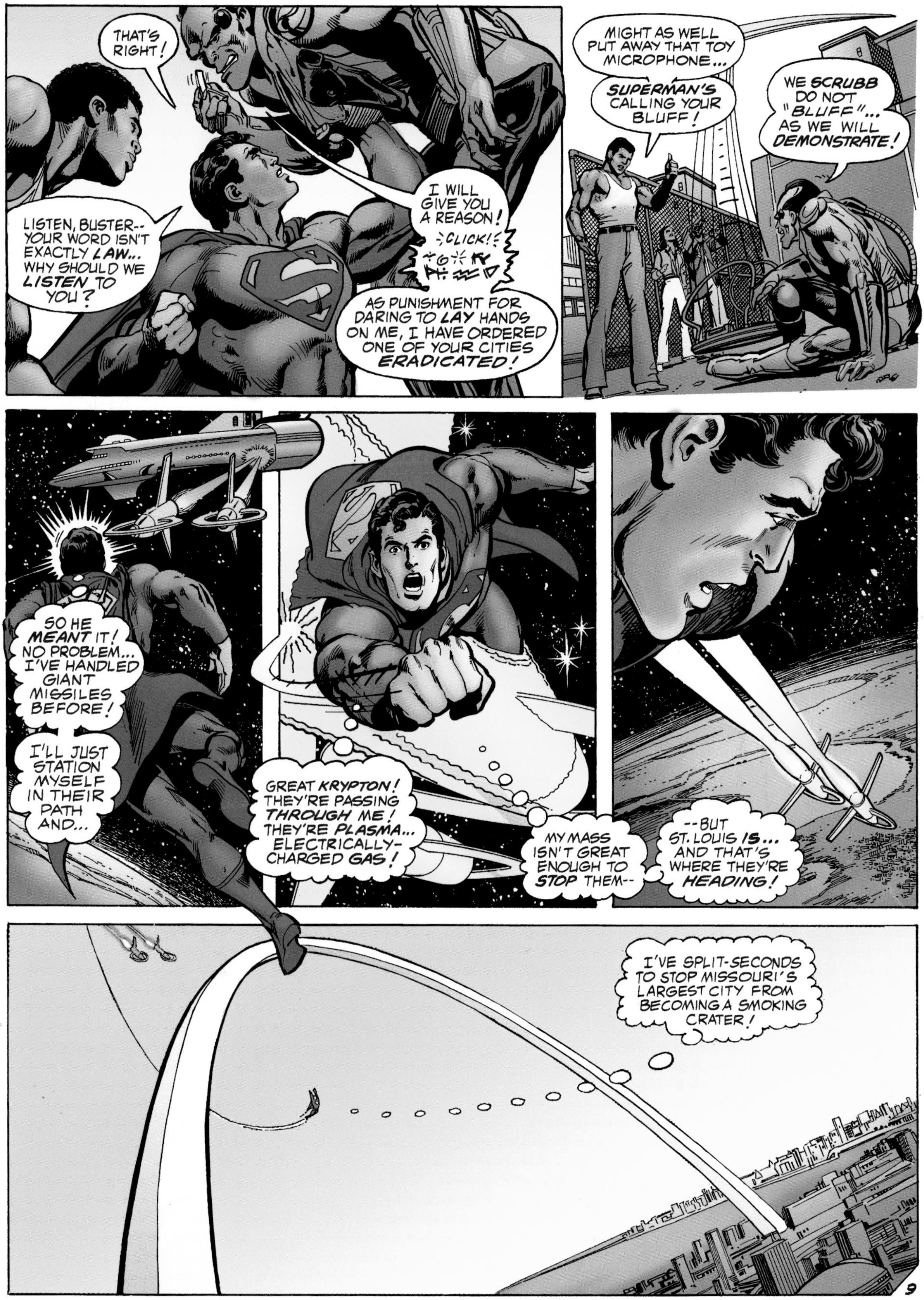

THAT'S RIGHT!
LISTEN, BUSTER-- YOUR WORD ISN'T EXACTLY LAW... WHY SHOULD WE LISTEN TO YOU?
I WILL GIVE YOU A REASON!
CLICK!
AS PUNISHMENT FOR DARING TO LAY HANDS ON ME, I HAVE ORDERED ONE OF YOUR CITIES ERADICATED!
MIGHT AS WELL PUT AWAY THAT TOY MICROPHONE...
SUPERMAN'S CALLING YOUR BLUFF!
WE SCRUBB DO NOT "BLUFF"... AS WE WILL DEMONSTRATE!
SO HE MEANT IT! NO PROBLEM... I'VE HANDLED GIANT MISSILES BEFORE!
I'LL JUST STATION MYSELF IN THEIR PATH AND...
GREAT KRYPTON! THEY'RE PASSING THROUGH ME! THEY'RE PLASMA... ELECTRICALLY-CHARGED GAS!
MY MASS ISN'T GREAT ENOUGH TO STOP THEM--
--BUT ST. LOUIS IS... AND THAT'S WHERE THEY'RE HEADING!
I'VE SPLIT-SECONDS TO STOP MISSOURI'S LARGEST CITY FROM BECOMING A SMOKING CRATER!

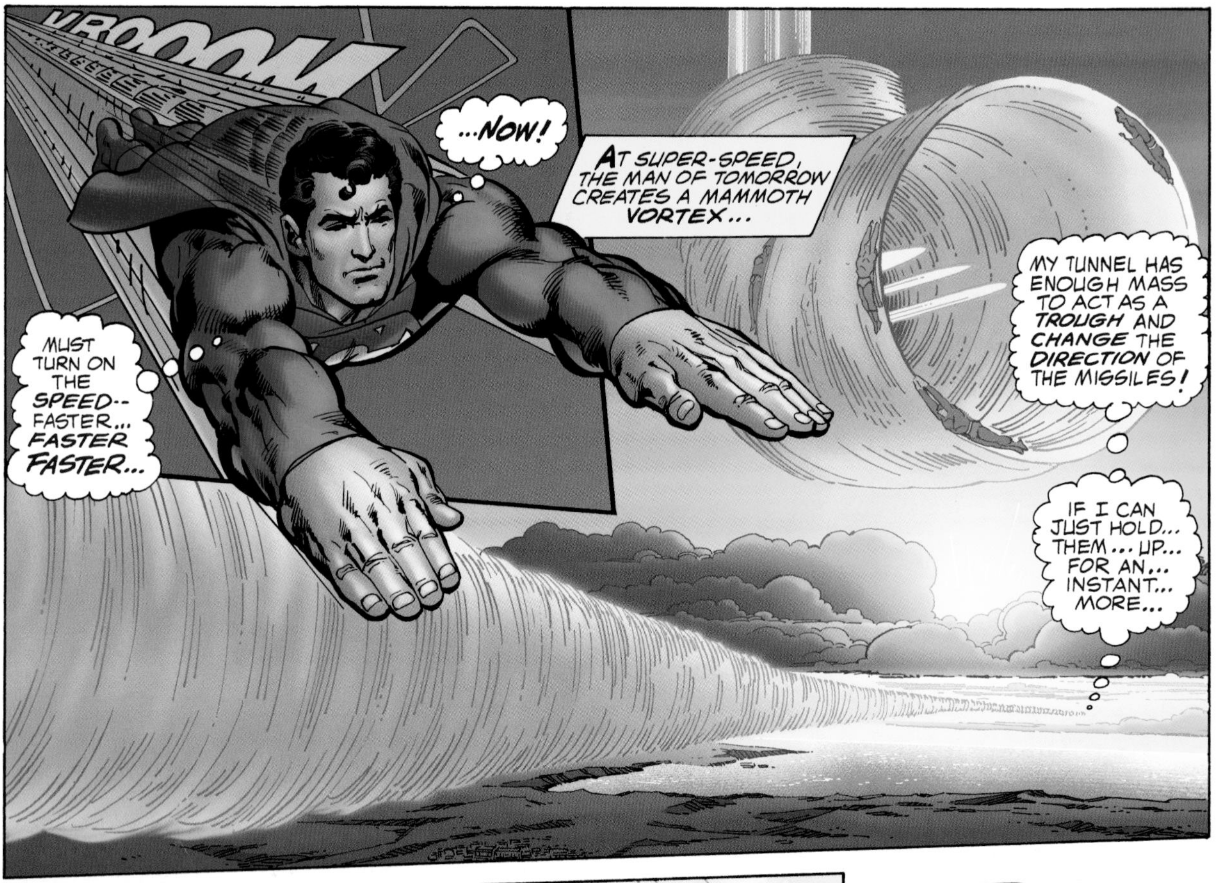
VROOOM
...NOW!
AT SUPER-SPEED, THE MAN OF TOMORROW CREATES A MAMMOTH VORTEX...
MUST TURN ON THE SPEED-- FASTER... FASTER FASTER...
MY TUNNEL HAS ENOUGH MASS TO ACT AS A TROUGH AND CHANGE THE DIRECTION OF THE MISSILES!
IF I CAN JUST HOLD... THEM... UP... FOR AN... INSTANT... MORE...

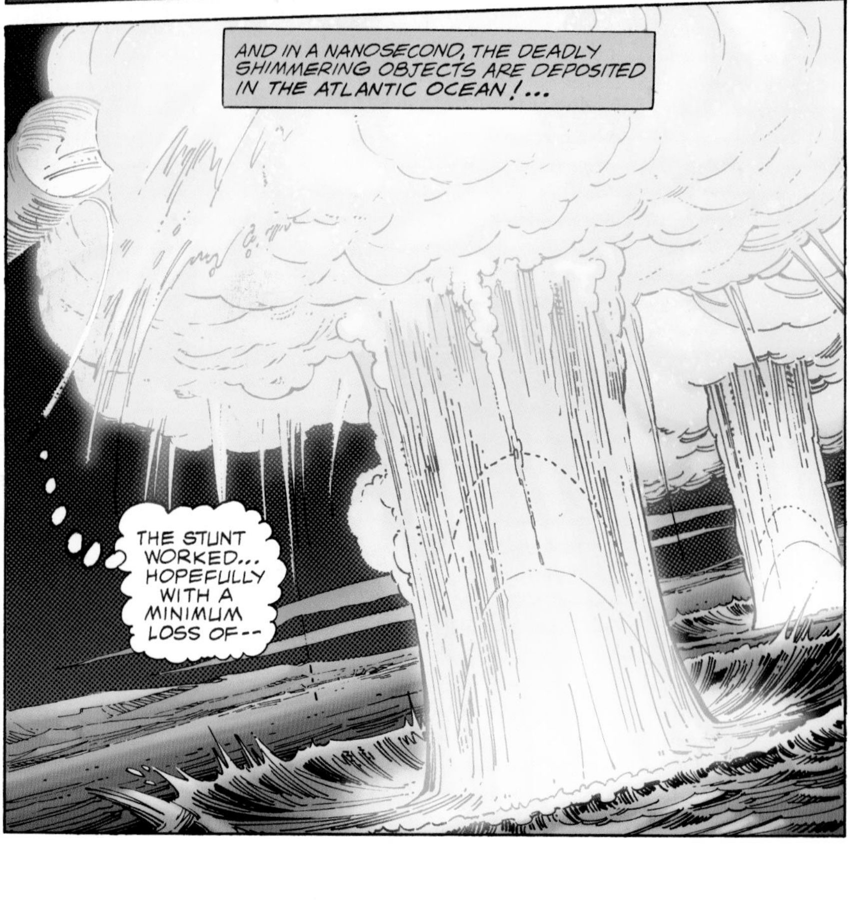
AND IN A NANOSECOND, THE DEADLY SHIMMERING OBJECTS ARE DEPOSITED IN THE ATLANTIC OCEAN!...
THE STUNT WORKED... HOPEFULLY WITH A MINIMUM LOSS OF--

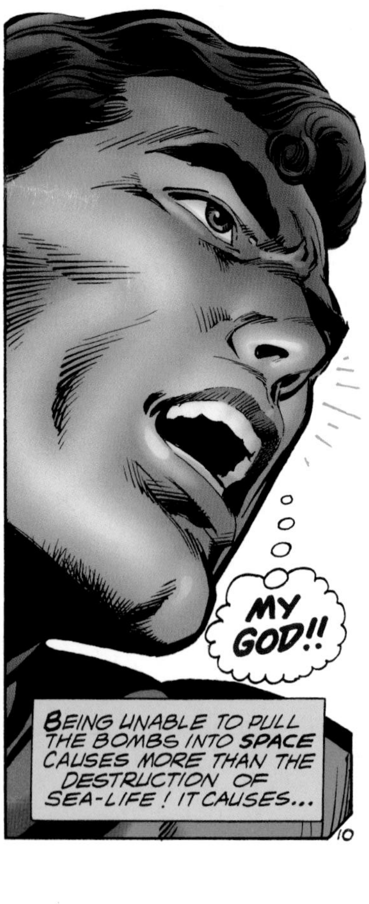
MY GOD!!
BEING UNABLE TO PULL THE BOMBS INTO SPACE CAUSES MORE THAN THE DESTRUCTION OF SEA-LIFE! IT CAUSES...

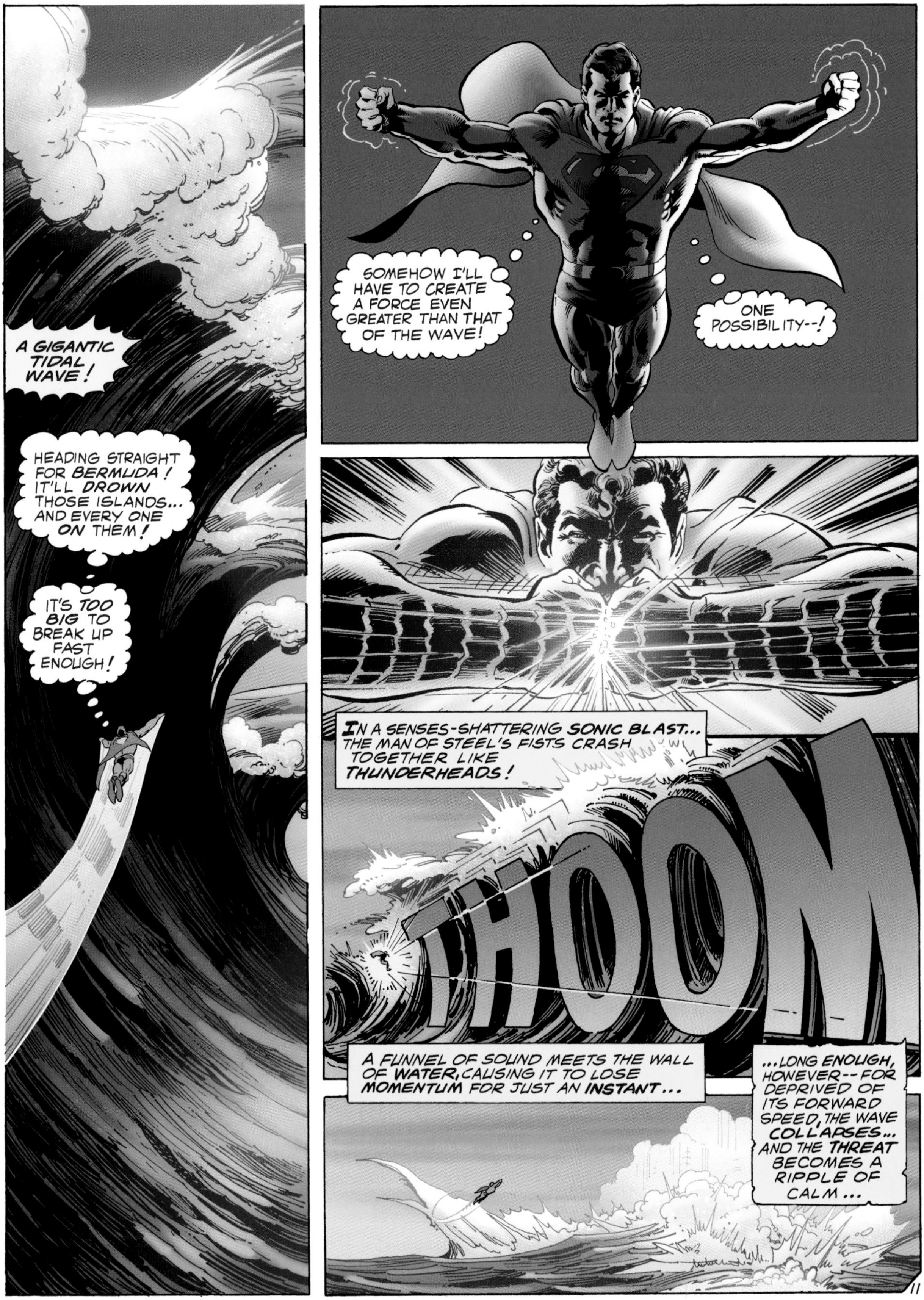

A GIGANTIC TIDAL WAVE!
HEADING STRAIGHT FOR BERMUDA! IT'LL DROWN THOSE ISLANDS... AND EVERY ONE ON THEM!
IT'S TOO BIG TO BREAK UP FAST ENOUGH!
SOMEHOW I'LL HAVE TO CREATE A FORCE EVEN GREATER THAN THAT OF THE WAVE!
ONE POSSIBILITY--!
IN A SENSES-SHATTERING SONIC BLAST... THE MAN OF STEEL'S FISTS CRASH TOGETHER LIKE THUNDERHEADS!
THOOM
A FUNNEL OF SOUND MEETS THE WALL OF WATER, CAUSING IT TO LOSE MOMENTUM FOR JUST AN INSTANT...
...LONG ENOUGH, HOWEVER--FOR DEPRIVED OF ITS FORWARD SPEED, THE WAVE COLLAPSES... AND THE THREAT BECOMES A RIPPLE OF CALM...
11

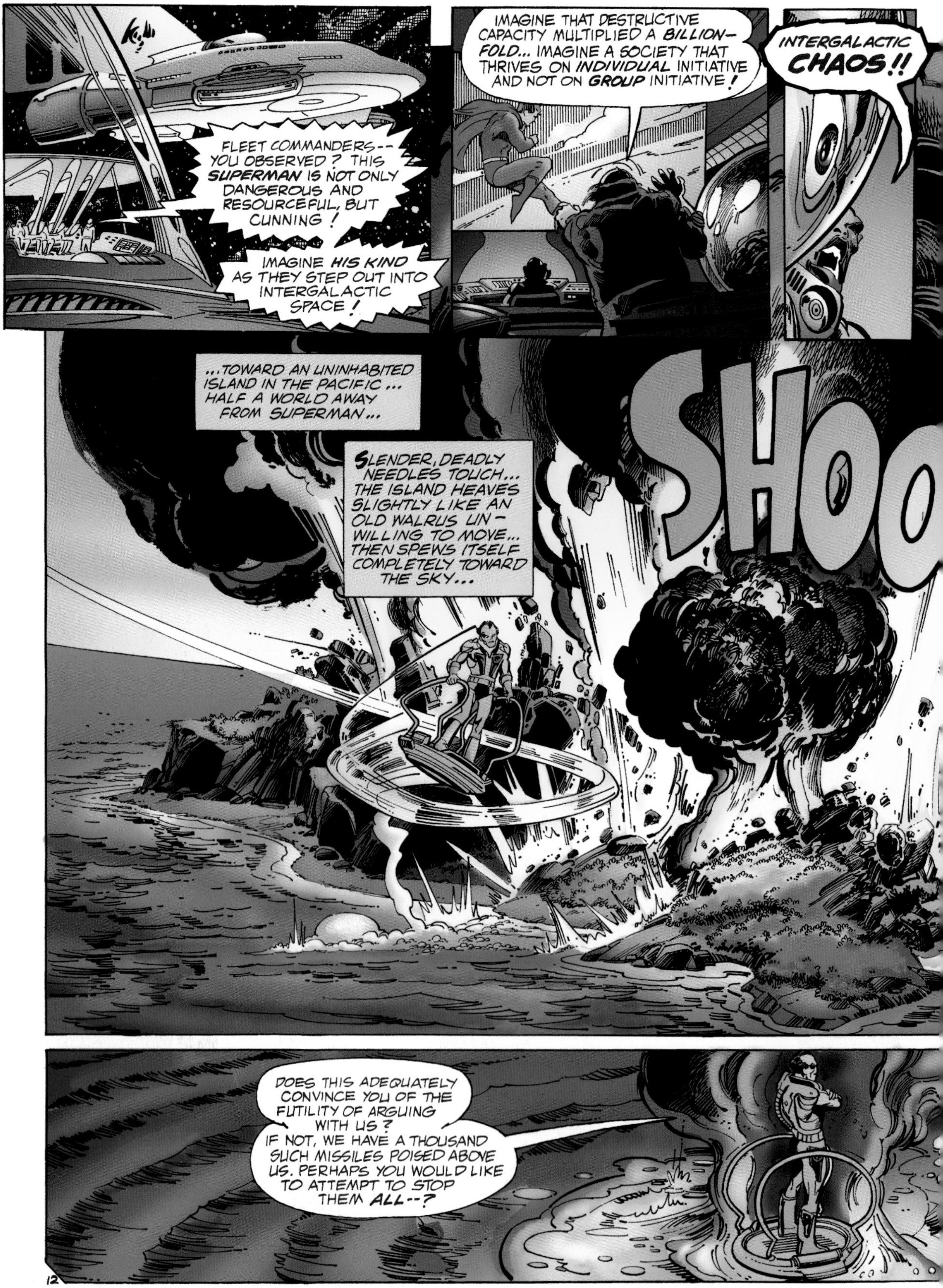
FLEET COMMANDERS-- YOU OBSERVED? THIS SUPERMAN IS NOT ONLY DANGEROUS AND RESOURCEFUL, BUT CUNNING!
IMAGINE HIS KIND AS THEY STEP OUT INTO INTERGALACTIC SPACE!
IMAGINE THAT DESTRUCTIVE CAPACITY MULTIPLIED A BILLION-FOLD... IMAGINE A SOCIETY THAT THRIVES ON INDIVIDUAL INITIATIVE AND NOT ON GROUP INITIATIVE!
INTERGALACTIC CHAOS!!
...TOWARD AN UNINHABITED ISLAND IN THE PACIFIC... HALF A WORLD AWAY FROM SUPERMAN...
SLENDER, DEADLY NEEDLES TOUCH... THE ISLAND HEAVES SLIGHTLY LIKE AN OLD WALRUS UN-WILLING TO MOVE... THEN SPEWS ITSELF COMPLETELY TOWARD THE SKY...
SHOO
DOES THIS ADEQUATELY CONVINCE YOU OF THE FUTILITY OF ARGUING WITH US? IF NOT, WE HAVE A THOUSAND SUCH MISSILES POISED ABOVE US. PERHAPS YOU WOULD LIKE TO ATTEMPT TO STOP THEM ALL--?

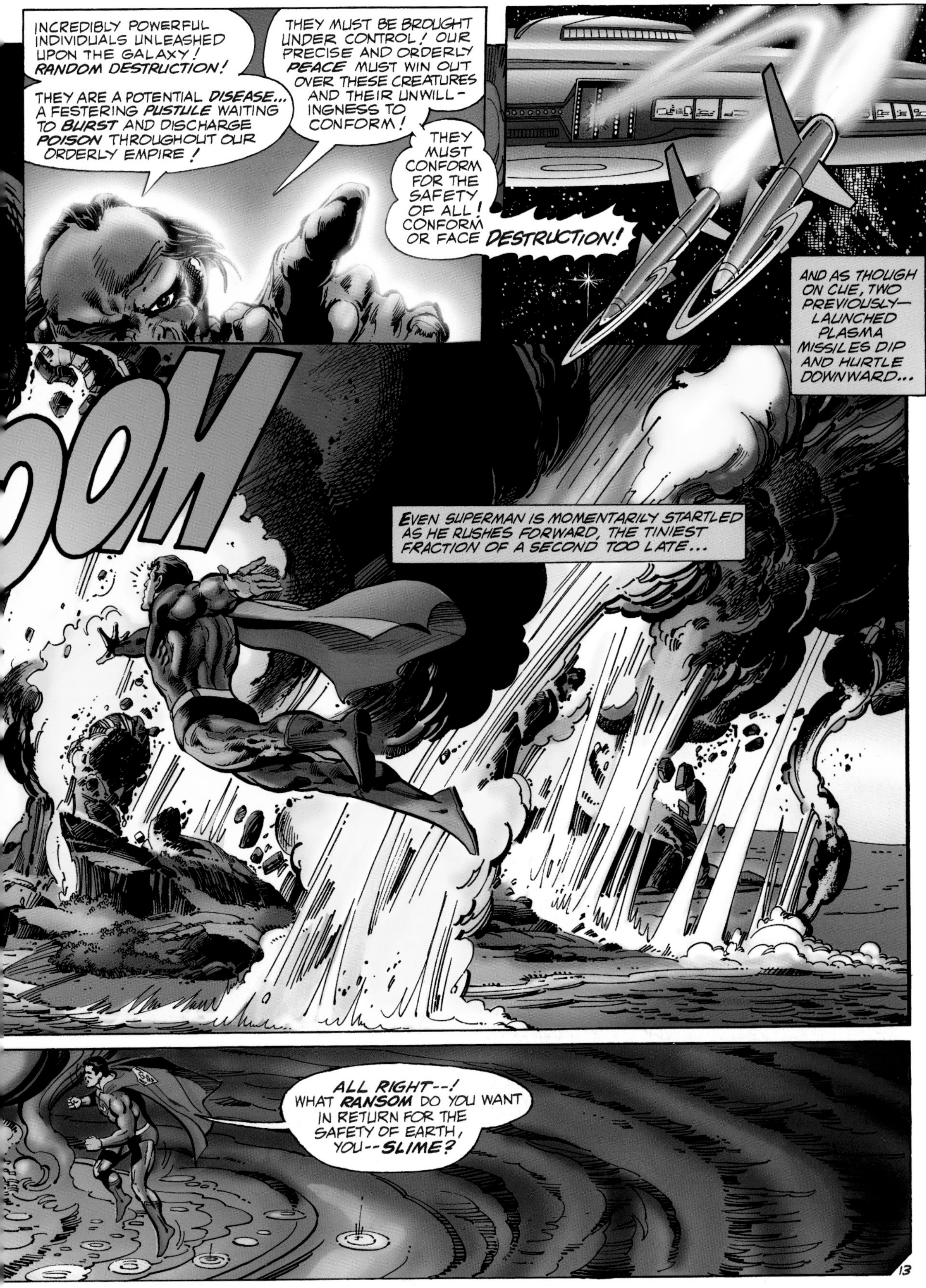

INCREDIBLY POWERFUL INDIVIDUALS UNLEASHED UPON THE GALAXY! RANDOM DESTRUCTION!
THEY ARE A POTENTIAL DISEASE... A FESTERING PUSTULE WAITING TO BURST AND DISCHARGE POISON THROUGHOUT OUR ORDERLY EMPIRE!
THEY MUST BE BROUGHT UNDER CONTROL! OUR PRECISE AND ORDERLY PEACE MUST WIN OUT OVER THESE CREATURES AND THEIR UNWILL-INGNESS TO CONFORM!
THEY MUST CONFORM FOR THE SAFETY OF ALL! CONFORM OR FACE DESTRUCTION!
AND AS THOUGH ON CUE, TWO PREVIOUSLY— LAUNCHED PLASMA MISSILES DIP AND HURTLE DOWNWARD...
OOM
EVEN SUPERMAN IS MOMENTARILY STARTLED AS HE RUSHES FORWARD, THE TINIEST FRACTION OF A SECOND TOO LATE...
ALL RIGHT--! WHAT RANSOM DO YOU WANT IN RETURN FOR THE SAFETY OF EARTH, YOU--SLIME?

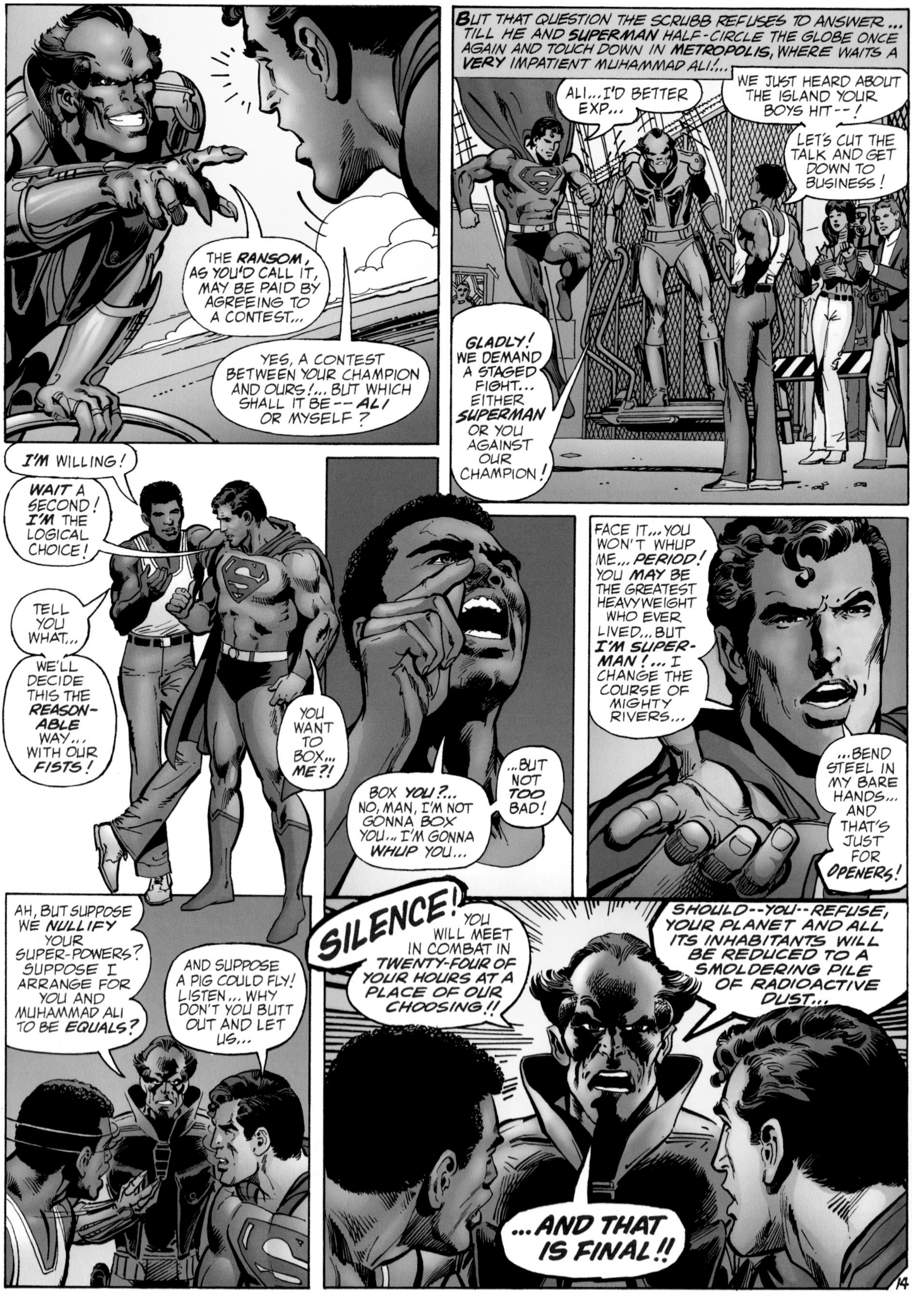

THE RANSOM, AS YOU'D CALL IT, MAY BE PAID BY AGREEING TO A CONTEST...
YES, A CONTEST BETWEEN YOUR CHAMPION AND OURS!... BUT WHICH SHALL IT BE--ALI OR MYSELF?
BUT THAT QUESTION THE SCRUBB REFUSES TO ANSWER... TILL HE AND SUPERMAN HALF-CIRCLE THE GLOBE ONCE AGAIN AND TOUCH DOWN IN METROPOLIS, WHERE WAITS A VERY IMPATIENT MUHAMMAD ALI!...
ALI...I'D BETTER EXP...
WE JUST HEARD ABOUT THE ISLAND YOUR BOYS HIT--!
LET'S CUT THE TALK AND GET DOWN TO BUSINESS!
GLADLY! WE DEMAND A STAGED FIGHT... EITHER SUPERMAN OR YOU AGAINST OUR CHAMPION!
I'M WILLING!
WAIT A SECOND! I'M THE LOGICAL CHOICE!
TELL YOU WHAT...
WE'LL DECIDE THIS THE REASON-ABLE WAY... WITH OUR FISTS!
YOU WANT TO BOX... ME?!
BOX YOU?... NO, MAN, I'M NOT GONNA BOX YOU... I'M GONNA WHUP YOU...
...BUT NOT TOO BAD!
FACE IT... YOU WON'T WHUP ME... PERIOD! YOU MAY BE THE GREATEST HEAVYWEIGHT WHO EVER LIVED... BUT I'M SUPER-MAN!... I CHANGE THE COURSE OF MIGHTY RIVERS...
...BEND STEEL IN MY BARE HANDS... AND THAT'S JUST FOR OPENERS!
AH, BUT SUPPOSE WE NULLIFY YOUR SUPER-POWERS? SUPPOSE I ARRANGE FOR YOU AND MUHAMMAD ALI TO BE EQUALS?
AND SUPPOSE A PIG COULD FLY! LISTEN... WHY DON'T YOU BUTT OUT AND LET US...
SILENCE!
YOU WILL MEET IN COMBAT IN TWENTY-FOUR OF YOUR HOURS AT A PLACE OF OUR CHOOSING!!
SHOULD--YOU--REFUSE, YOUR PLANET AND ALL ITS INHABITANTS WILL BE REDUCED TO A SMOLDERING PILE OF RADIOACTIVE DUST...
...AND THAT IS FINAL!!

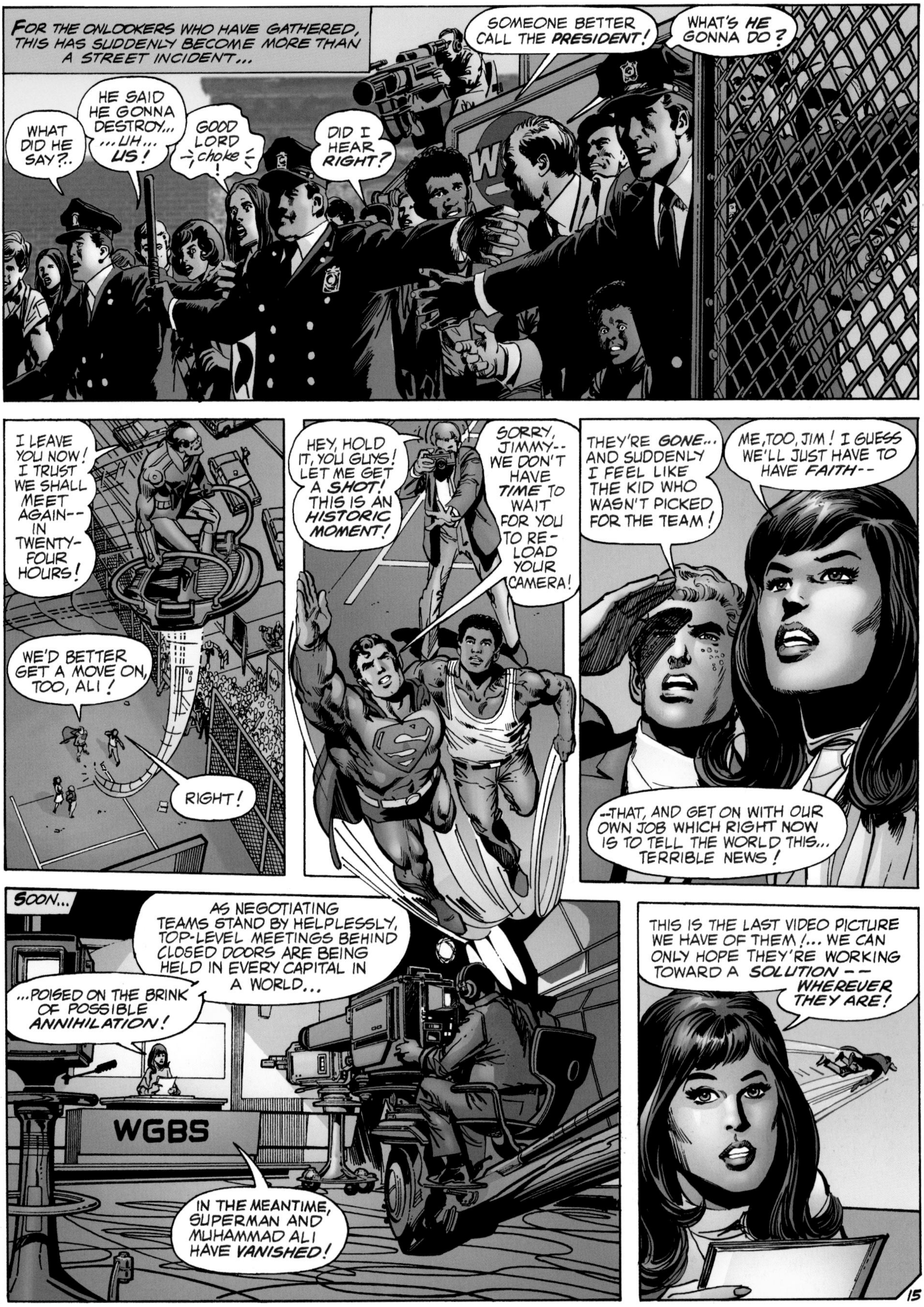

FOR THE ONLOOKERS WHO HAVE GATHERED, THIS HAS SUDDENLY BECOME MORE THAN A STREET INCIDENT...
SOMEONE BETTER CALL THE PRESIDENT!
WHAT'S HE GONNA DO?
WHAT DID HE SAY?..
HE SAID HE GONNA DESTROY... ...UH... US!
GOOD LORD choke!
DID I HEAR RIGHT?
I LEAVE YOU NOW! I TRUST WE SHALL MEET AGAIN-- IN TWENTY-FOUR HOURS!
WE'D BETTER GET A MOVE ON, TOO, ALI!
RIGHT!
HEY, HOLD IT, YOU GUYS! LET ME GET A SHOT! THIS IS AN HISTORIC MOMENT!
SORRY, JIMMY-- WE DON'T HAVE TIME TO WAIT FOR YOU TO RE-LOAD YOUR CAMERA!
THEY'RE GONE... AND SUDDENLY I FEEL LIKE THE KID WHO WASN'T PICKED FOR THE TEAM!
ME, TOO, JIM! I GUESS WE'LL JUST HAVE TO HAVE FAITH--
--THAT, AND GET ON WITH OUR OWN JOB WHICH RIGHT NOW IS TO TELL THE WORLD THIS... TERRIBLE NEWS!
SOON...
AS NEGOTIATING TEAMS STAND BY HELPLESSLY, TOP-LEVEL MEETINGS BEHIND CLOSED DOORS ARE BEING HELD IN EVERY CAPITAL IN A WORLD...
...POISED ON THE BRINK OF POSSIBLE ANNIHILATION!
WGBS
IN THE MEANTIME, SUPERMAN AND MUHAMMAD ALI HAVE VANISHED!
THIS IS THE LAST VIDEO PICTURE WE HAVE OF THEM!... WE CAN ONLY HOPE THEY'RE WORKING TOWARD A SOLUTION -- WHEREVER THEY ARE!

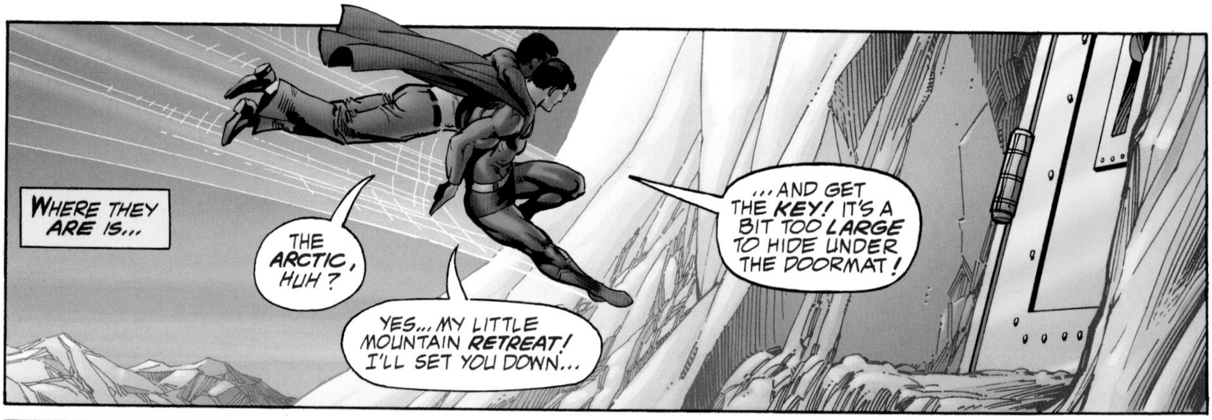
WHERE THEY ARE IS...
THE ARCTIC, HUH?
YES... MY LITTLE MOUNTAIN RETREAT! I'LL SET YOU DOWN...
...AND GET THE KEY! IT'S A BIT TOO LARGE TO HIDE UNDER THE DOORMAT!

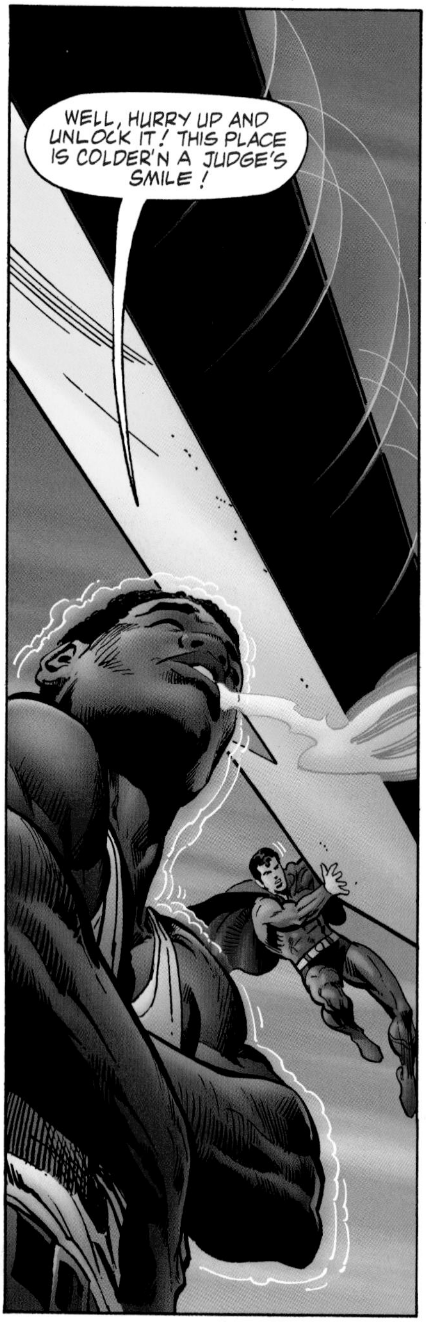
WELL, HURRY UP AND UNLOCK IT! THIS PLACE IS COLDER'N A JUDGE'S SMILE!

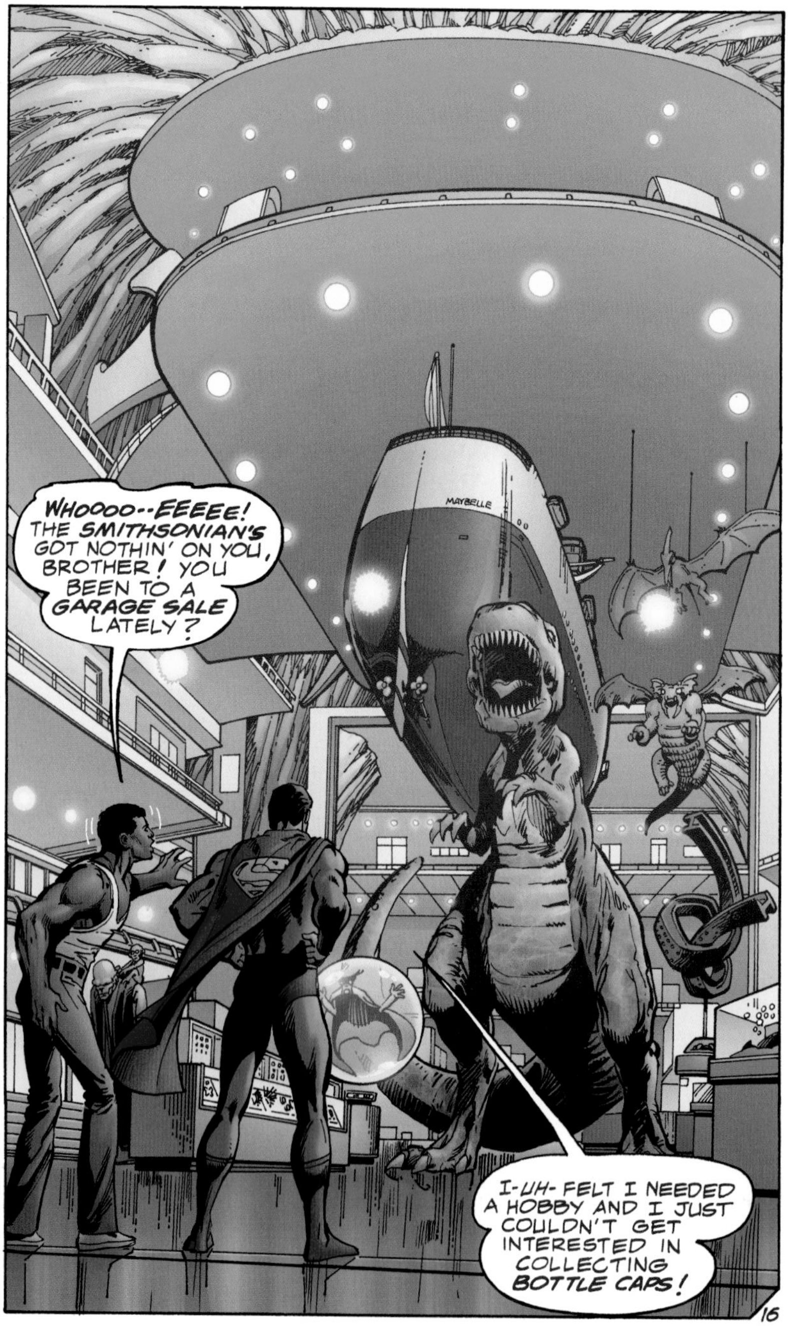
WHOOOO--EEEEE! THE SMITHSONIAN'S GOT NOTHIN' ON YOU, BROTHER! YOU BEEN TO A GARAGE SALE LATELY?
MAYBELLE
I-UH- FELT I NEEDED A HOBBY AND I JUST COULDN'T GET INTERESTED IN COLLECTING BOTTLE CAPS!

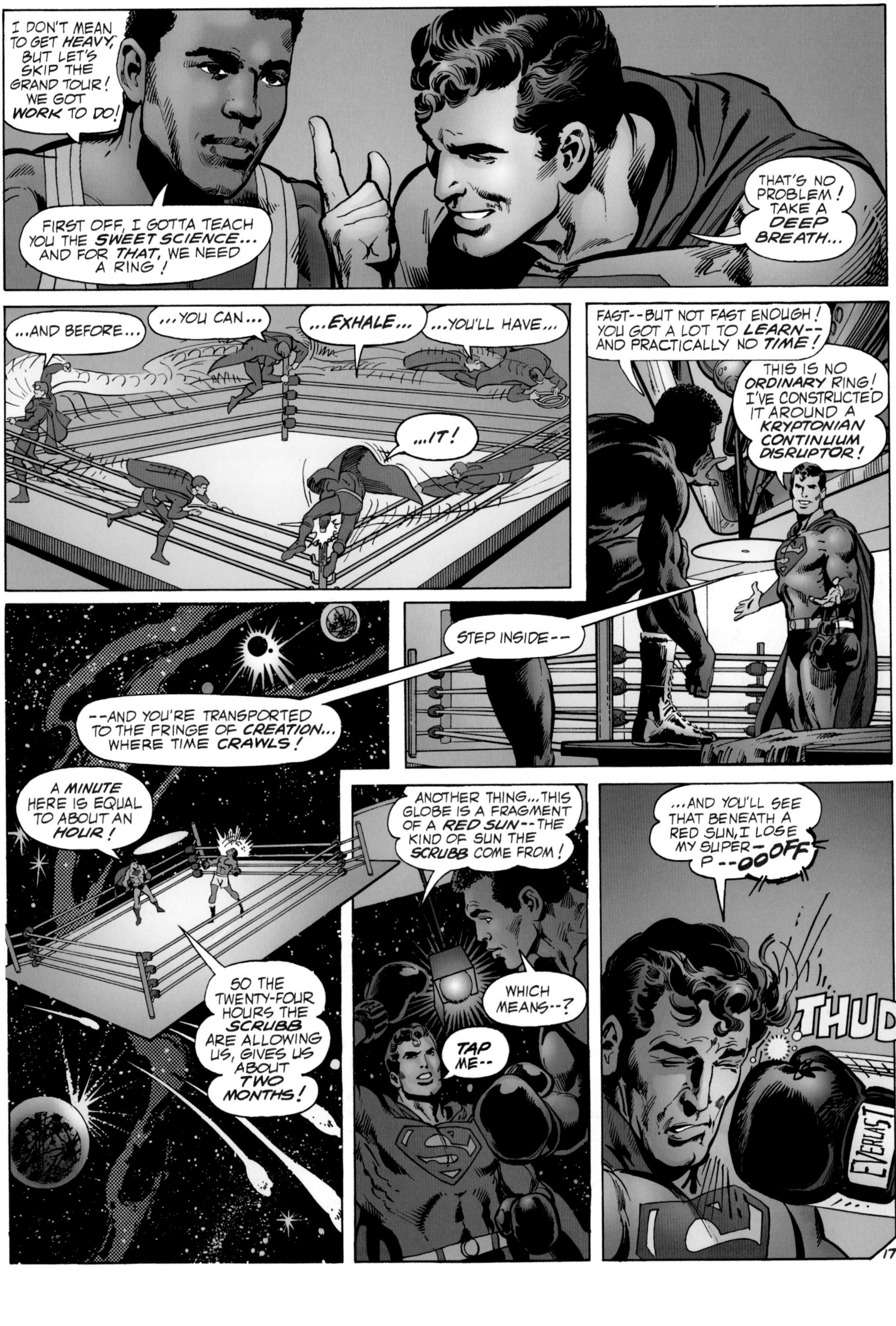
I DON'T MEAN TO GET HEAVY, BUT LET'S SKIP THE GRAND TOUR! WE GOT WORK TO DO!
FIRST OFF, I GOTTA TEACH YOU THE SWEET SCIENCE... AND FOR THAT, WE NEED A RING!
THAT'S NO PROBLEM! TAKE A DEEP BREATH...
...AND BEFORE...
...YOU CAN...
...EXHALE...
...YOU'LL HAVE...
...IT!
FAST--BUT NOT FAST ENOUGH! YOU GOT A LOT TO LEARN--AND PRACTICALLY NO TIME!
THIS IS NO ORDINARY RING! I'VE CONSTRUCTED IT AROUND A KRYPTONIAN CONTINUUM DISRUPTOR!
STEP INSIDE--
--AND YOU'RE TRANSPORTED TO THE FRINGE OF CREATION... WHERE TIME CRAWLS!
A MINUTE HERE IS EQUAL TO ABOUT AN HOUR!
SO THE TWENTY-FOUR HOURS THE SCRUBB ARE ALLOWING US, GIVES US ABOUT TWO MONTHS!
ANOTHER THING... THIS GLOBE IS A FRAGMENT OF A RED SUN--THE KIND OF SUN THE SCRUBB COME FROM!
WHICH MEANS--?
TAP ME--
...AND YOU'LL SEE THAT BENEATH A RED SUN, I LOSE MY SUPER-P--OOOFF
THUD
EVERLAST

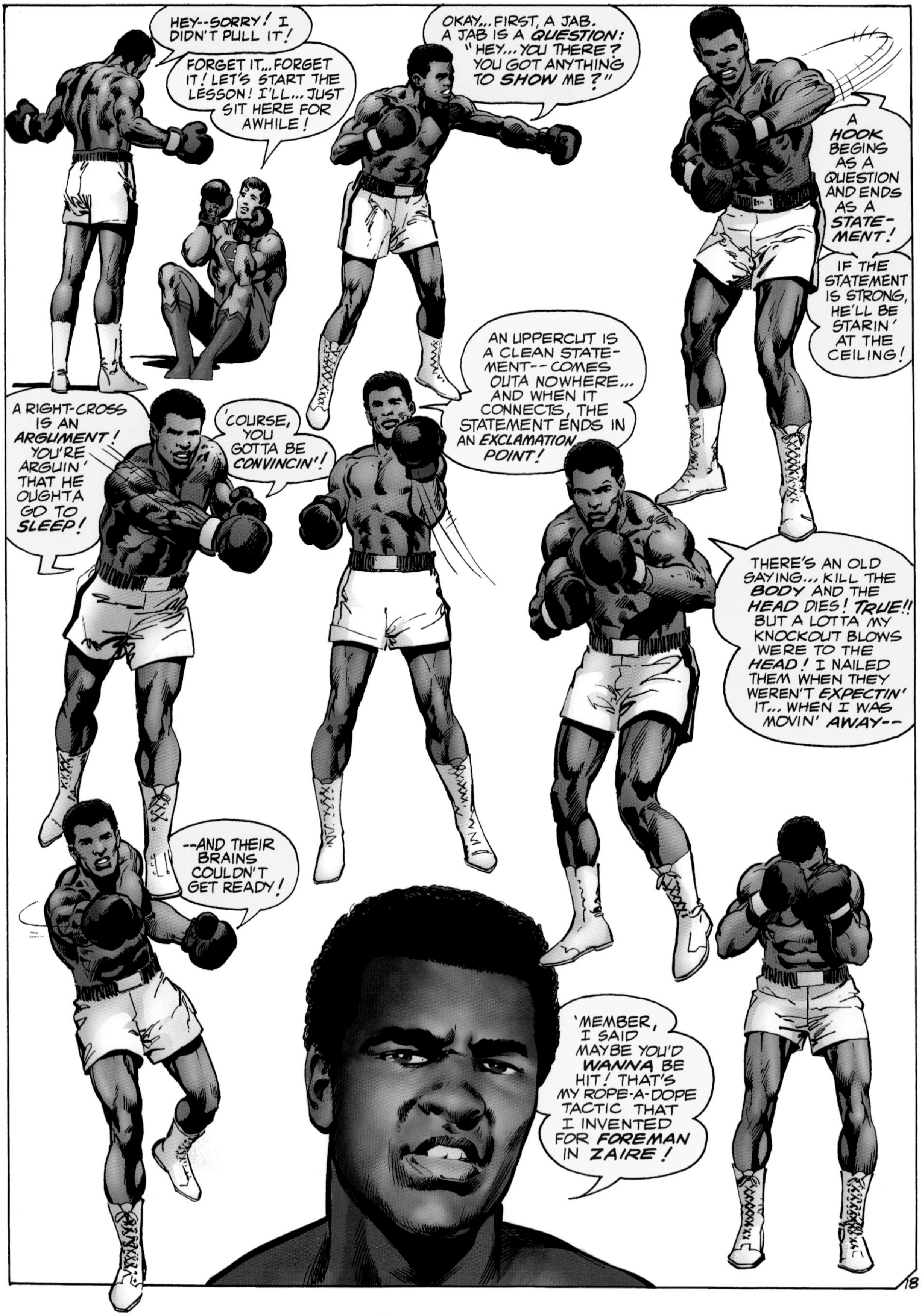
HEY--SORRY! I DIDN'T PULL IT!
FORGET IT...FORGET IT! LET'S START THE LESSON! I'LL... JUST SIT HERE FOR AWHILE!
OKAY... FIRST, A JAB. A JAB IS A QUESTION: "HEY... YOU THERE? YOU GOT ANYTHING TO SHOW ME?"
A HOOK BEGINS AS A QUESTION AND ENDS AS A STATEMENT!
IF THE STATEMENT IS STRONG, HE'LL BE STARIN' AT THE CEILING!
A RIGHT-CROSS IS AN ARGUMENT! YOU'RE ARGUIN' THAT HE OUGHTA GO TO SLEEP!
'COURSE, YOU GOTTA BE CONVINCIN'!
AN UPPERCUT IS A CLEAN STATEMENT-- COMES OUTA NOWHERE... AND WHEN IT CONNECTS, THE STATEMENT ENDS IN AN EXCLAMATION POINT!
THERE'S AN OLD SAYING... KILL THE BODY AND THE HEAD DIES! TRUE!! BUT A LOTTA MY KNOCKOUT BLOWS WERE TO THE HEAD! I NAILED THEM WHEN THEY WEREN'T EXPECTIN' IT... WHEN I WAS MOVIN' AWAY--
--AND THEIR BRAINS COULDN'T GET READY!
'MEMBER, I SAID MAYBE YOU'D WANNA BE HIT! THAT'S MY ROPE-A-DOPE TACTIC THAT I INVENTED FOR FOREMAN IN ZAIRE!

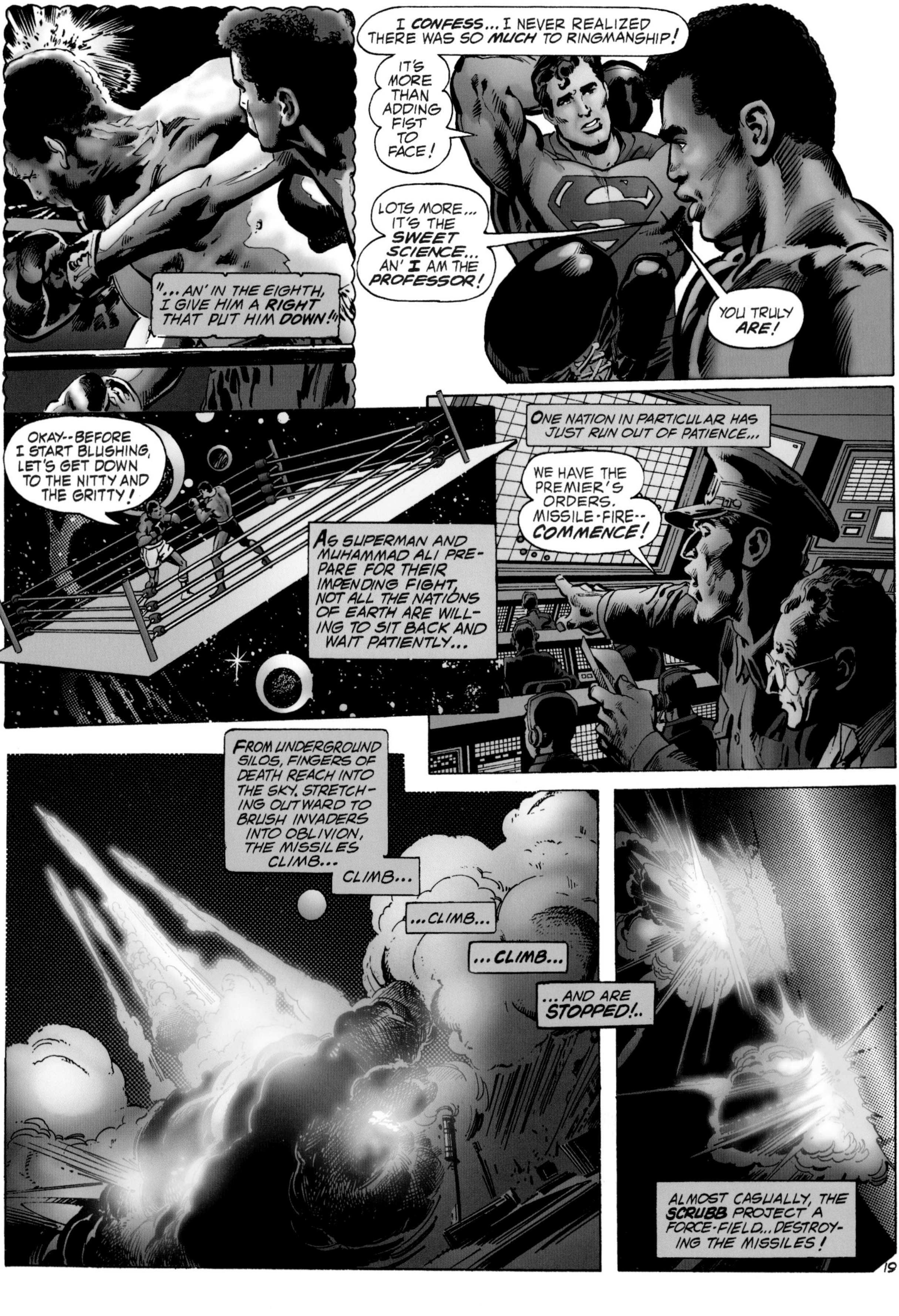
"...AN' IN THE EIGHTH, I GIVE HIM A RIGHT THAT PUT HIM DOWN!"
I CONFESS... I NEVER REALIZED THERE WAS SO MUCH TO RINGMANSHIP!
IT'S MORE THAN ADDING FIST TO FACE!
LOTS MORE... IT'S THE SWEET SCIENCE... AN' I AM THE PROFESSOR!
YOU TRULY ARE!
OKAY--BEFORE I START BLUSHING, LET'S GET DOWN TO THE NITTY AND THE GRITTY!
AS SUPERMAN AND MUHAMMAD ALI PREPARE FOR THEIR IMPENDING FIGHT, NOT ALL THE NATIONS OF EARTH ARE WILLING TO SIT BACK AND WAIT PATIENTLY...
ONE NATION IN PARTICULAR HAS JUST RUN OUT OF PATIENCE...
WE HAVE THE PREMIER'S ORDERS. MISSILE-FIRE--COMMENCE!
FROM UNDERGROUND SILOS, FINGERS OF DEATH REACH INTO THE SKY. STRETCHING OUTWARD TO BRUSH INVADERS INTO OBLIVION, THE MISSILES CLIMB...
CLIMB...
...CLIMB...
...CLIMB...
...AND ARE STOPPED!.
ALMOST CASUALLY, THE SCRUBB PROJECT A FORCE-FIELD...DESTROYING THE MISSILES!

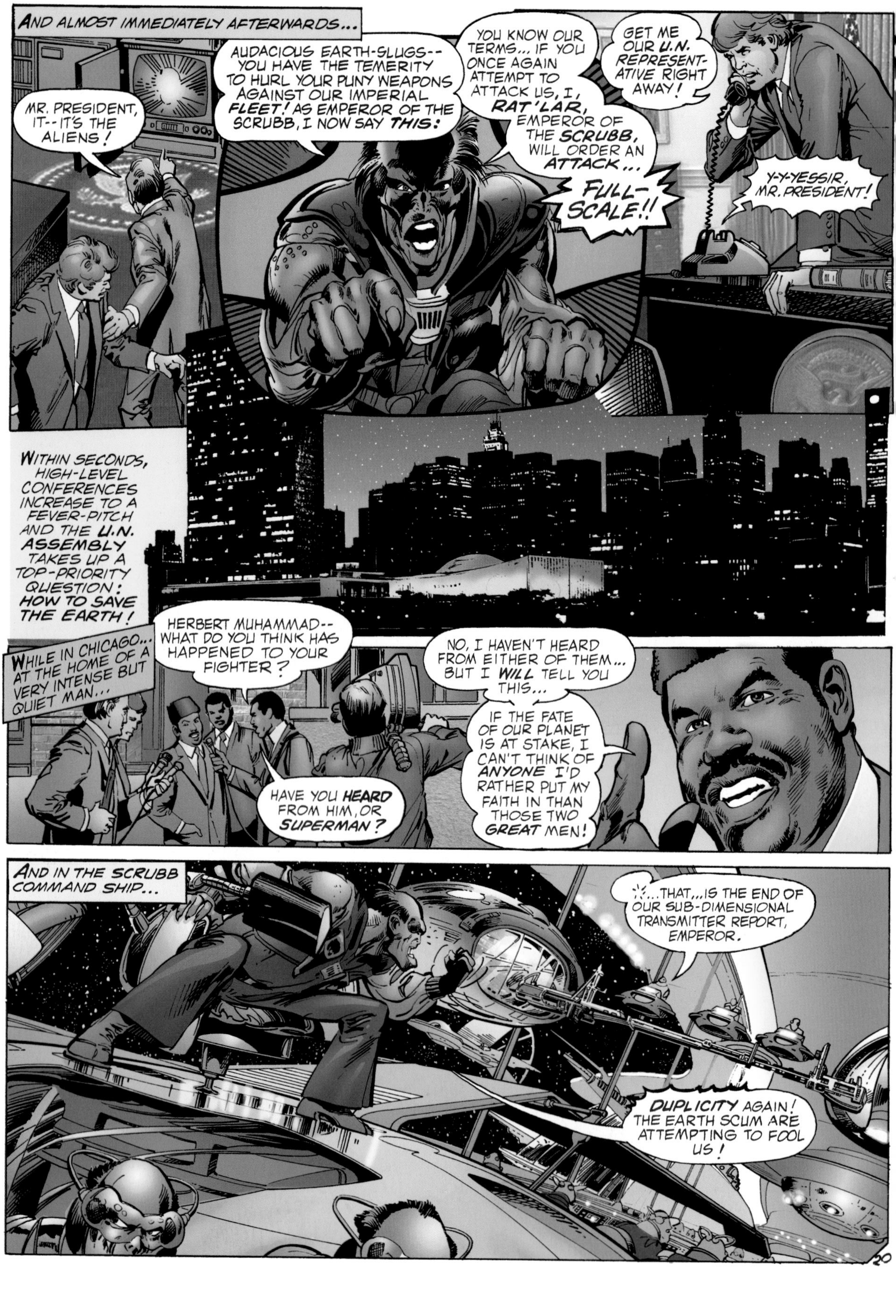
AND ALMOST IMMEDIATELY AFTERWARDS...
MR. PRESIDENT, IT-- IT'S THE ALIENS!
AUDACIOUS EARTH-SLUGS-- YOU HAVE THE TEMERITY TO HURL YOUR PUNY WEAPONS AGAINST OUR IMPERIAL FLEET! AS EMPEROR OF THE SCRUBB, I NOW SAY THIS:
YOU KNOW OUR TERMS... IF YOU ONCE AGAIN ATTEMPT TO ATTACK US, I, RAT'LAR, EMPEROR OF THE SCRUBB, WILL ORDER AN ATTACK...
FULL-SCALE!!
GET ME OUR U.N. REPRESENTATIVE RIGHT AWAY!
Y-Y-YESSIR, MR. PRESIDENT!
WITHIN SECONDS, HIGH-LEVEL CONFERENCES INCREASE TO A FEVER-PITCH AND THE U.N. ASSEMBLY TAKES UP A TOP-PRIORITY QUESTION: HOW TO SAVE THE EARTH!
WHILE IN CHICAGO... AT THE HOME OF A VERY INTENSE BUT QUIET MAN...
HERBERT MUHAMMAD-- WHAT DO YOU THINK HAS HAPPENED TO YOUR FIGHTER?
HAVE YOU HEARD FROM HIM, OR SUPERMAN?
NO, I HAVEN'T HEARD FROM EITHER OF THEM... BUT I WILL TELL YOU THIS...
IF THE FATE OF OUR PLANET IS AT STAKE, I CAN'T THINK OF ANYONE I'D RATHER PUT MY FAITH IN THAN THOSE TWO GREAT MEN!
AND IN THE SCRUBB COMMAND SHIP...
...THAT...IS THE END OF OUR SUB-DIMENSIONAL TRANSMITTER REPORT, EMPEROR.
DUPLICITY AGAIN! THE EARTH SCUM ARE ATTEMPTING TO FOOL US!
20

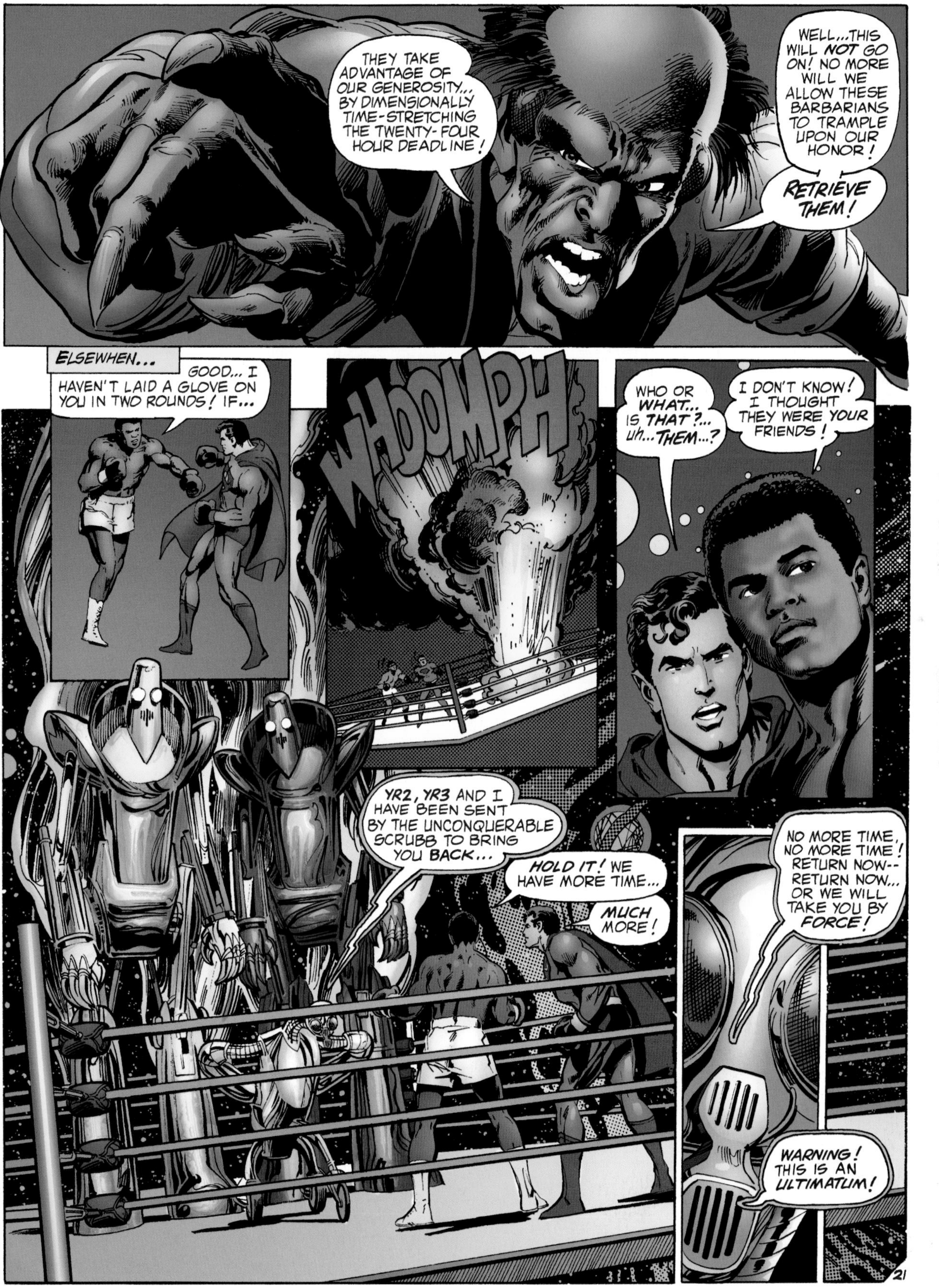
THEY TAKE ADVANTAGE OF OUR GENEROSITY... BY DIMENSIONALLY TIME-STRETCHING THE TWENTY-FOUR HOUR DEADLINE!
WELL... THIS WILL NOT GO ON! NO MORE WILL WE ALLOW THESE BARBARIANS TO TRAMPLE UPON OUR HONOR!
RETRIEVE THEM!
ELSEWHEN...
GOOD... I HAVEN'T LAID A GLOVE ON YOU IN TWO ROUNDS! IF...
WHOOMPH
WHO OR WHAT...? IS THAT?... uh... THEM...?
I DON'T KNOW! I THOUGHT THEY WERE YOUR FRIENDS!
YR2, YR3 AND I HAVE BEEN SENT BY THE UNCONQUERABLE SCRUBB TO BRING YOU BACK...
HOLD IT! WE HAVE MORE TIME...
MUCH MORE!
NO MORE TIME, NO MORE TIME! RETURN NOW-- RETURN NOW... OR WE WILL TAKE YOU BY FORCE!
WARNING! THIS IS AN ULTIMATUM!

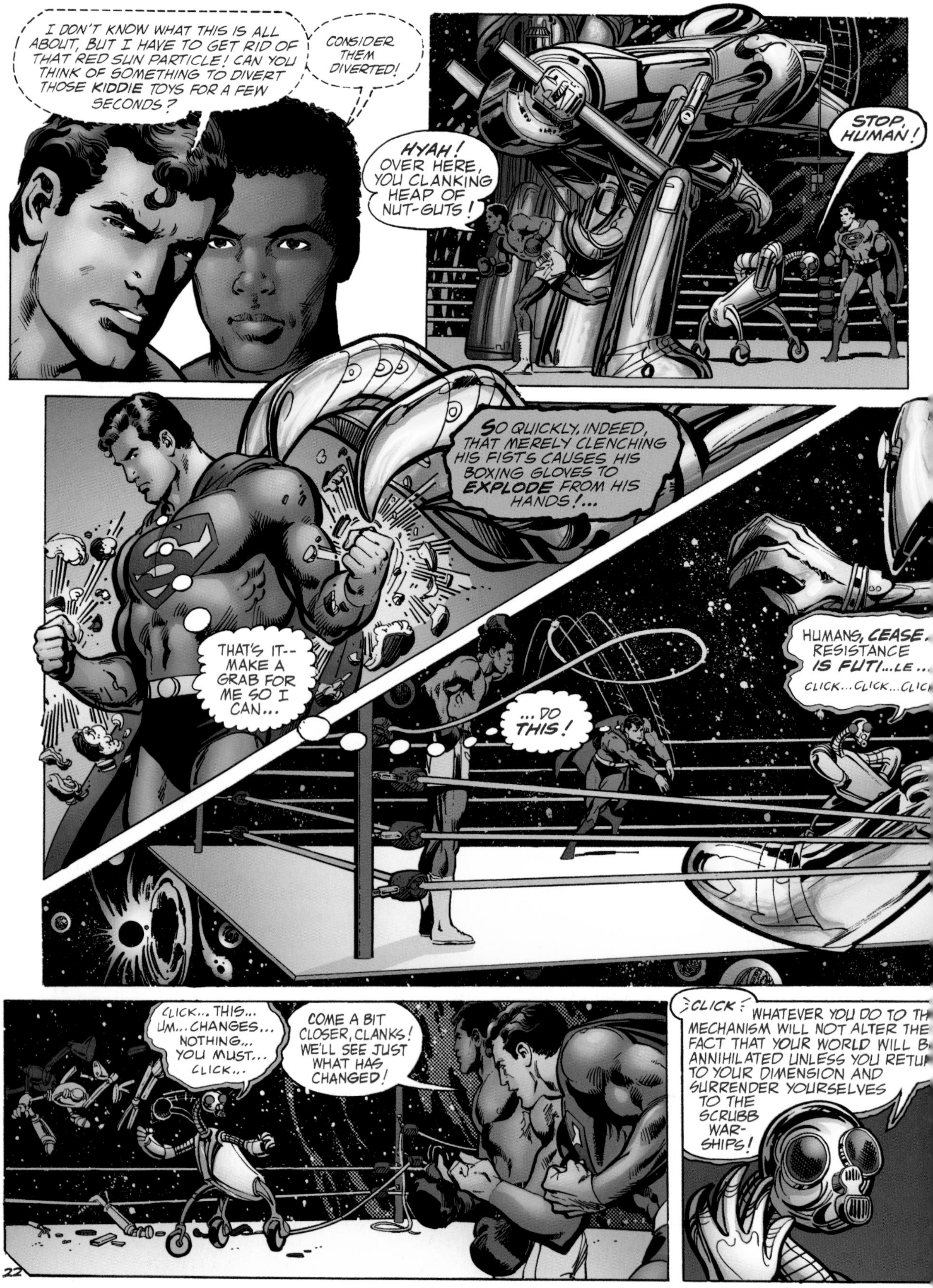
I DON'T KNOW WHAT THIS IS ALL ABOUT, BUT I HAVE TO GET RID OF THAT RED SUN PARTICLE! CAN YOU THINK OF SOMETHING TO DIVERT THOSE KIDDIE TOYS FOR A FEW SECONDS?
CONSIDER THEM DIVERTED!
HYAH! OVER HERE, YOU CLANKING HEAP OF NUT-GUTS!
STOP, HUMAN!
SO QUICKLY, INDEED, THAT MERELY CLENCHING HIS FISTS CAUSES HIS BOXING GLOVES TO EXPLODE FROM HIS HANDS!...
THAT'S IT-- MAKE A GRAB FOR ME SO I CAN...
...DO THIS!
HUMANS, CEASE. RESISTANCE IS FUTI...LE...
CLICK...CLICK...CLIC
CLICK... THIS... UM...CHANGES... NOTHING... YOU MUST... CLICK...
COME A BIT CLOSER, CLANKS! WE'LL SEE JUST WHAT HAS CHANGED!
CLICK! WHATEVER YOU DO TO TH MECHANISM WILL NOT ALTER THE FACT THAT YOUR WORLD WILL B ANNIHILATED UNLESS YOU RETUR TO YOUR DIMENSION AND SURRENDER YOURSELVES TO THE SCRUBB WAR-SHIPS!

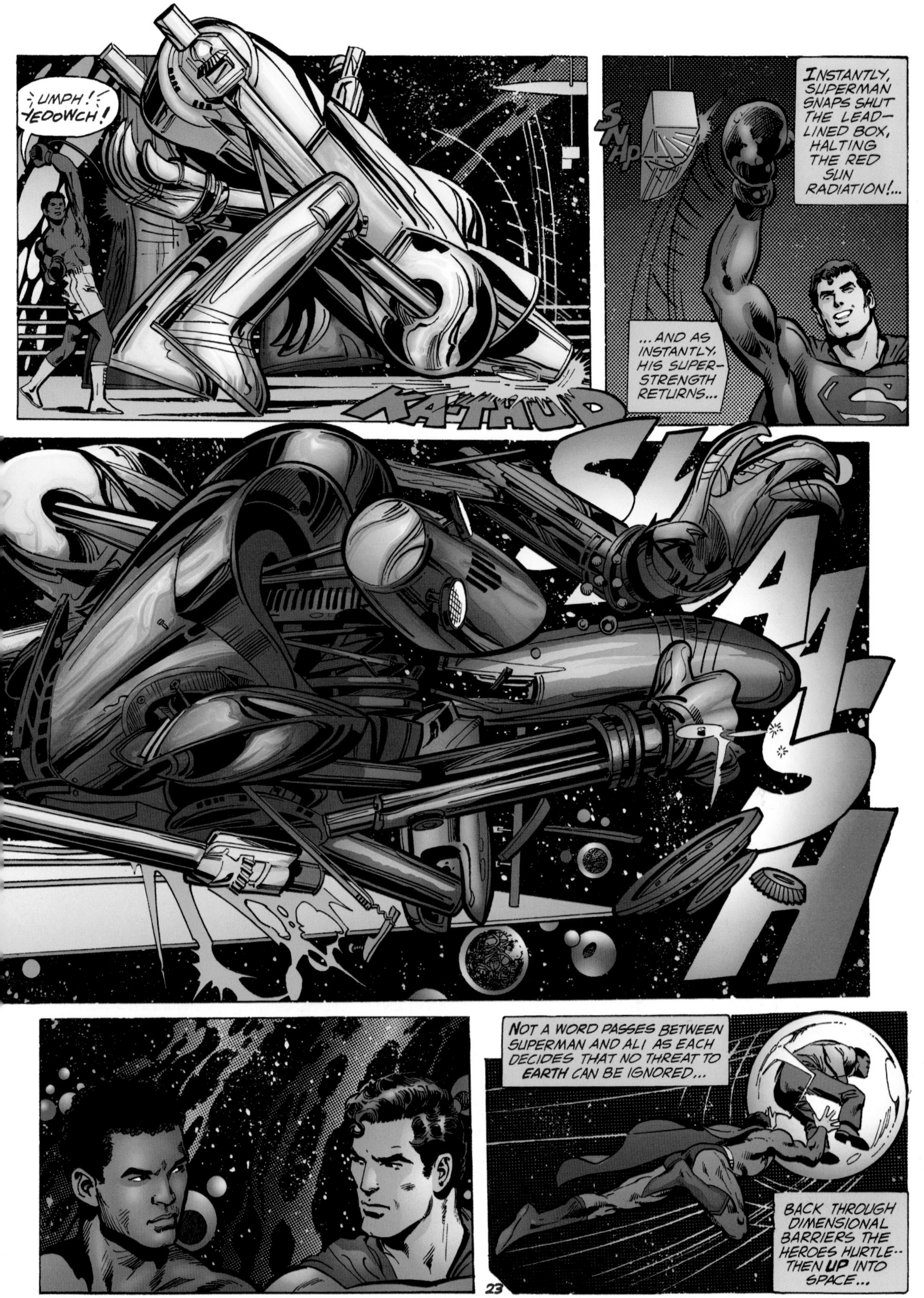
UMPH!
YEOOWCH!
KA-THUD
SNAP
INSTANTLY, SUPERMAN SNAPS SHUT THE LEAD-LINED BOX, HALTING THE RED SUN RADIATION!...
...AND AS INSTANTLY, HIS SUPER-STRENGTH RETURNS...
SMASH
NOT A WORD PASSES BETWEEN SUPERMAN AND ALI AS EACH DECIDES THAT NO THREAT TO EARTH CAN BE IGNORED...
BACK THROUGH DIMENSIONAL BARRIERS THE HEROES HURTLE-- THEN UP INTO SPACE...

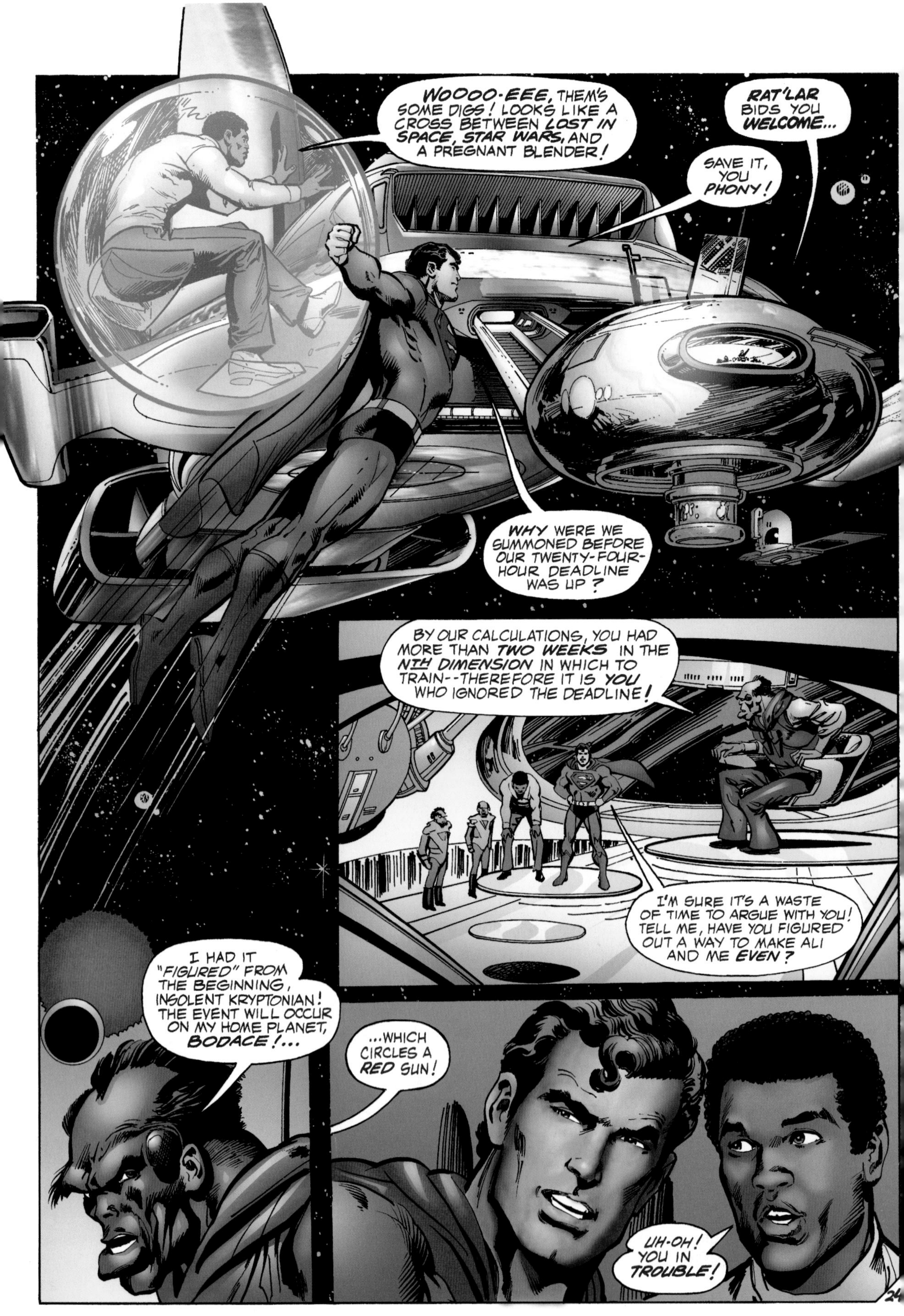

WOOOO-EEE, THEM'S SOME DIGS! LOOKS LIKE A CROSS BETWEEN LOST IN SPACE, STAR WARS, AND A PREGNANT BLENDER!
RAT'LAR BIDS YOU WELCOME...
SAVE IT, YOU PHONY!
WHY WERE WE SUMMONED BEFORE OUR TWENTY-FOUR-HOUR DEADLINE WAS UP?
BY OUR CALCULATIONS, YOU HAD MORE THAN TWO WEEKS IN THE NTH DIMENSION IN WHICH TO TRAIN--THEREFORE IT IS YOU WHO IGNORED THE DEADLINE!
I'M SURE IT'S A WASTE OF TIME TO ARGUE WITH YOU! TELL ME, HAVE YOU FIGURED OUT A WAY TO MAKE ALI AND ME EVEN?
I HAD IT "FIGURED" FROM THE BEGINNING, INSOLENT KRYPTONIAN! THE EVENT WILL OCCUR ON MY HOME PLANET, BODACE!...
...WHICH CIRCLES A RED SUN!
UH-OH! YOU IN TROUBLE!

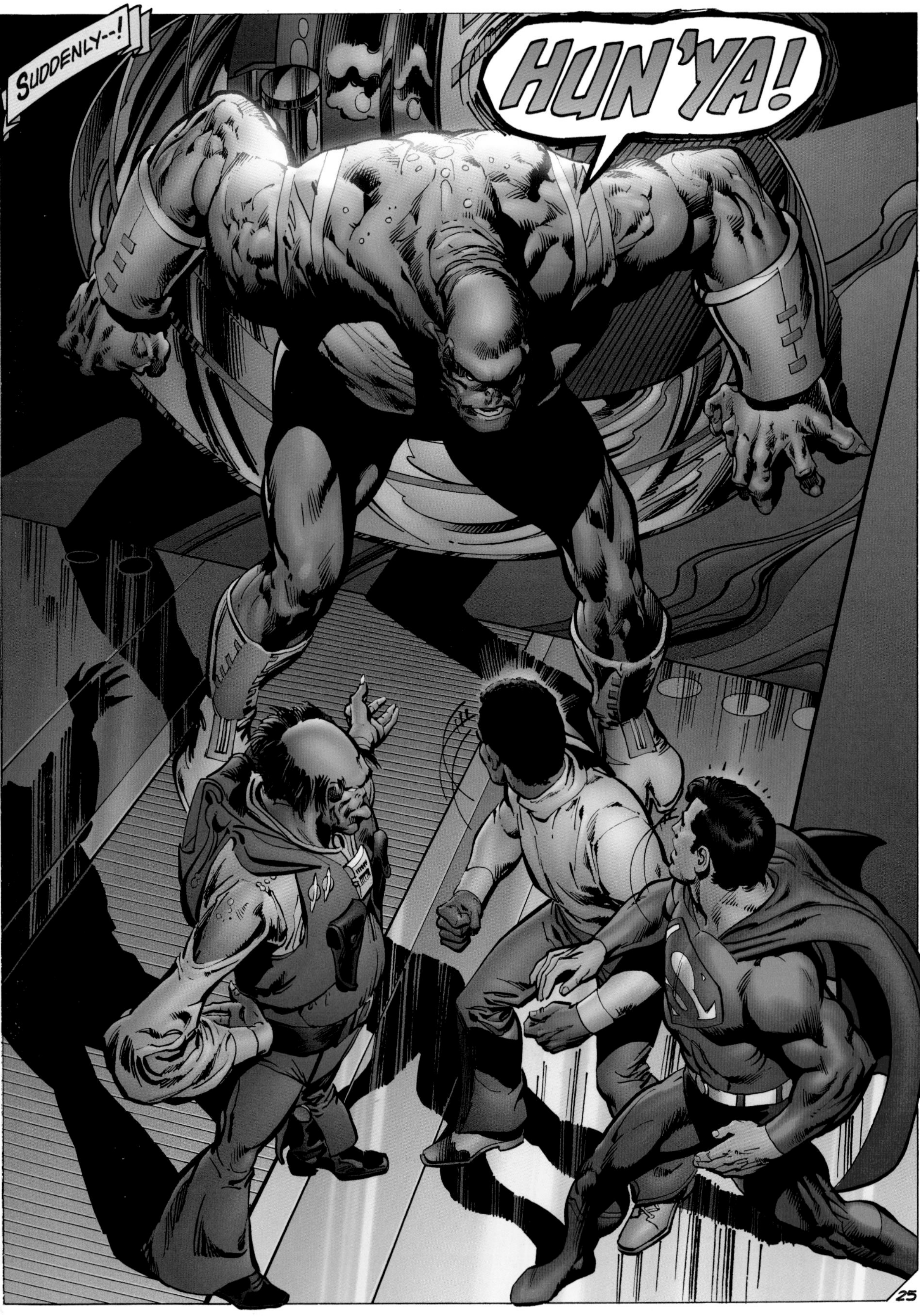
SUDDENLY--!
HUN'YA!

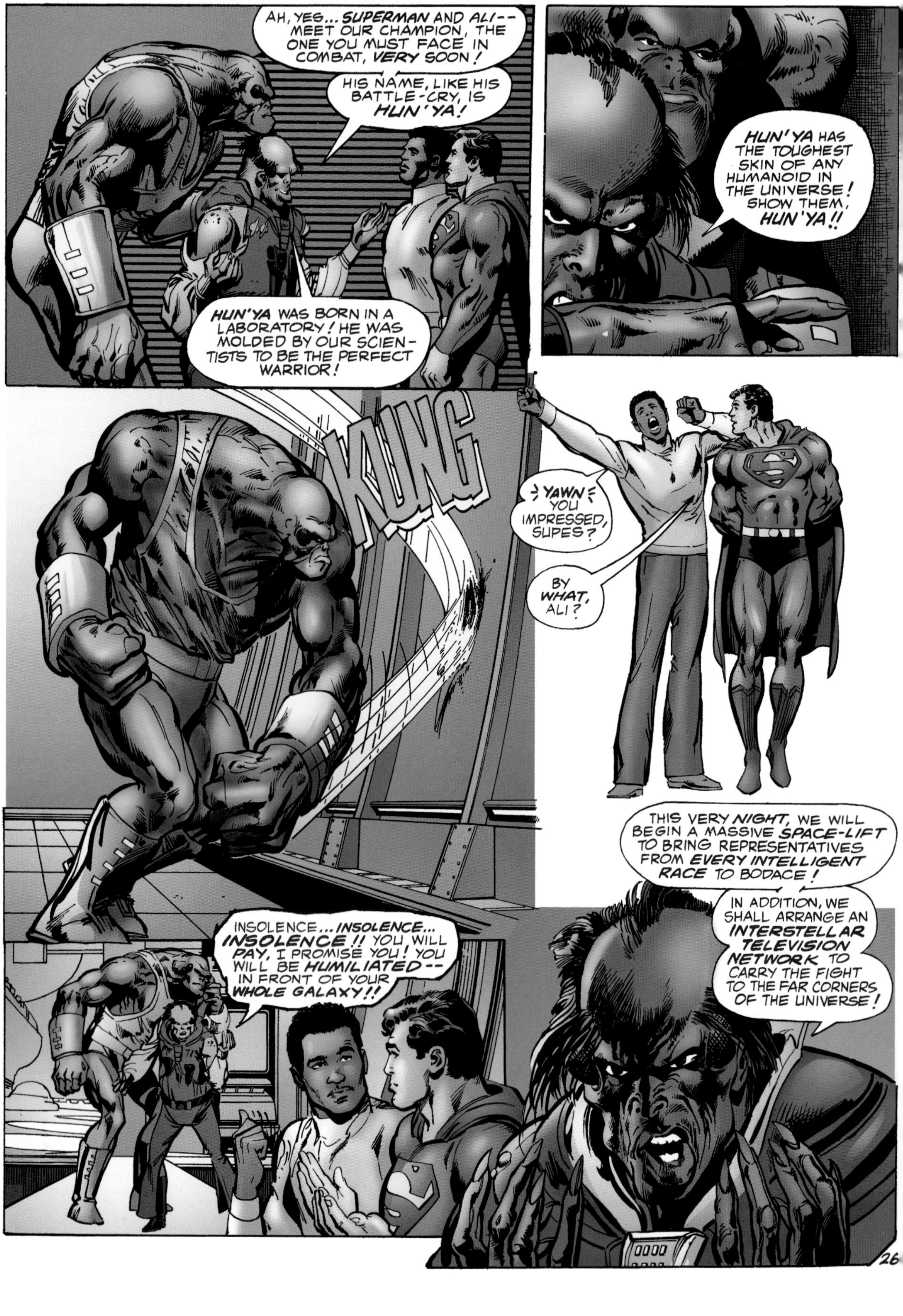
AH, YES... SUPERMAN AND ALI-- MEET OUR CHAMPION, THE ONE YOU MUST FACE IN COMBAT, VERY SOON!
HIS NAME, LIKE HIS BATTLE-CRY, IS HUN'YA!
HUN'YA WAS BORN IN A LABORATORY! HE WAS MOLDED BY OUR SCIENTISTS TO BE THE PERFECT WARRIOR!
HUN'YA HAS THE TOUGHEST SKIN OF ANY HUMANOID IN THE UNIVERSE! SHOW THEM, HUN'YA!!
KUNG
YAWN YOU IMPRESSED, SUPES?
BY WHAT, ALI?
THIS VERY NIGHT, WE WILL BEGIN A MASSIVE SPACE-LIFT TO BRING REPRESENTATIVES FROM EVERY INTELLIGENT RACE TO BODACE!
IN ADDITION, WE SHALL ARRANGE AN INTERSTELLAR TELEVISION NETWORK TO CARRY THE FIGHT TO THE FAR CORNERS OF THE UNIVERSE!
INSOLENCE... INSOLENCE... INSOLENCE!! YOU WILL PAY, I PROMISE YOU! YOU WILL BE HUMILIATED-- IN FRONT OF YOUR WHOLE GALAXY!!

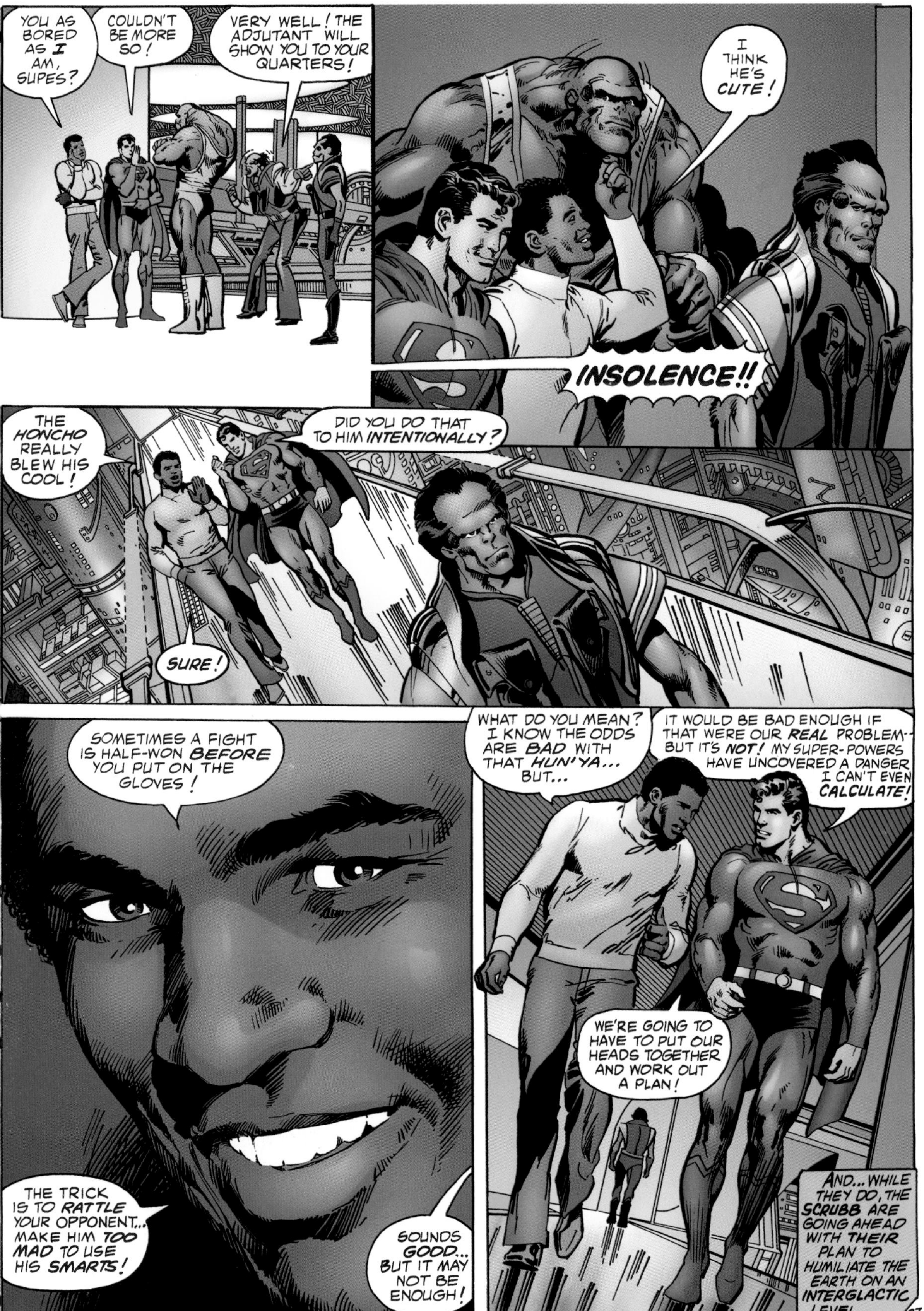
YOU AS BORED AS I AM, SUPES?
COULDN'T BE MORE SO!
VERY WELL! THE ADJUTANT WILL SHOW YOU TO YOUR QUARTERS!
I THINK HE'S CUTE!
INSOLENCE!!
THE HONCHO REALLY BLEW HIS COOL!
DID YOU DO THAT TO HIM INTENTIONALLY?
SURE!
SOMETIMES A FIGHT IS HALF-WON BEFORE YOU PUT ON THE GLOVES!
THE TRICK IS TO RATTLE YOUR OPPONENT... MAKE HIM TOO MAD TO USE HIS SMARTS!
SOUNDS GOOD... BUT IT MAY NOT BE ENOUGH!
WHAT DO YOU MEAN? I KNOW THE ODDS ARE BAD WITH THAT HUN'YA... BUT...
IT WOULD BE BAD ENOUGH IF THAT WERE OUR REAL PROBLEM-- BUT IT'S NOT! MY SUPER-POWERS HAVE UNCOVERED A DANGER I CAN'T EVEN CALCULATE!
WE'RE GOING TO HAVE TO PUT OUR HEADS TOGETHER AND WORK OUT A PLAN!
AND... WHILE THEY DO, THE SCRUBB ARE GOING AHEAD WITH THEIR PLAN TO HUMILIATE THE EARTH ON AN INTERGLACTIC LEVEL...

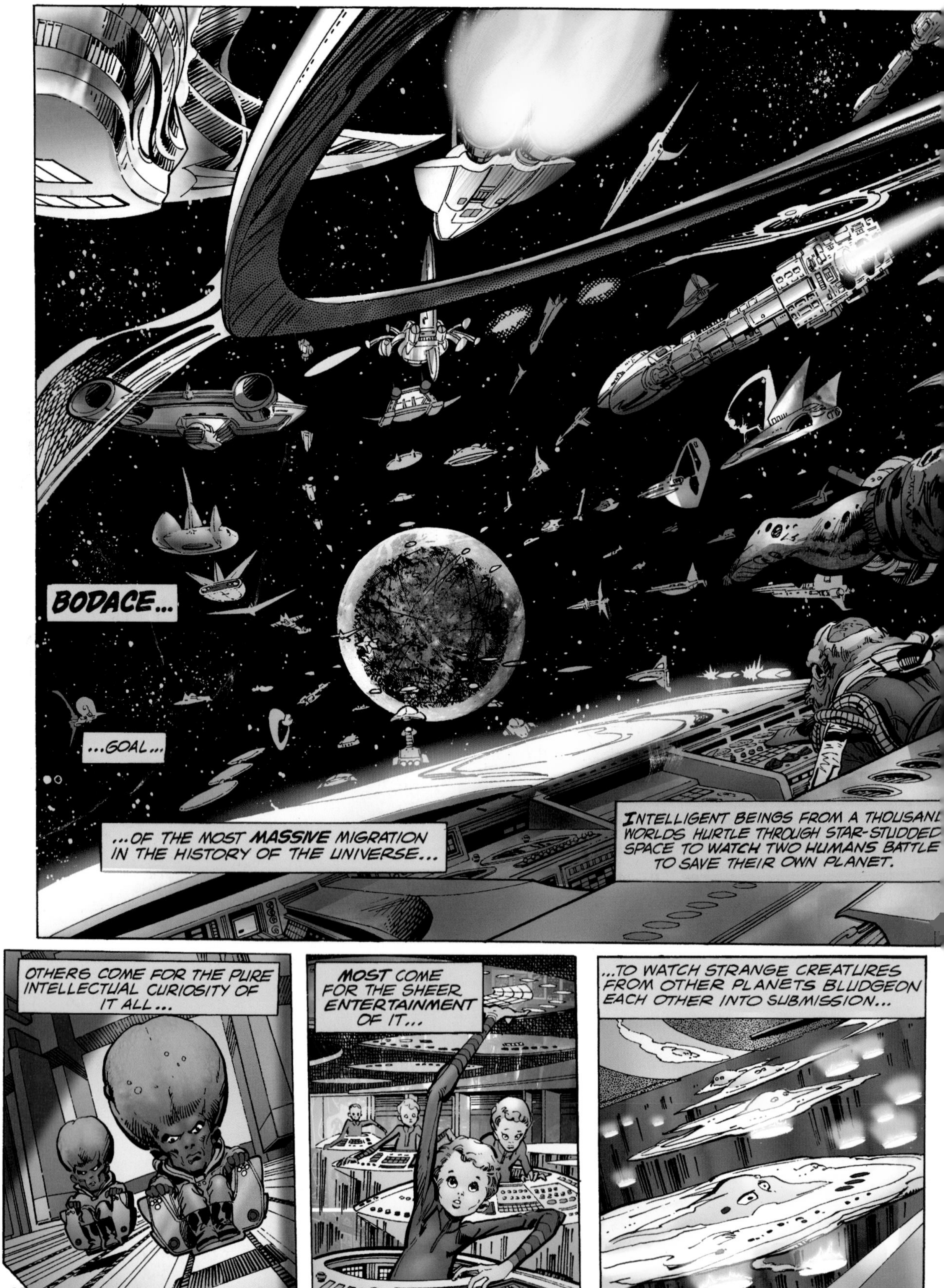
BODACE...
...GOAL...
...OF THE MOST MASSIVE MIGRATION IN THE HISTORY OF THE UNIVERSE...
INTELLIGENT BEINGS FROM A THOUSAND WORLDS HURTLE THROUGH STAR-STUDDED SPACE TO WATCH TWO HUMANS BATTLE TO SAVE THEIR OWN PLANET.
OTHERS COME FOR THE PURE INTELLECTUAL CURIOSITY OF IT ALL...
MOST COME FOR THE SHEER ENTERTAINMENT OF IT...
...TO WATCH STRANGE CREATURES FROM OTHER PLANETS BLUDGEON EACH OTHER INTO SUBMISSION...

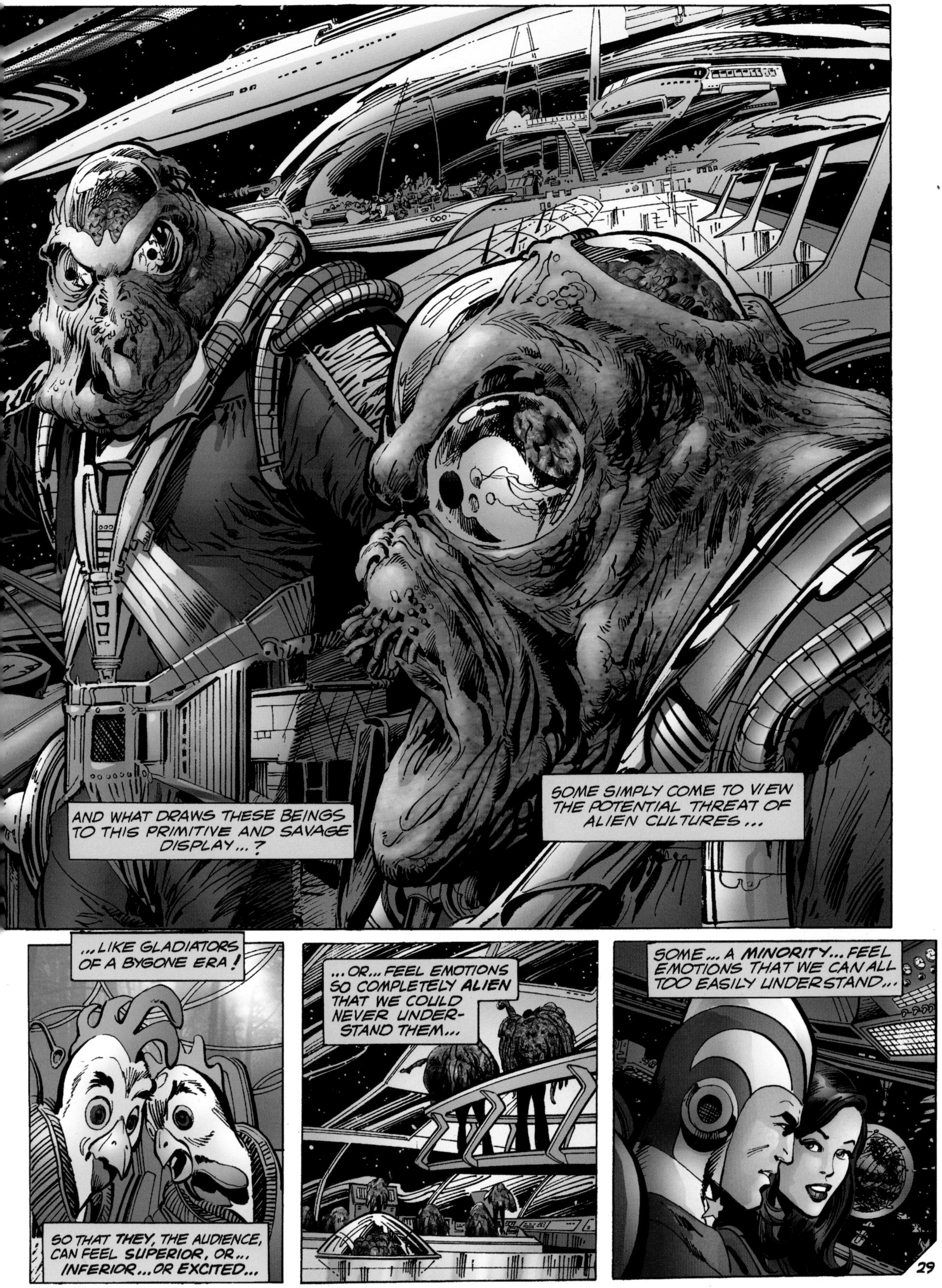
AND WHAT DRAWS THESE BEINGS TO THIS PRIMITIVE AND SAVAGE DISPLAY...?
SOME SIMPLY COME TO VIEW THE POTENTIAL THREAT OF ALIEN CULTURES...
...LIKE GLADIATORS OF A BYGONE ERA!
SO THAT THEY, THE AUDIENCE, CAN FEEL SUPERIOR, OR... INFERIOR...OR EXCITED...
...OR...FEEL EMOTIONS SO COMPLETELY ALIEN THAT WE COULD NEVER UNDER-STAND THEM...
SOME...A MINORITY...FEEL EMOTIONS THAT WE CAN ALL TOO EASILY UNDERSTAND...

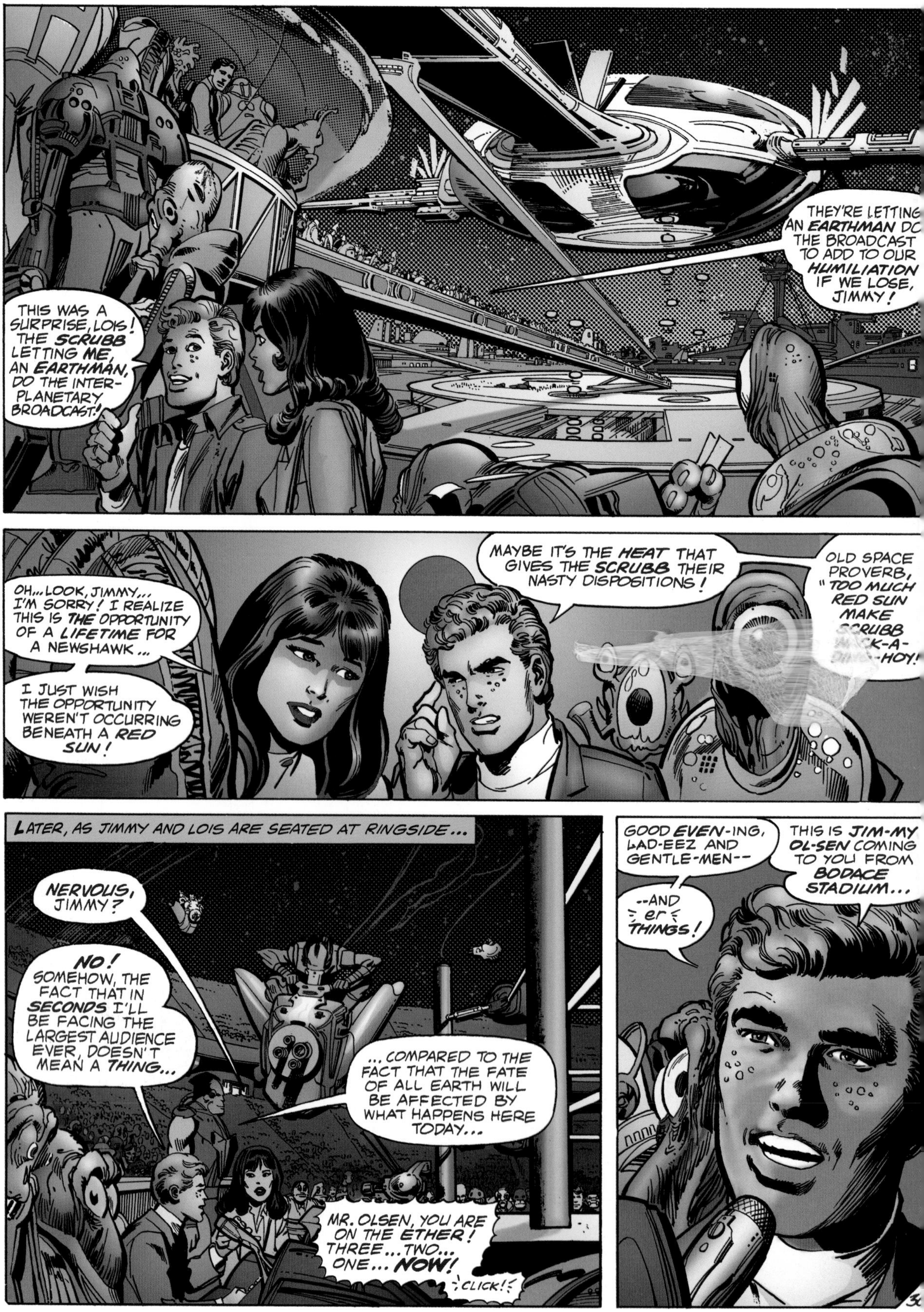
THIS WAS A SURPRISE, LOIS! THE SCRUBB LETTING ME, AN EARTHMAN, DO THE INTER-PLANETARY BROADCAST!
THEY'RE LETTING AN EARTHMAN DO THE BROADCAST TO ADD TO OUR HUMILIATION IF WE LOSE, JIMMY!
OH... LOOK, JIMMY... I'M SORRY! I REALIZE THIS IS THE OPPORTUNITY OF A LIFETIME FOR A NEWSHAWK...
I JUST WISH THE OPPORTUNITY WEREN'T OCCURRING BENEATH A RED SUN!
MAYBE IT'S THE HEAT THAT GIVES THE SCRUBB THEIR NASTY DISPOSITIONS!
OLD SPACE PROVERB, "TOO MUCH RED SUN MAKE SCRUBB
LATER, AS JIMMY AND LOIS ARE SEATED AT RINGSIDE...
NERVOUS, JIMMY?
NO! SOMEHOW, THE FACT THAT IN SECONDS I'LL BE FACING THE LARGEST AUDIENCE EVER, DOESN'T MEAN A THING...
...COMPARED TO THE FACT THAT THE FATE OF ALL EARTH WILL BE AFFECTED BY WHAT HAPPENS HERE TODAY...
MR. OLSEN, YOU ARE ON THE ETHER! THREE... TWO... ONE... NOW!
CLICK!
GOOD EVEN-ING, LAD-EEZ AND GENTLE-MEN--
--AND er THINGS!
THIS IS JIM-MY OL-SEN COMING TO YOU FROM BODACE STADIUM...

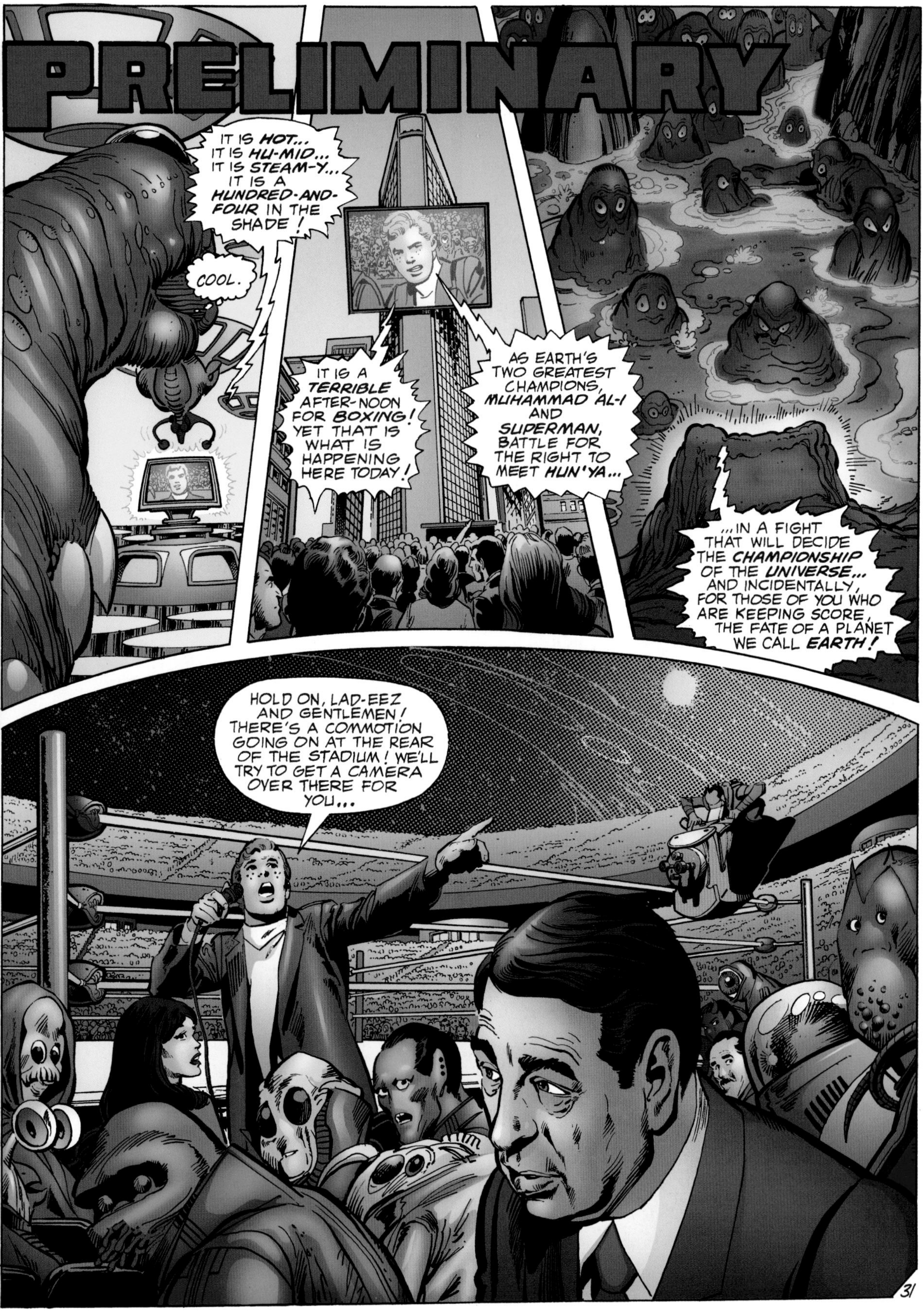
PRELIMINARY
IT IS HOT... IT IS HU-MID... IT IS STEAM-Y... IT IS A HUNDRED-AND-FOUR IN THE SHADE!
COOL.
IT IS A TERRIBLE AFTER-NOON FOR BOXING! YET THAT IS WHAT IS HAPPENING HERE TODAY!
AS EARTH'S TWO GREATEST CHAMPIONS, MUHAMMAD AL-I AND SUPERMAN, BATTLE FOR THE RIGHT TO MEET HUN'YA...
...IN A FIGHT THAT WILL DECIDE THE CHAMPIONSHIP OF THE UNIVERSE... AND INCIDENTALLY, FOR THOSE OF YOU WHO ARE KEEPING SCORE, THE FATE OF A PLANET WE CALL EARTH!
HOLD ON, LAD-EEZ AND GENTLEMEN! THERE'S A COMMOTION GOING ON AT THE REAR OF THE STADIUM! WE'LL TRY TO GET A CAMERA OVER THERE FOR YOU...

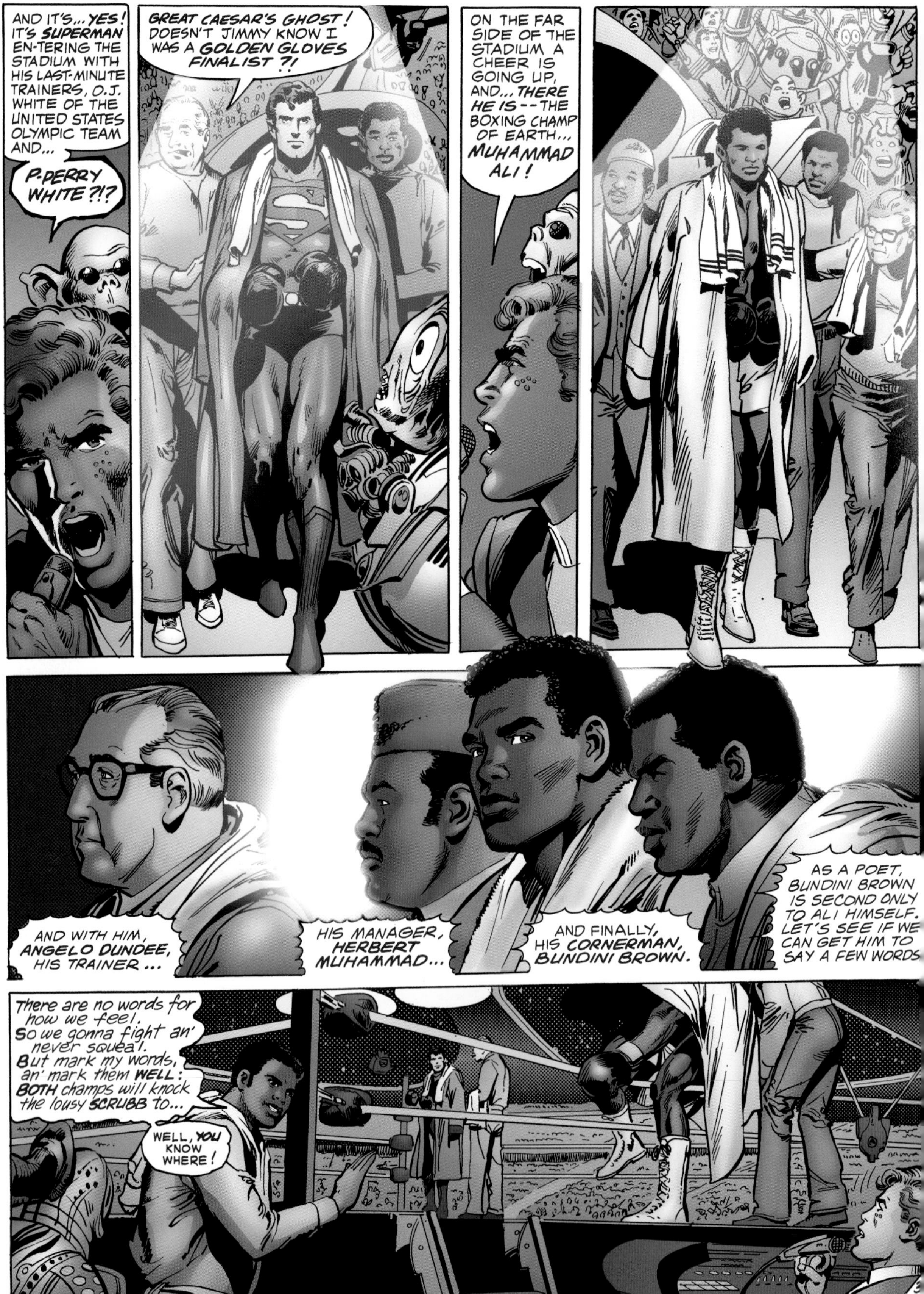
AND IT'S... YES! IT'S SUPERMAN EN-TERING THE STADIUM WITH HIS LAST-MINUTE TRAINERS, O.J. WHITE OF THE UNITED STATES OLYMPIC TEAM AND...
P. PERRY WHITE ?!?
GREAT CAESAR'S GHOST! DOESN'T JIMMY KNOW I WAS A GOLDEN GLOVES FINALIST ?!
ON THE FAR SIDE OF THE STADIUM A CHEER IS GOING UP, AND... THERE HE IS -- THE BOXING CHAMP OF EARTH... MUHAMMAD ALI!
AND WITH HIM, ANGELO DUNDEE, HIS TRAINER ...
HIS MANAGER, HERBERT MUHAMMAD...
AND FINALLY, HIS CORNERMAN, BUNDINI BROWN.
AS A POET, BUNDINI BROWN IS SECOND ONLY TO ALI HIMSELF. LET'S SEE IF WE CAN GET HIM TO SAY A FEW WORDS.
There are no words for how we feel. So we gonna fight an' never squeal. But mark my words, an' mark them WELL: BOTH champs will knock the lousy SCRUBB to...
WELL, YOU KNOW WHERE!

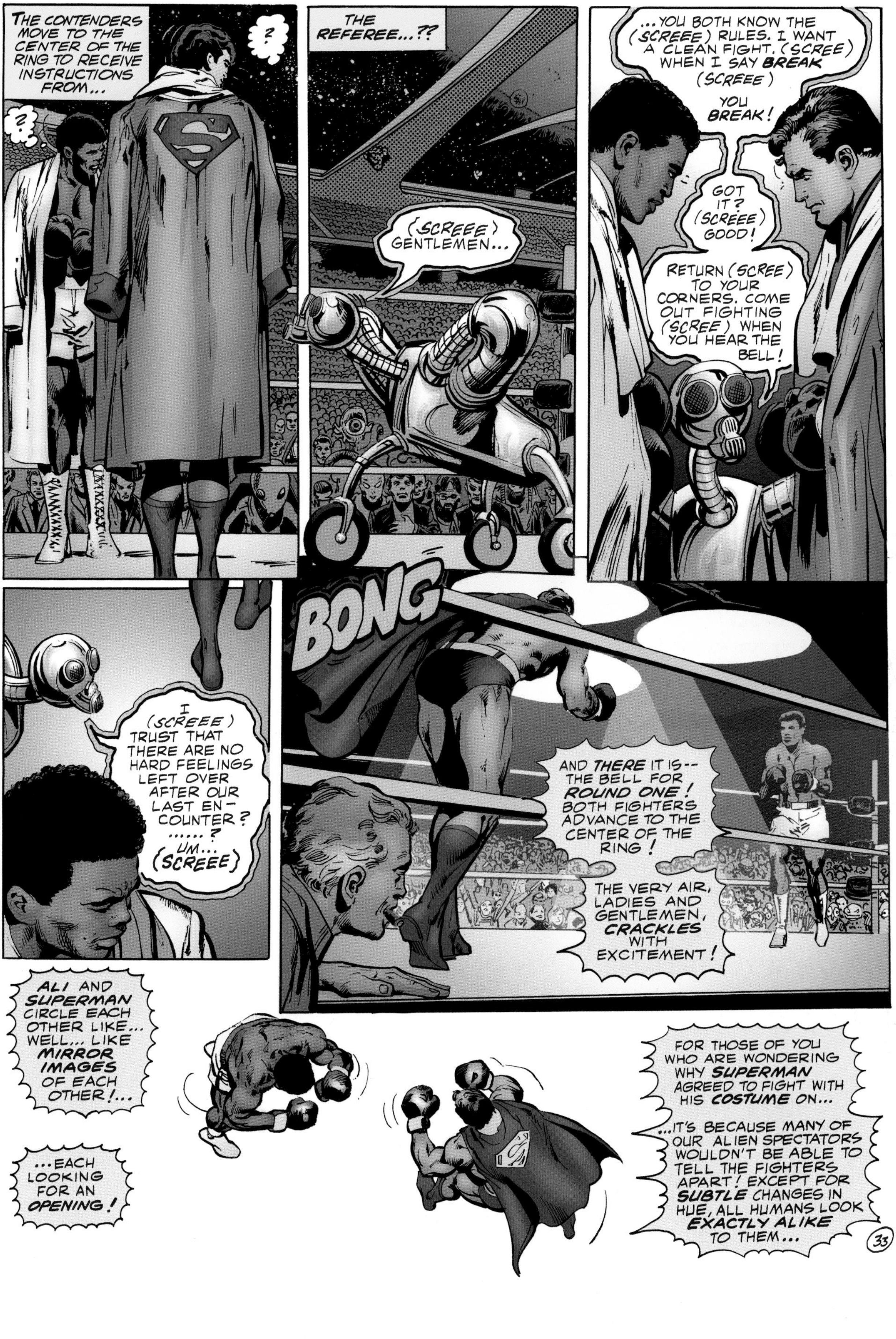
THE CONTENDERS MOVE TO THE CENTER OF THE RING TO RECEIVE INSTRUCTIONS FROM...
?
?
THE REFEREE...??
(SCREEE) GENTLEMEN...
...YOU BOTH KNOW THE (SCREEE) RULES. I WANT A CLEAN FIGHT. (SCREE) WHEN I SAY BREAK (SCREEE)
YOU BREAK!
GOT IT? (SCREEE) GOOD!
RETURN (SCREE) TO YOUR CORNERS. COME OUT FIGHTING (SCREE) WHEN YOU HEAR THE BELL!
I (SCREEE) TRUST THAT THERE ARE NO HARD FEELINGS LEFT OVER AFTER OUR LAST EN-COUNTER? ......? UM... (SCREEE)
BONG
AND THERE IT IS-- THE BELL FOR ROUND ONE! BOTH FIGHTERS ADVANCE TO THE CENTER OF THE RING!
THE VERY AIR, LADIES AND GENTLEMEN, CRACKLES WITH EXCITEMENT!
ALI AND SUPERMAN CIRCLE EACH OTHER LIKE... WELL... LIKE MIRROR IMAGES OF EACH OTHER!...
...EACH LOOKING FOR AN OPENING!
FOR THOSE OF YOU WHO ARE WONDERING WHY SUPERMAN AGREED TO FIGHT WITH HIS COSTUME ON...
...IT'S BECAUSE MANY OF OUR ALIEN SPECTATORS WOULDN'T BE ABLE TO TELL THE FIGHTERS APART! EXCEPT FOR SUBTLE CHANGES IN HUE, ALL HUMANS LOOK EXACTLY ALIKE TO THEM...

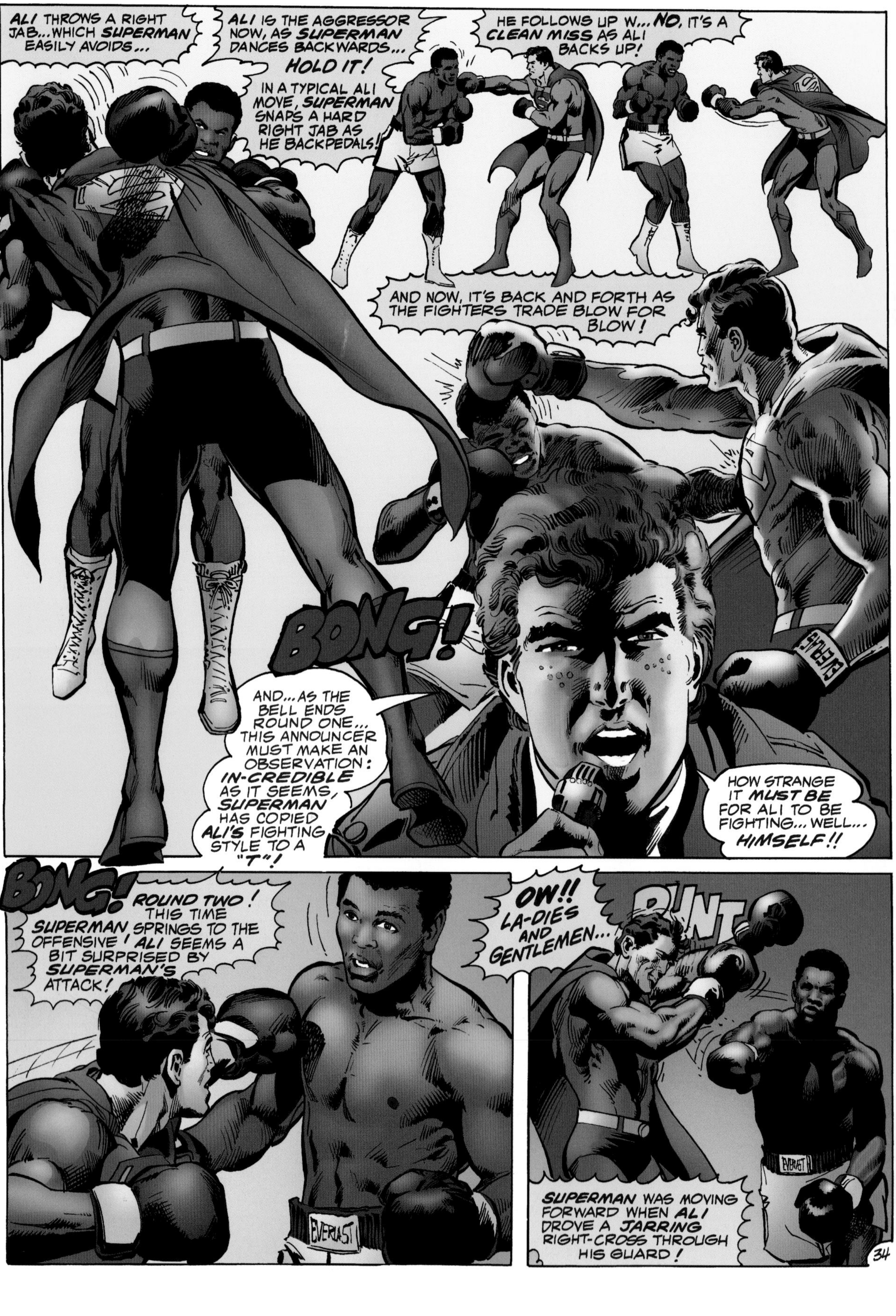

ALI THROWS A RIGHT JAB...WHICH SUPERMAN EASILY AVOIDS...
ALI IS THE AGGRESSOR NOW, AS SUPERMAN DANCES BACKWARDS... HOLD IT!
IN A TYPICAL ALI MOVE, SUPERMAN SNAPS A HARD RIGHT JAB AS HE BACKPEDALS!
HE FOLLOWS UP W... NO, IT'S A CLEAN MISS AS ALI BACKS UP!
AND NOW, IT'S BACK AND FORTH AS THE FIGHTERS TRADE BLOW FOR BLOW!
BONG!
AND... AS THE BELL ENDS ROUND ONE... THIS ANNOUNCER MUST MAKE AN OBSERVATION: IN-CREDIBLE AS IT SEEMS, SUPERMAN HAS COPIED ALI'S FIGHTING STYLE TO A "T"!
HOW STRANGE IT MUST BE FOR ALI TO BE FIGHTING... WELL... HIMSELF!!
BONG!
ROUND TWO! THIS TIME SUPERMAN SPRINGS TO THE OFFENSIVE! ALI SEEMS A BIT SURPRISED BY SUPERMAN'S ATTACK!
EVERLAST
OW!! LA-DIES AND GENTLEMEN...
EVERLAST
SUPERMAN WAS MOVING FORWARD WHEN ALI DROVE A JARRING RIGHT-CROSS THROUGH HIS GUARD!

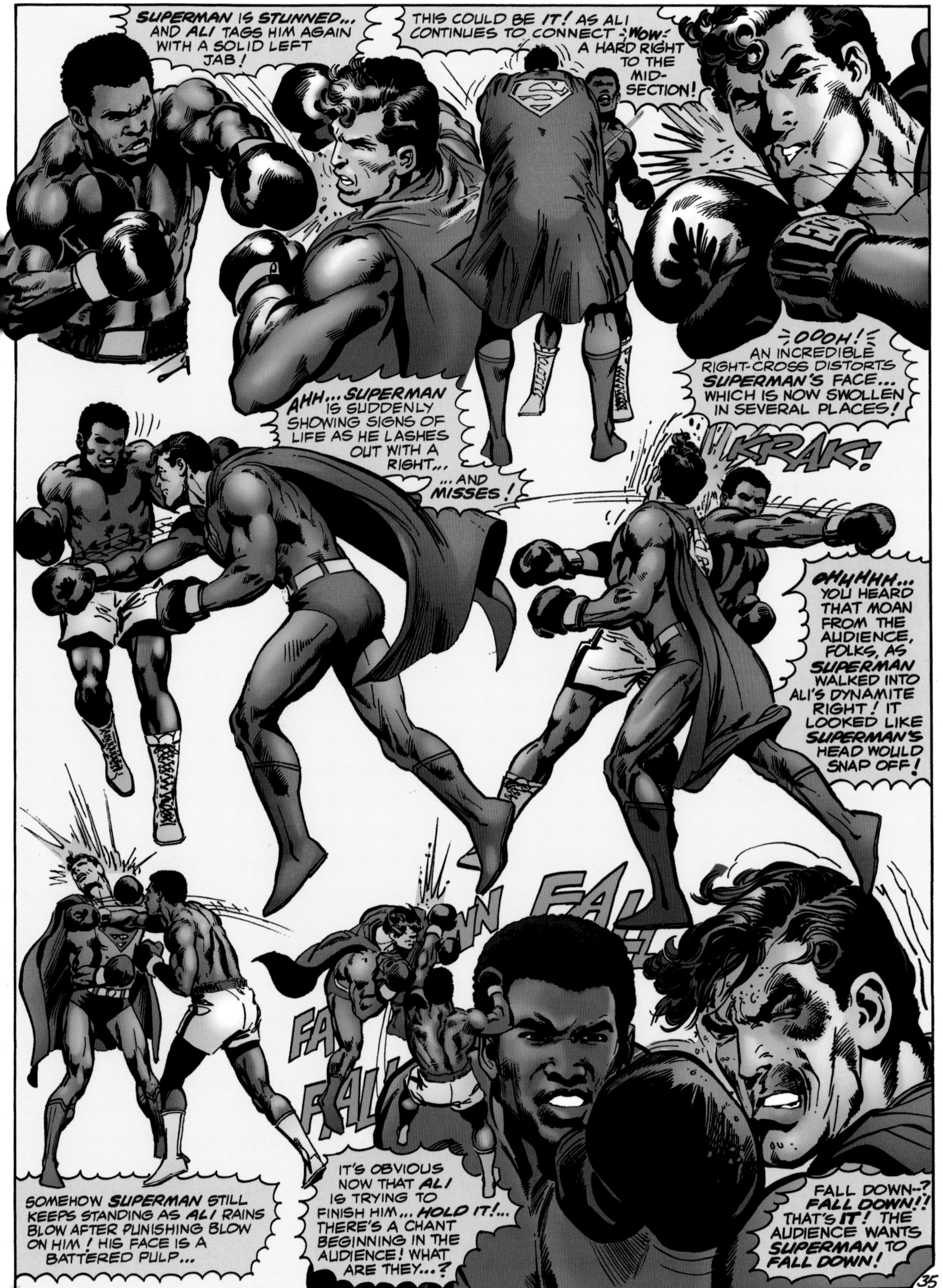
SUPERMAN IS STUNNED... AND ALI TAGS HIM AGAIN WITH A SOLID LEFT JAB!
THIS COULD BE IT! AS ALI CONTINUES TO CONNECT: WOW: A HARD RIGHT TO THE MID-SECTION!
OOOH! AN INCREDIBLE RIGHT-CROSS DISTORTS SUPERMAN'S FACE... WHICH IS NOW SWOLLEN IN SEVERAL PLACES!
AHH... SUPERMAN IS SUDDENLY SHOWING SIGNS OF LIFE AS HE LASHES OUT WITH A RIGHT... ...AND MISSES!
KRAK!
OHHHHH... YOU HEARD THAT MOAN FROM THE AUDIENCE, FOLKS, AS SUPERMAN WALKED INTO ALI'S DYNAMITE RIGHT! IT LOOKED LIKE SUPERMAN'S HEAD WOULD SNAP OFF!
SOMEHOW SUPERMAN STILL KEEPS STANDING AS ALI RAINS BLOW AFTER PUNISHING BLOW ON HIM! HIS FACE IS A BATTERED PULP...
IT'S OBVIOUS NOW THAT ALI IS TRYING TO FINISH HIM... HOLD IT!... THERE'S A CHANT BEGINNING IN THE AUDIENCE! WHAT ARE THEY...?
FALL DOWN..? FALL DOWN!! THAT'S IT! THE AUDIENCE WANTS SUPERMAN TO FALL DOWN!

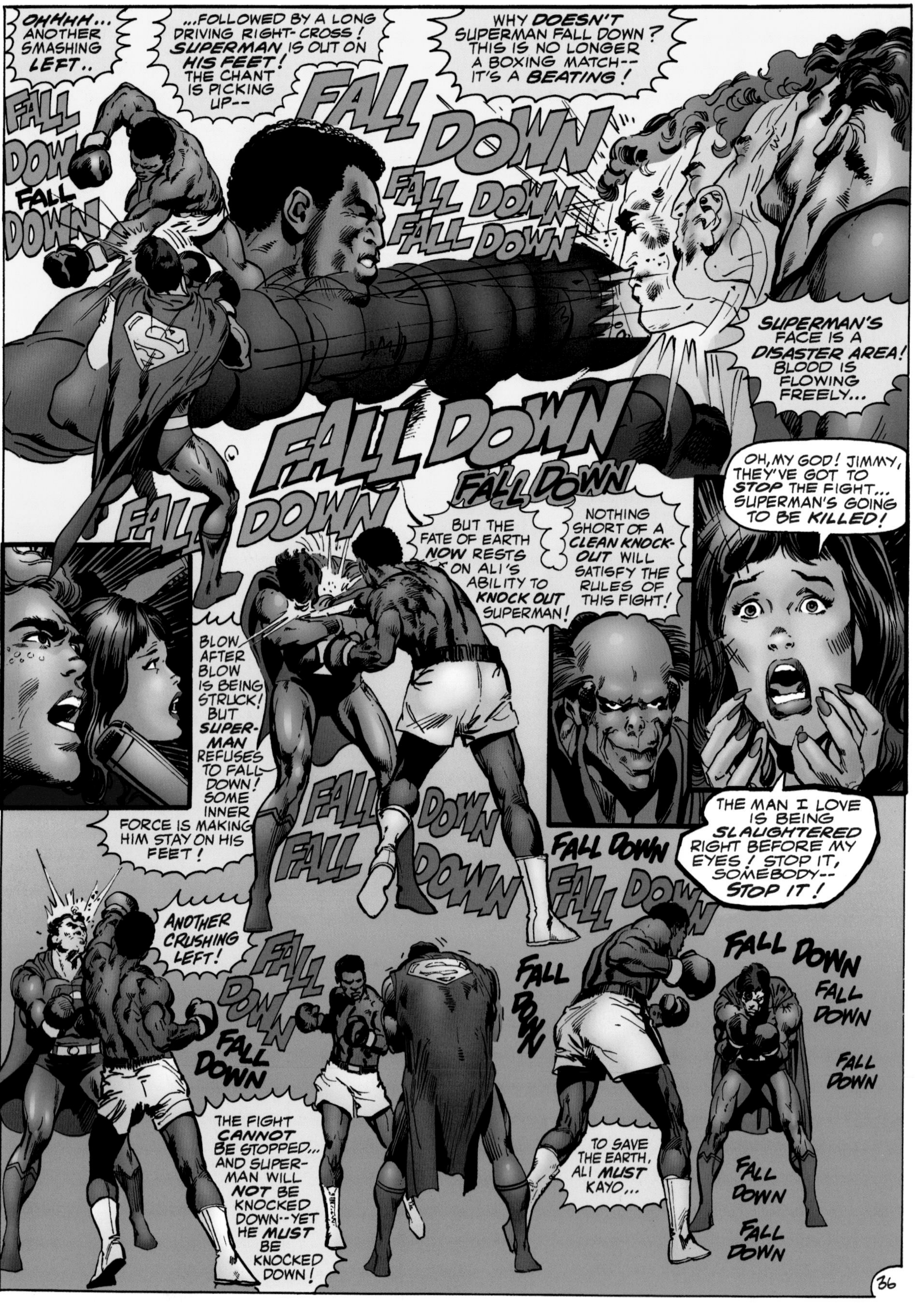
OHHHH... ANOTHER SMASHING LEFT..
...FOLLOWED BY A LONG DRIVING RIGHT-CROSS! SUPERMAN IS OUT ON HIS FEET! THE CHANT IS PICKING UP--
WHY DOESN'T SUPERMAN FALL DOWN? THIS IS NO LONGER A BOXING MATCH-- IT'S A BEATING!
FALL DOWN FALL DOWN
FALL DOWN FALL DOWN FALL DOWN
SUPERMAN'S FACE IS A DISASTER AREA! BLOOD IS FLOWING FREELY...
FALL DOWN FALL DOWN FALL DOWN
OH, MY GOD! JIMMY, THEY'VE GOT TO STOP THE FIGHT... SUPERMAN'S GOING TO BE KILLED!
BUT THE FATE OF EARTH NOW RESTS ON ALI'S ABILITY TO KNOCK OUT SUPERMAN!
NOTHING SHORT OF A CLEAN KNOCK-OUT WILL SATISFY THE RULES OF THIS FIGHT!
BLOW AFTER BLOW IS BEING STRUCK! BUT SUPERMAN REFUSES TO FALL DOWN! SOME INNER FORCE IS MAKING HIM STAY ON HIS FEET!
FALL DOWN FALL DOWN
THE MAN I LOVE IS BEING SLAUGHTERED RIGHT BEFORE MY EYES! STOP IT, SOMEBODY-- STOP IT!
FALL DOWN FALL DOWN
ANOTHER CRUSHING LEFT!
FALL DOWN FALL DOWN
FALL DOWN
FALL DOWN FALL DOWN FALL DOWN
THE FIGHT CANNOT BE STOPPED... AND SUPERMAN WILL NOT BE KNOCKED DOWN--YET HE MUST BE KNOCKED DOWN!
TO SAVE THE EARTH, ALI MUST KAYO...
FALL DOWN FALL DOWN

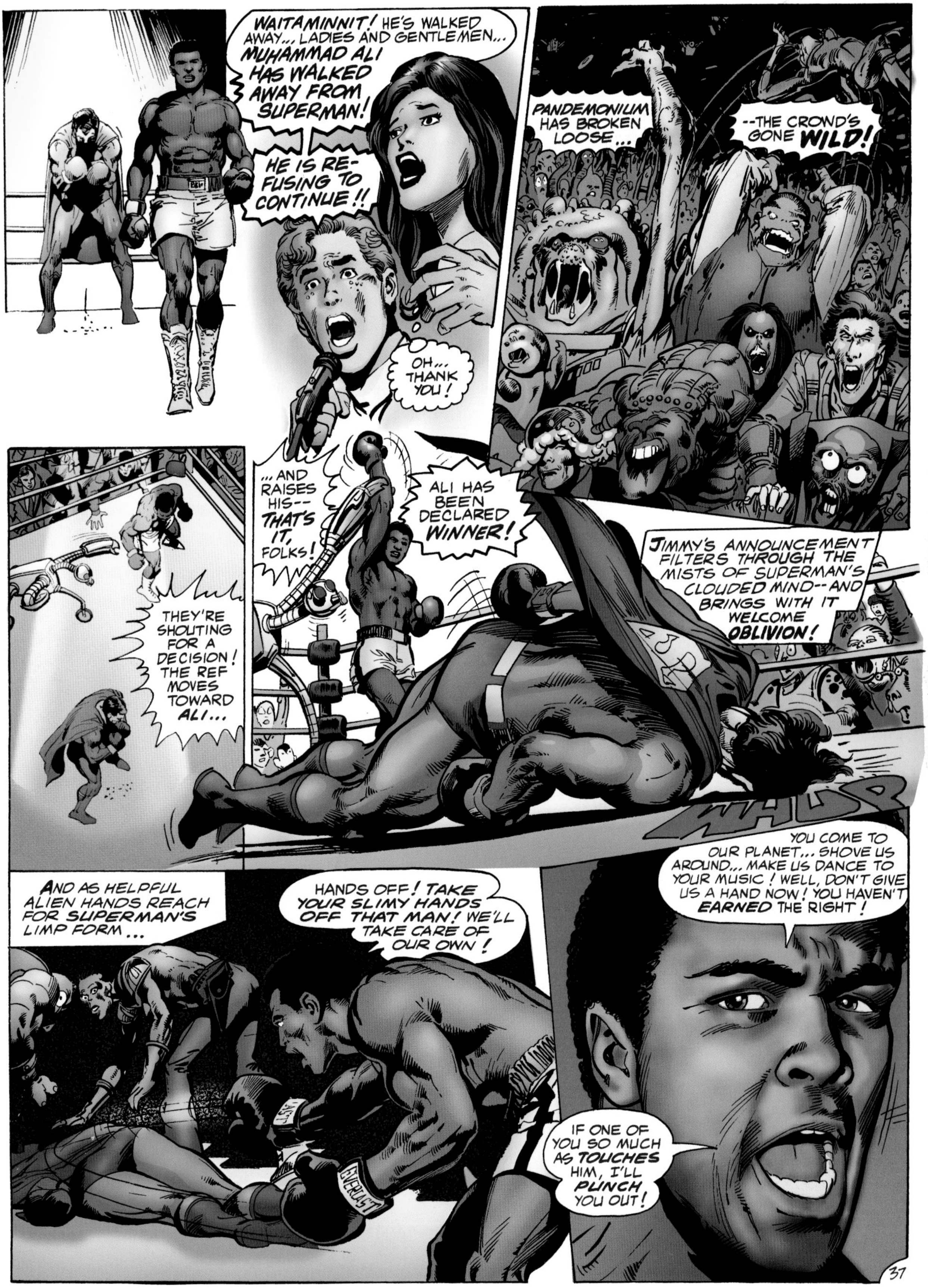

WAITAMINNIT! HE'S WALKED AWAY... LADIES AND GENTLEMEN... MUHAMMAD ALI HAS WALKED AWAY FROM SUPERMAN!
HE IS RE-FUSING TO CONTINUE!!
OH... THANK YOU!
PANDEMONIUM HAS BROKEN LOOSE...
--THE CROWD'S GONE WILD!
THEY'RE SHOUTING FOR A DECISION! THE REF MOVES TOWARD ALI...
...AND RAISES HIS-- THAT'S IT, FOLKS!
ALI HAS BEEN DECLARED WINNER!
JIMMY'S ANNOUNCEMENT FILTERS THROUGH THE MISTS OF SUPERMAN'S CLOUDED MIND--AND BRINGS WITH IT WELCOME OBLIVION!
WHUD
AND AS HELPFUL ALIEN HANDS REACH FOR SUPERMAN'S LIMP FORM...
HANDS OFF! TAKE YOUR SLIMY HANDS OFF THAT MAN! WE'LL TAKE CARE OF OUR OWN!
YOU COME TO OUR PLANET... SHOVE US AROUND... MAKE US DANCE TO YOUR MUSIC! WELL, DON'T GIVE US A HAND NOW! YOU HAVEN'T EARNED THE RIGHT!
IF ONE OF YOU SO MUCH AS TOUCHES HIM, I'LL PUNCH YOU OUT!

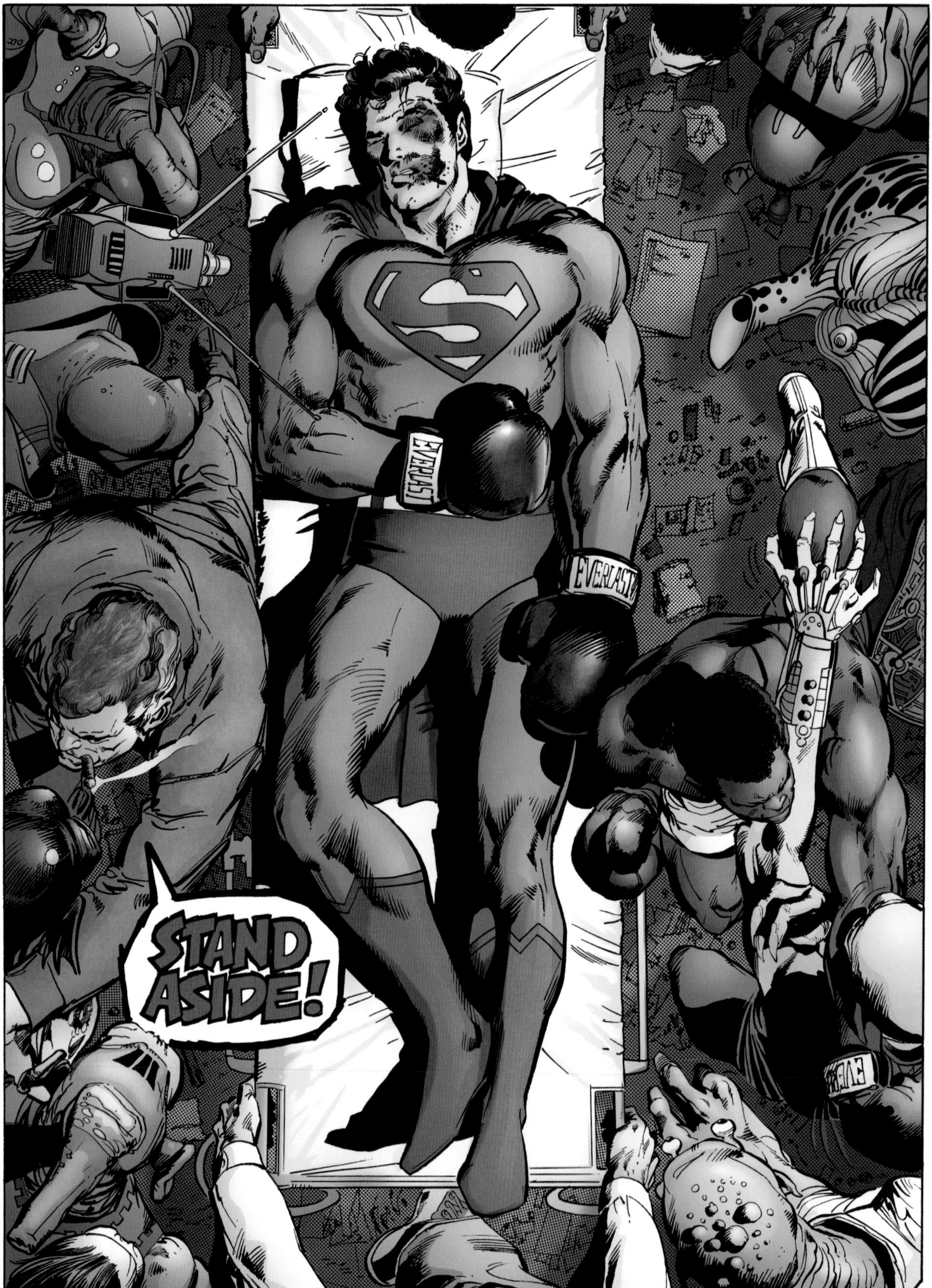
STAND ASIDE!

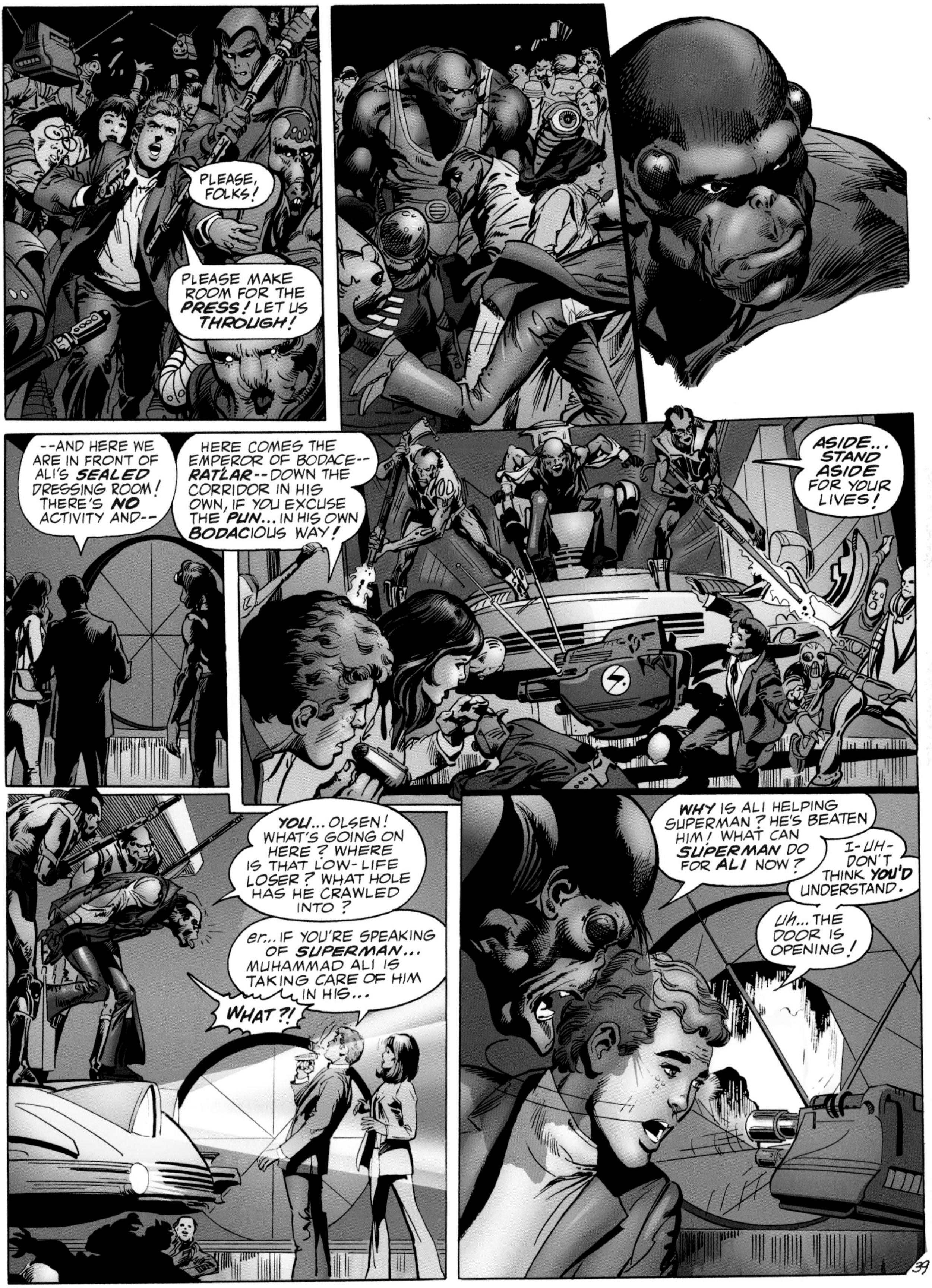
PLEASE, FOLKS!
PLEASE MAKE ROOM FOR THE PRESS! LET US THROUGH!
--AND HERE WE ARE IN FRONT OF ALI'S SEALED DRESSING ROOM! THERE'S NO ACTIVITY AND--
HERE COMES THE EMPEROR OF BODACE-- RATLAR--DOWN THE CORRIDOR IN HIS OWN, IF YOU EXCUSE THE PUN... IN HIS OWN BODACIOUS WAY!
ASIDE... STAND ASIDE FOR YOUR LIVES!
YOU... OLSEN! WHAT'S GOING ON HERE? WHERE IS THAT LOW-LIFE LOSER? WHAT HOLE HAS HE CRAWLED INTO?
er... IF YOU'RE SPEAKING OF SUPERMAN... MUHAMMAD ALI IS TAKING CARE OF HIM IN HIS...
WHAT?!
WHY IS ALI HELPING SUPERMAN? HE'S BEATEN HIM! WHAT CAN SUPERMAN DO FOR ALI NOW?
I-UH- DON'T THINK YOU'D UNDERSTAND.
Uh... THE DOOR IS OPENING!

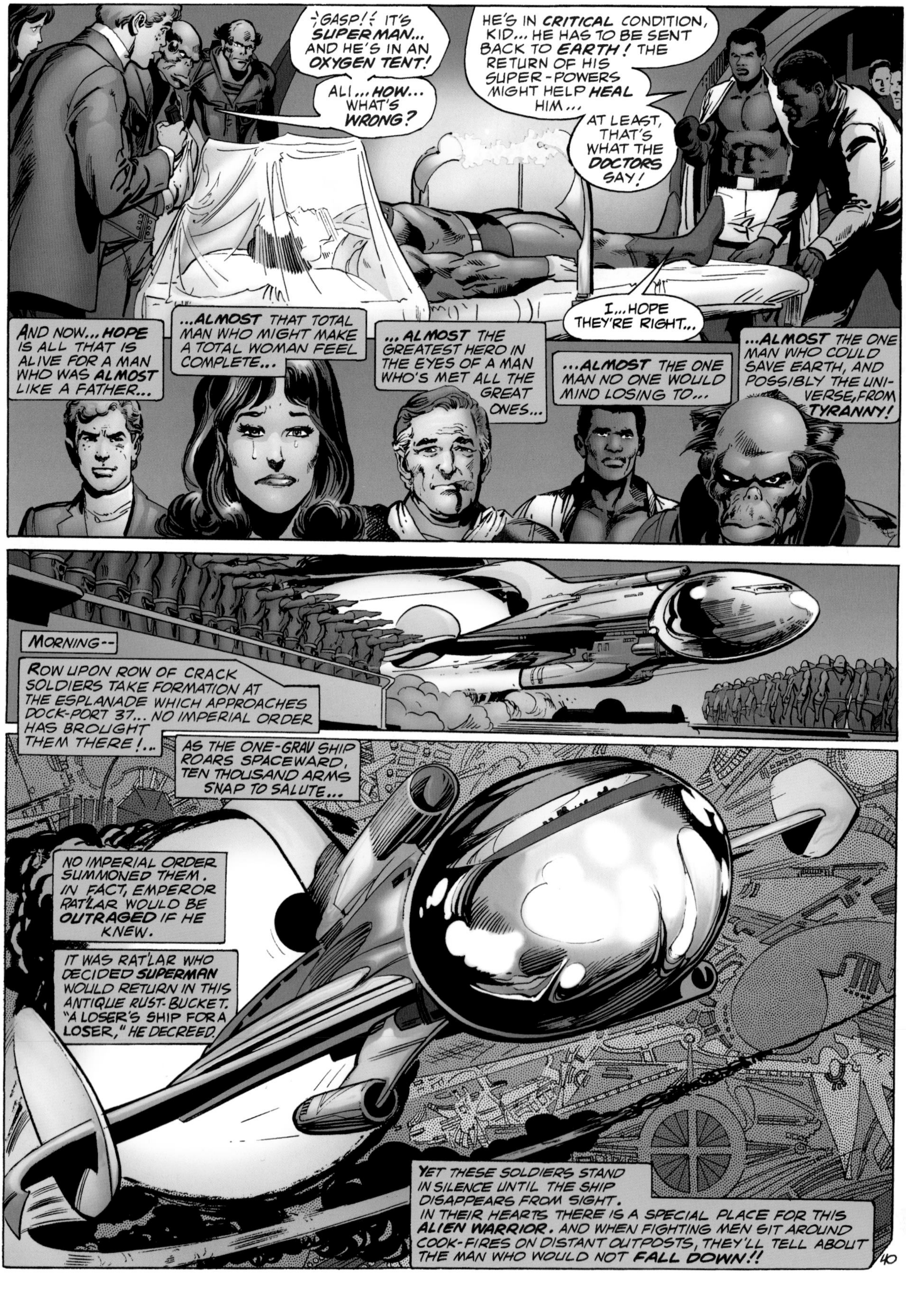
GASP! IT'S SUPERMAN... AND HE'S IN AN OXYGEN TENT!
ALI... HOW... WHAT'S WRONG?
HE'S IN CRITICAL CONDITION, KID... HE HAS TO BE SENT BACK TO EARTH! THE RETURN OF HIS SUPER-POWERS MIGHT HELP HEAL HIM...
AT LEAST, THAT'S WHAT THE DOCTORS SAY!
I... HOPE THEY'RE RIGHT...
AND NOW... HOPE IS ALL THAT IS ALIVE FOR A MAN WHO WAS ALMOST LIKE A FATHER...
...ALMOST THAT TOTAL MAN WHO MIGHT MAKE A TOTAL WOMAN FEEL COMPLETE...
...ALMOST THE GREATEST HERO IN THE EYES OF A MAN WHO'S MET ALL THE GREAT ONES...
...ALMOST THE ONE MAN NO ONE WOULD MIND LOSING TO...
...ALMOST THE ONE MAN WHO COULD SAVE EARTH, AND POSSIBLY THE UNIVERSE, FROM TYRANNY!
MORNING--
ROW UPON ROW OF CRACK SOLDIERS TAKE FORMATION AT THE ESPLANADE WHICH APPROACHES DOCK-PORT 37... NO IMPERIAL ORDER HAS BROUGHT THEM THERE!..
AS THE ONE-GRAV SHIP ROARS SPACEWARD, TEN THOUSAND ARMS SNAP TO SALUTE...
NO IMPERIAL ORDER SUMMONED THEM. IN FACT, EMPEROR RAT'LAR WOULD BE OUTRAGED IF HE KNEW.
IT WAS RAT'LAR WHO DECIDED SUPERMAN WOULD RETURN IN THIS ANTIQUE RUST-BUCKET. "A LOSER'S SHIP FOR A LOSER," HE DECREED.
YET THESE SOLDIERS STAND IN SILENCE UNTIL THE SHIP DISAPPEARS FROM SIGHT. IN THEIR HEARTS THERE IS A SPECIAL PLACE FOR THIS ALIEN WARRIOR. AND WHEN FIGHTING MEN SIT AROUND COOK-FIRES ON DISTANT OUTPOSTS, THEY'LL TELL ABOUT THE MAN WHO WOULD NOT FALL DOWN!!

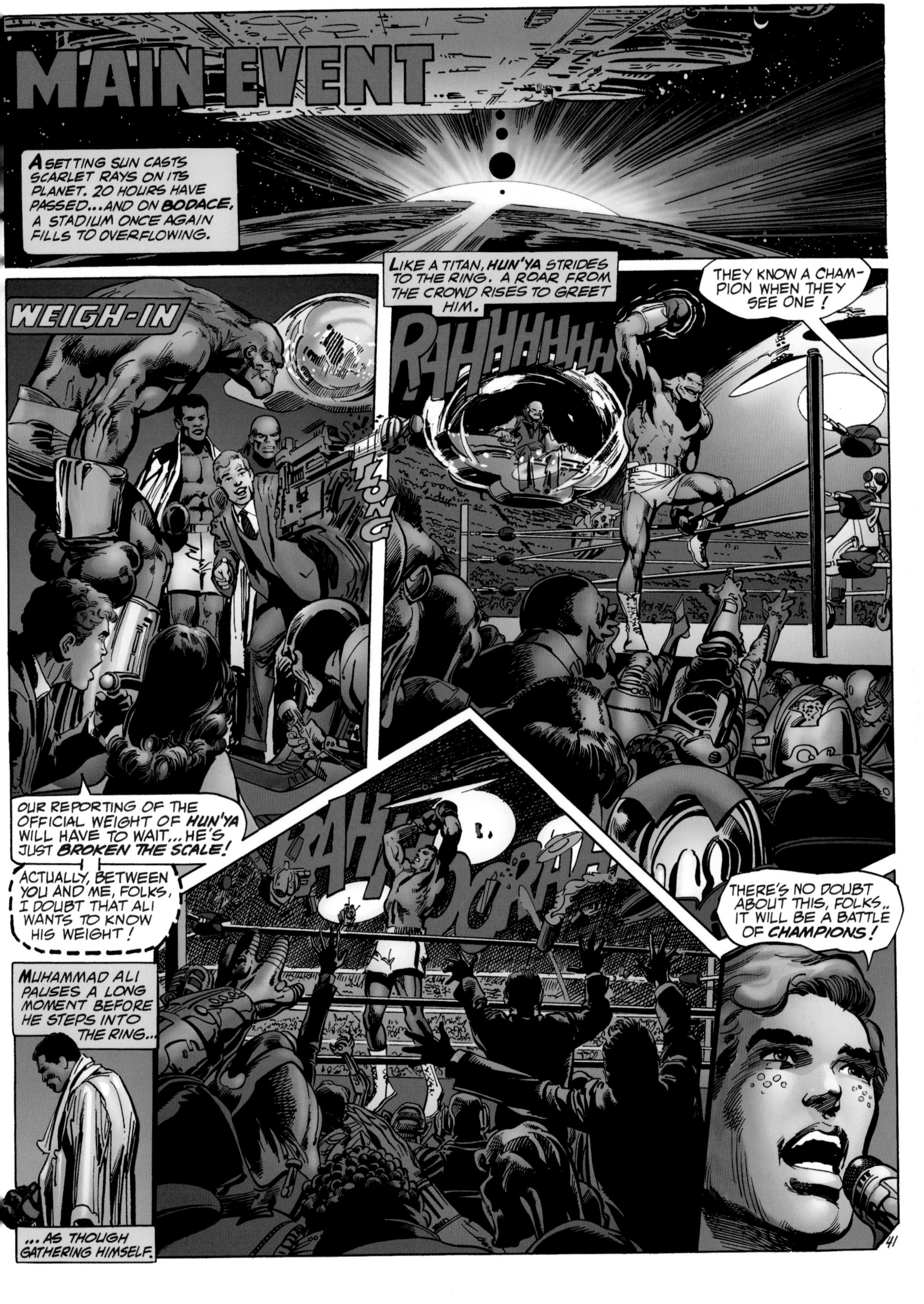
MAIN EVENT
A SETTING SUN CASTS SCARLET RAYS ON ITS PLANET. 20 HOURS HAVE PASSED...AND ON BODACE, A STADIUM ONCE AGAIN FILLS TO OVERFLOWING.
WEIGH-IN
TONG
OUR REPORTING OF THE OFFICIAL WEIGHT OF HUN'YA WILL HAVE TO WAIT... HE'S JUST BROKEN THE SCALE!
ACTUALLY, BETWEEN YOU AND ME, FOLKS, I DOUBT THAT ALI WANTS TO KNOW HIS WEIGHT!
LIKE A TITAN, HUN'YA STRIDES TO THE RING. A ROAR FROM THE CROWD RISES TO GREET HIM.
RAHHHHHH
THEY KNOW A CHAMPION WHEN THEY SEE ONE!
MUHAMMAD ALI PAUSES A LONG MOMENT BEFORE HE STEPS INTO THE RING...
...AS THOUGH GATHERING HIMSELF.
THERE'S NO DOUBT ABOUT THIS, FOLKS.. IT WILL BE A BATTLE OF CHAMPIONS!

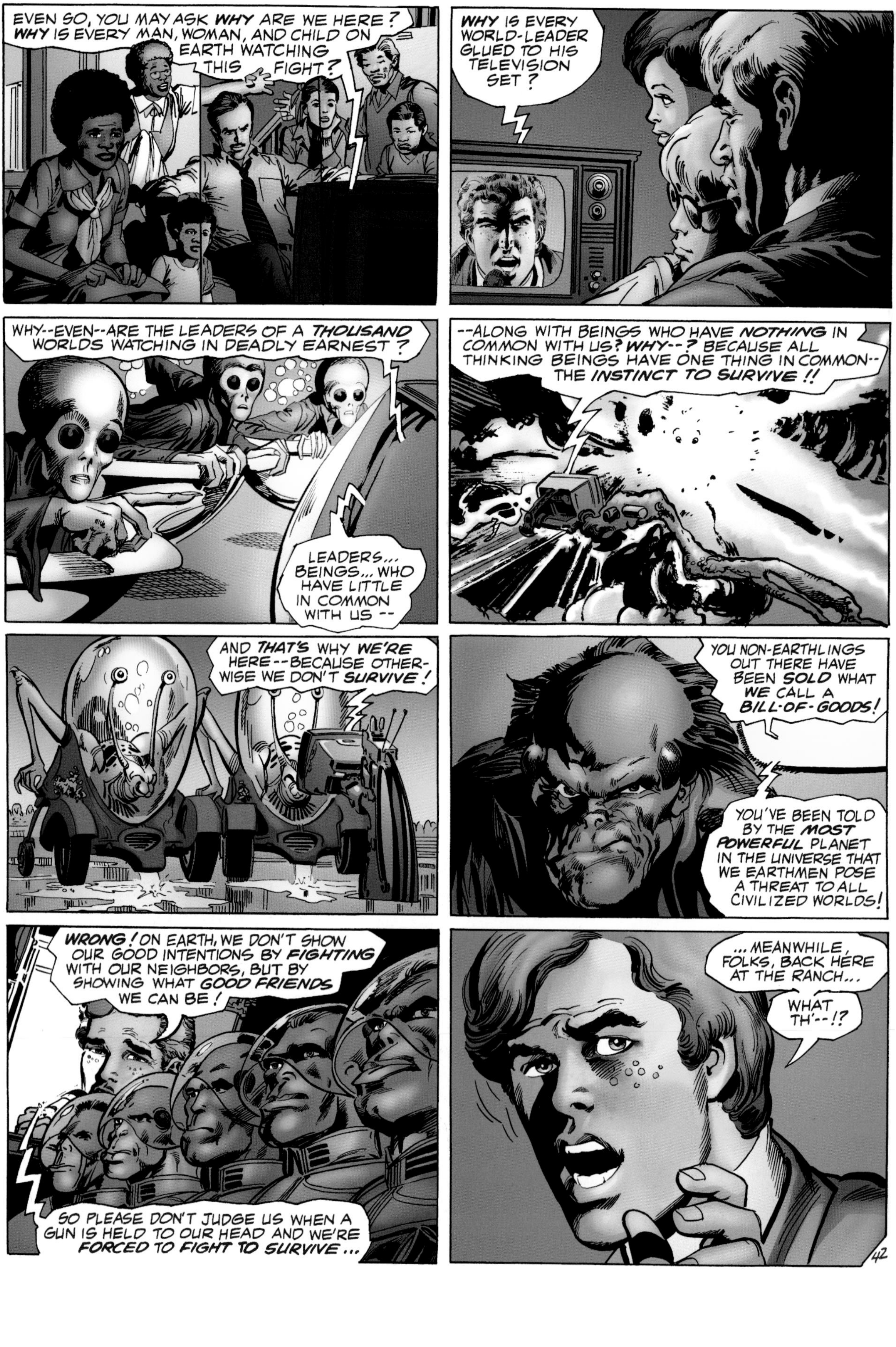
EVEN SO, YOU MAY ASK WHY ARE WE HERE? WHY IS EVERY MAN, WOMAN, AND CHILD ON EARTH WATCHING THIS FIGHT?
WHY IS EVERY WORLD-LEADER GLUED TO HIS TELEVISION SET?
WHY--EVEN--ARE THE LEADERS OF A THOUSAND WORLDS WATCHING IN DEADLY EARNEST?
LEADERS... BEINGS... WHO HAVE LITTLE IN COMMON WITH US--
--ALONG WITH BEINGS WHO HAVE NOTHING IN COMMON WITH US? WHY--? BECAUSE ALL THINKING BEINGS HAVE ONE THING IN COMMON-- THE INSTINCT TO SURVIVE!!
AND THAT'S WHY WE'RE HERE--BECAUSE OTHERWISE WE DON'T SURVIVE!
YOU NON-EARTHLINGS OUT THERE HAVE BEEN SOLD WHAT WE CALL A BILL-OF-GOODS!
YOU'VE BEEN TOLD BY THE MOST POWERFUL PLANET IN THE UNIVERSE THAT WE EARTHMEN POSE A THREAT TO ALL CIVILIZED WORLDS!
WRONG! ON EARTH, WE DON'T SHOW OUR GOOD INTENTIONS BY FIGHTING WITH OUR NEIGHBORS, BUT BY SHOWING WHAT GOOD FRIENDS WE CAN BE!
SO PLEASE DON'T JUDGE US WHEN A GUN IS HELD TO OUR HEAD AND WE'RE FORCED TO FIGHT TO SURVIVE...
...MEANWHILE, FOLKS, BACK HERE AT THE RANCH...
WHAT TH'--!?
42

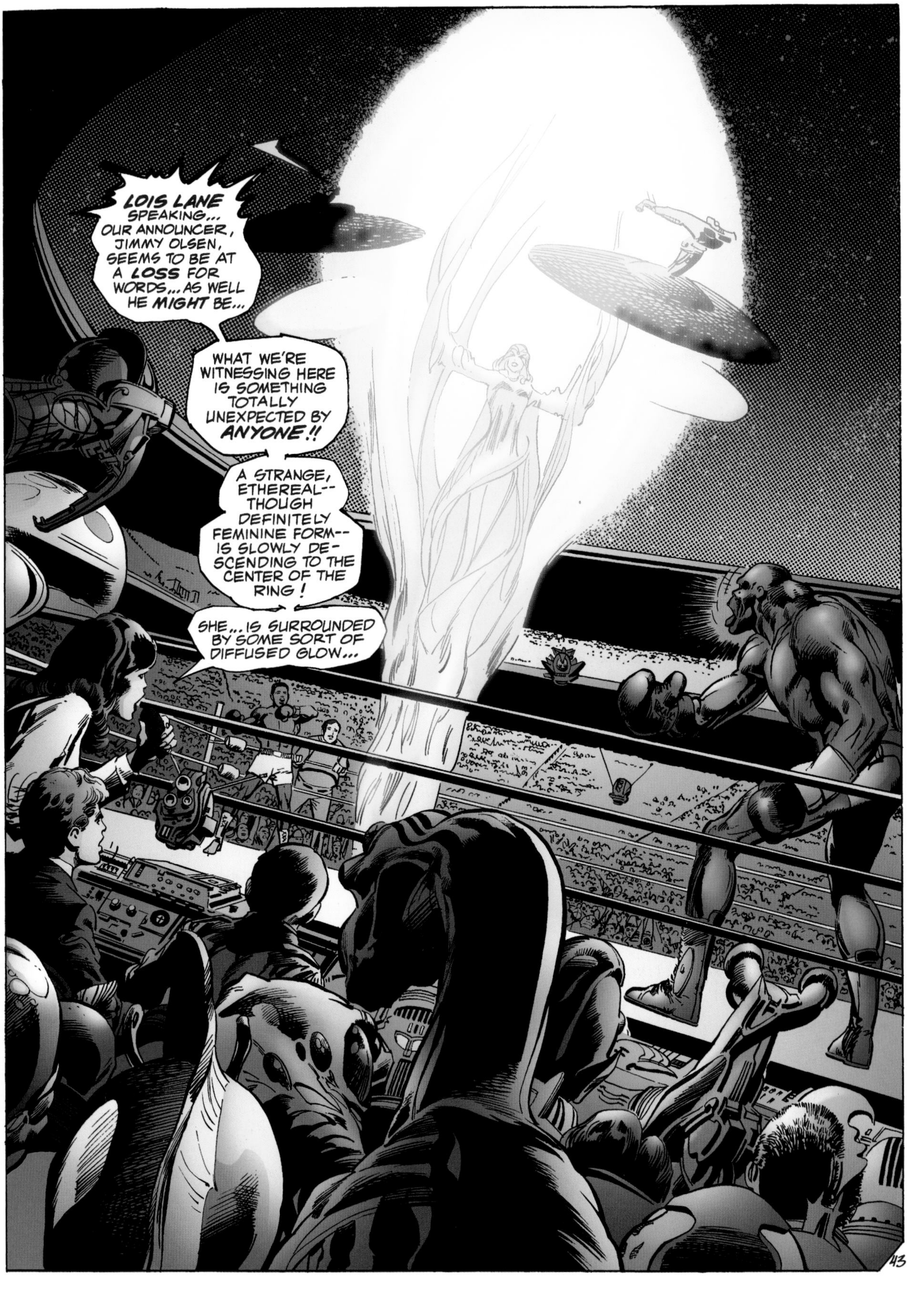
LOIS LANE SPEAKING... OUR ANNOUNCER, JIMMY OLSEN, SEEMS TO BE AT A LOSS FOR WORDS... AS WELL HE MIGHT BE...
WHAT WE'RE WITNESSING HERE IS SOMETHING TOTALLY UNEXPECTED BY ANYONE!!
A STRANGE, ETHEREAL-- THOUGH DEFINITELY FEMININE FORM-- IS SLOWLY DE-SCENDING TO THE CENTER OF THE RING!
SHE... IS SURROUNDED BY SOME SORT OF DIFFUSED GLOW...

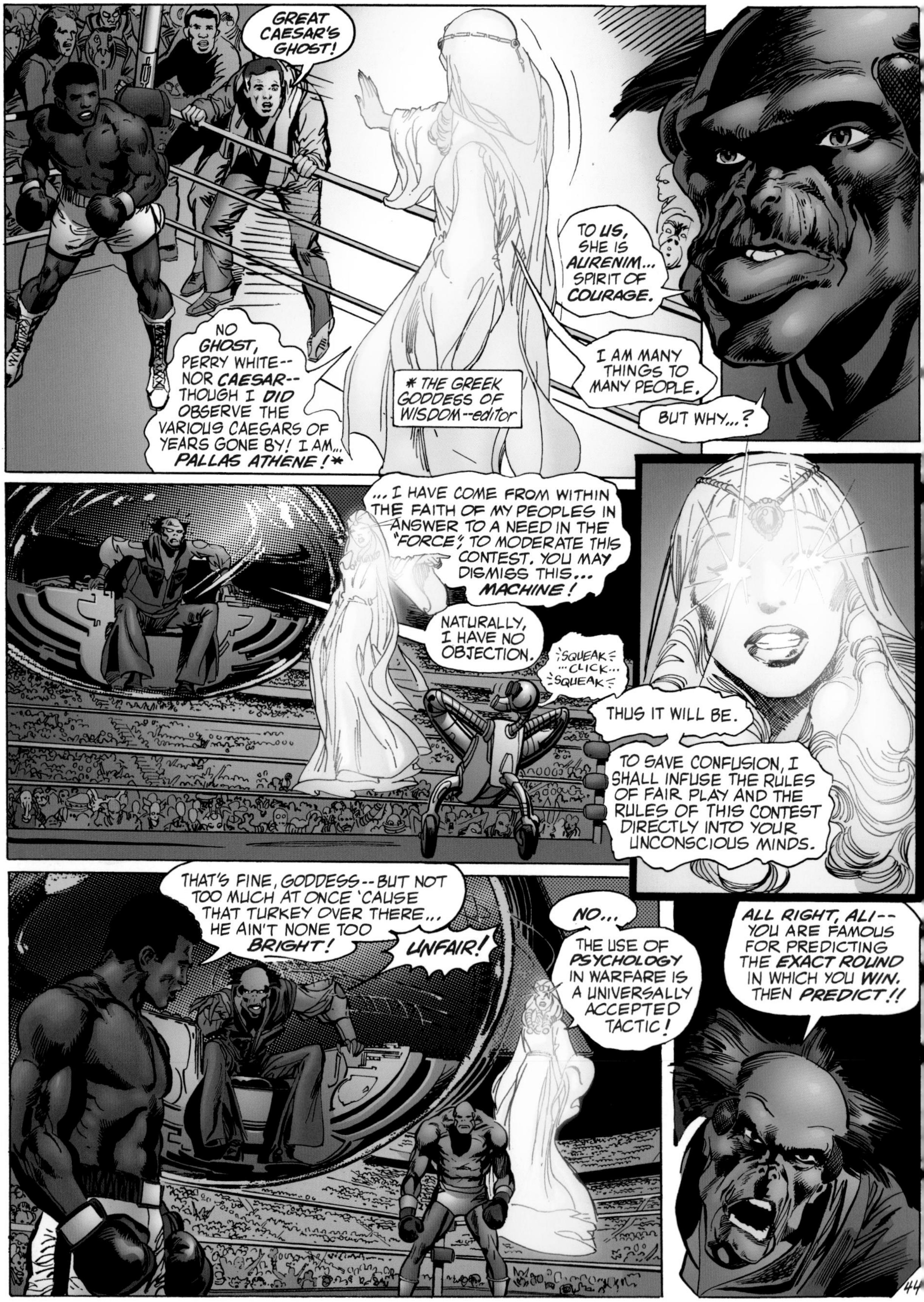

GREAT CAESAR'S GHOST!
NO GHOST, PERRY WHITE-- NOR CAESAR-- THOUGH I DID OBSERVE THE VARIOUS CAESARS OF YEARS GONE BY! I AM... PALLAS ATHENE!*
* THE GREEK GODDESS OF WISDOM--editor
TO US, SHE IS AURENIM... SPIRIT OF COURAGE.
I AM MANY THINGS TO MANY PEOPLE.
BUT WHY...?
... I HAVE COME FROM WITHIN THE FAITH OF MY PEOPLES IN ANSWER TO A NEED IN THE "FORCE" TO MODERATE THIS CONTEST. YOU MAY DISMISS THIS... MACHINE!
NATURALLY, I HAVE NO OBJECTION.
SQUEAK ...CLICK... SQUEAK
THUS IT WILL BE.
TO SAVE CONFUSION, I SHALL INFUSE THE RULES OF FAIR PLAY AND THE RULES OF THIS CONTEST DIRECTLY INTO YOUR UNCONSCIOUS MINDS.
THAT'S FINE, GODDESS-- BUT NOT TOO MUCH AT ONCE 'CAUSE THAT TURKEY OVER THERE... HE AIN'T NONE TOO BRIGHT!
UNFAIR!
NO...
THE USE OF PSYCHOLOGY IN WARFARE IS A UNIVERSALLY ACCEPTED TACTIC!
ALL RIGHT, ALI-- YOU ARE FAMOUS FOR PREDICTING THE EXACT ROUND IN WHICH YOU WIN. THEN PREDICT!!

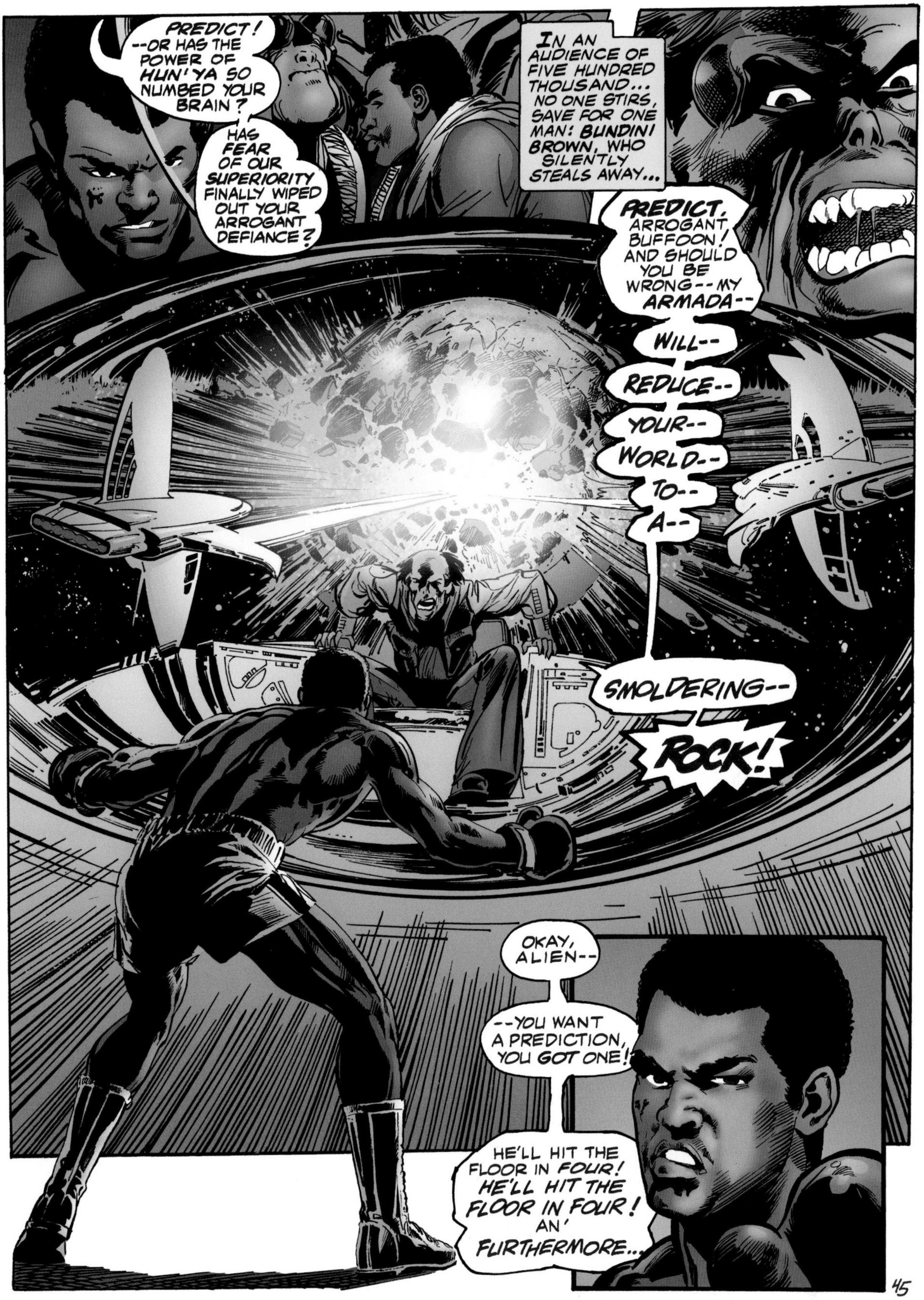
PREDICT! --OR HAS THE POWER OF HUN'YA SO NUMBED YOUR BRAIN?
HAS FEAR OF OUR SUPERIORITY FINALLY WIPED OUT YOUR ARROGANT DEFIANCE?
IN AN AUDIENCE OF FIVE HUNDRED THOUSAND... NO ONE STIRS, SAVE FOR ONE MAN: BUNDINI BROWN, WHO SILENTLY STEALS AWAY...
PREDICT, ARROGANT BUFFOON! AND SHOULD YOU BE WRONG--MY ARMADA--
WILL--
REDUCE--
YOUR--
WORLD--
TO--
A--
SMOLDERING--
ROCK!
OKAY, ALIEN--
--YOU WANT A PREDICTION, YOU GOT ONE!
HE'LL HIT THE FLOOR IN FOUR! HE'LL HIT THE FLOOR IN FOUR! AN' FURTHERMORE...

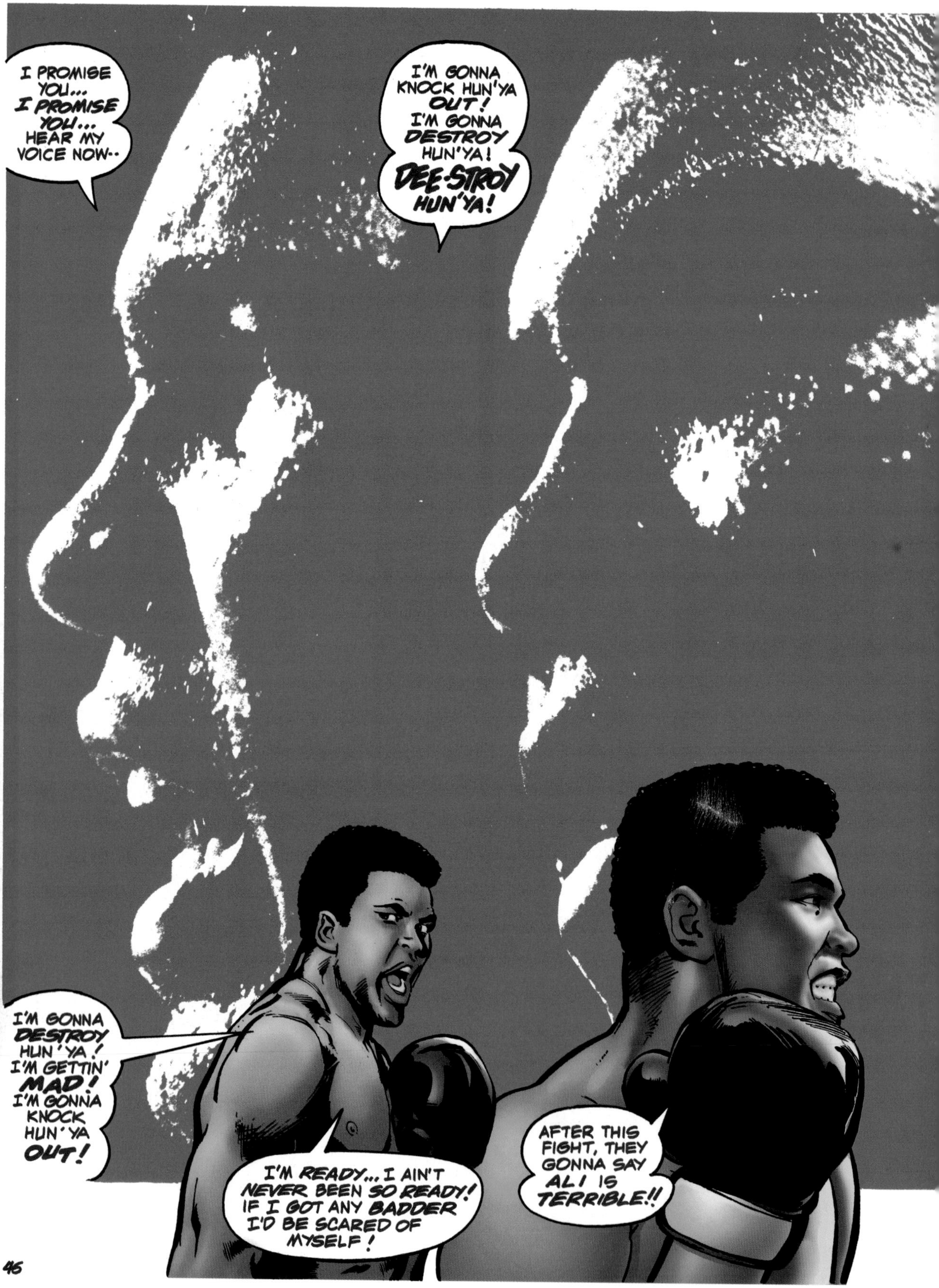
I PROMISE YOU... I PROMISE YOU... HEAR MY VOICE NOW..
I'M GONNA KNOCK HUN'YA OUT! I'M GONNA DESTROY HUN'YA! DEE-STROY HUN'YA!
I'M GONNA DESTROY HUN'YA! I'M GETTIN' MAD! I'M GONNA KNOCK HUN'YA OUT!
I'M READY... I AIN'T NEVER BEEN SO READY! IF I GOT ANY BADDER I'D BE SCARED OF MYSELF!
AFTER THIS FIGHT, THEY GONNA SAY ALI IS TERRIBLE!!

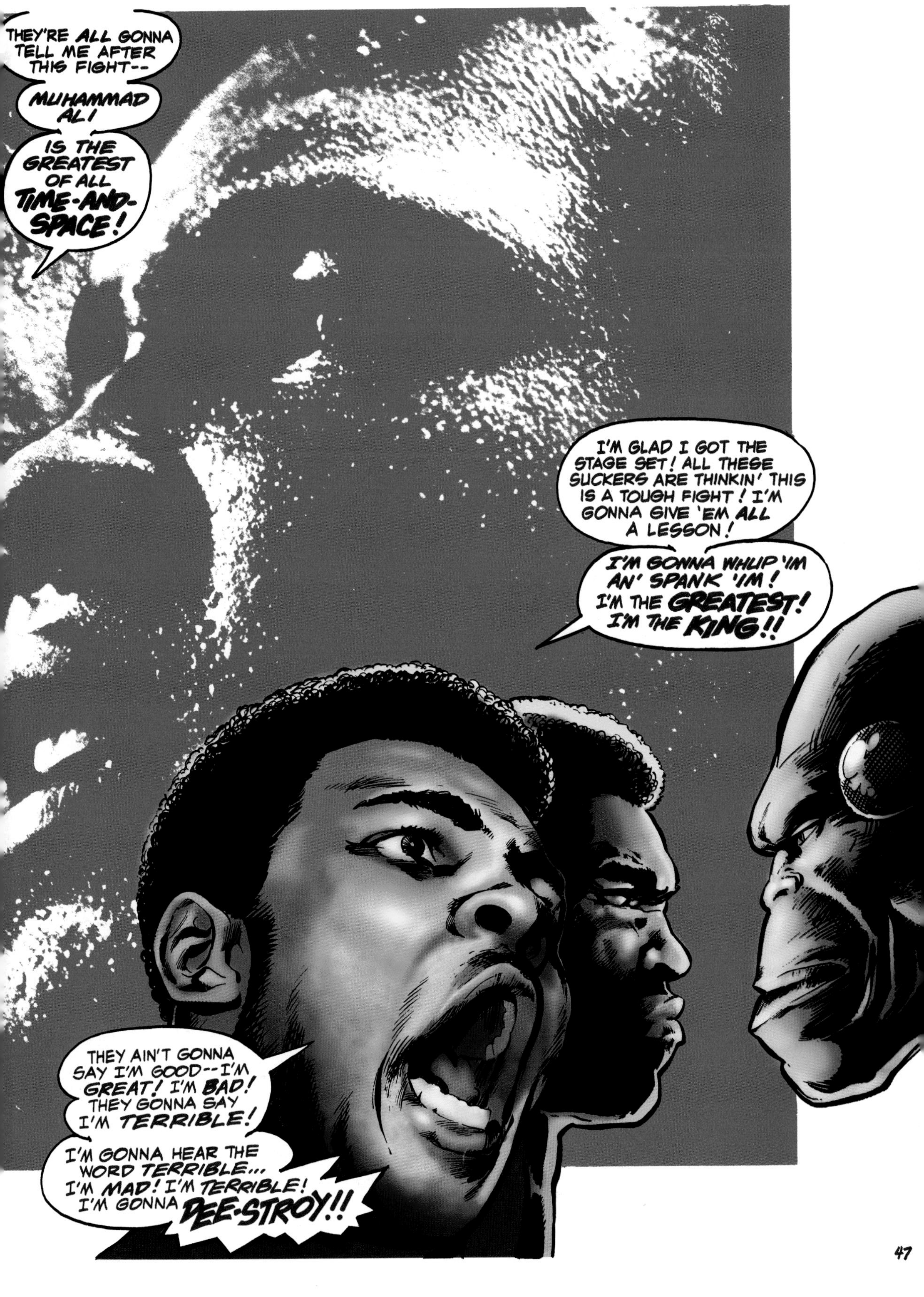
THEY'RE ALL GONNA TELL ME AFTER THIS FIGHT--
MUHAMMAD ALI
IS THE GREATEST OF ALL TIME-AND-SPACE!
I'M GLAD I GOT THE STAGE SET! ALL THESE SUCKERS ARE THINKIN' THIS IS A TOUGH FIGHT! I'M GONNA GIVE 'EM ALL A LESSON!
I'M GONNA WHUP 'IM AN' SPANK 'IM! I'M THE GREATEST! I'M THE KING!!
THEY AIN'T GONNA SAY I'M GOOD--I'M GREAT! I'M BAD! THEY GONNA SAY I'M TERRIBLE!
I'M GONNA HEAR THE WORD TERRIBLE... I'M MAD! I'M TERRIBLE! I'M GONNA DEE-STROY!!

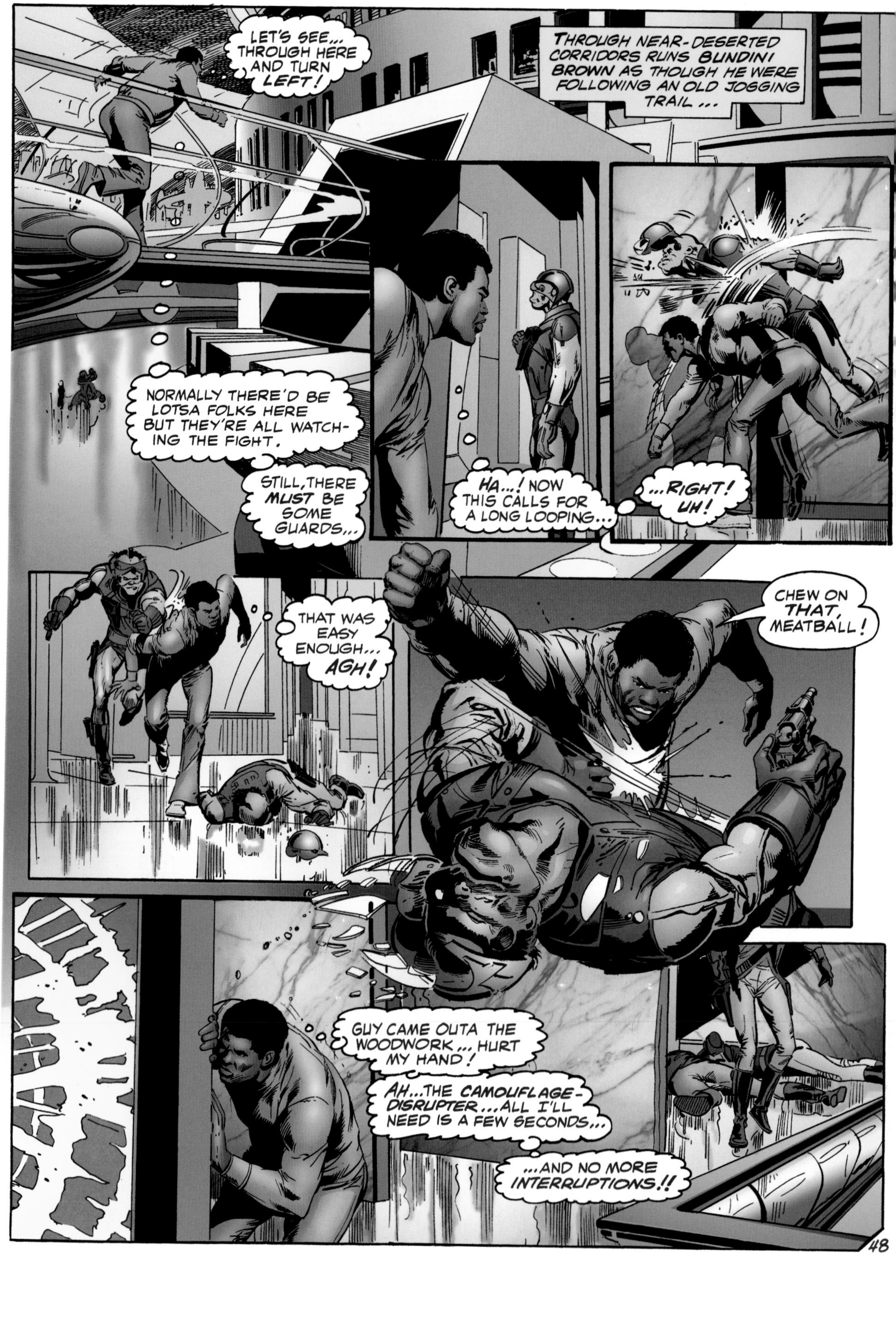
LET'S SEE... THROUGH HERE AND TURN LEFT!
THROUGH NEAR-DESERTED CORRIDORS RUNS BUNDINI BROWN AS THOUGH HE WERE FOLLOWING AN OLD JOGGING TRAIL...
NORMALLY THERE'D BE LOTSA FOLKS HERE BUT THEY'RE ALL WATCHING THE FIGHT.
STILL, THERE MUST BE SOME GUARDS...
HA...! NOW THIS CALLS FOR A LONG LOOPING...
...RIGHT! UH!
THAT WAS EASY ENOUGH... AGH!
CHEW ON THAT, MEATBALL!
GUY CAME OUTA THE WOODWORK... HURT MY HAND!
AH... THE CAMOUFLAGE-DISRUPTER... ALL I'LL NEED IS A FEW SECONDS...
...AND NO MORE INTERRUPTIONS!!

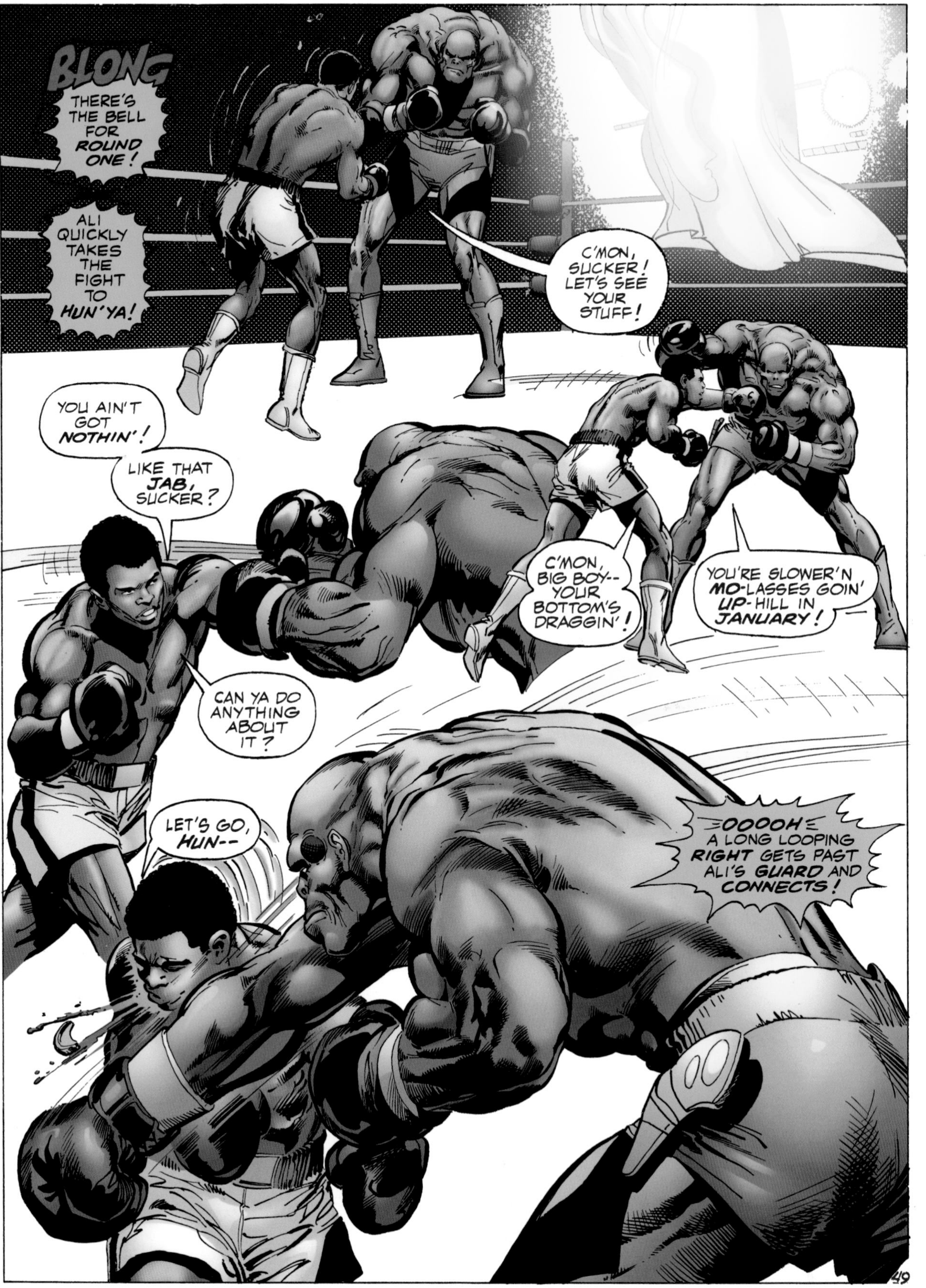
BLONG
THERE'S THE BELL FOR ROUND ONE!
ALI QUICKLY TAKES THE FIGHT TO HUN'YA!
C'MON, SUCKER! LET'S SEE YOUR STUFF!
C'MON, BIG BOY-- YOUR BOTTOM'S DRAGGIN'!
YOU'RE SLOWER'N MO-LASSES GOIN' UP-HILL IN JANUARY!
YOU AIN'T GOT NOTHIN'!
LIKE THAT JAB, SUCKER?
CAN YA DO ANYTHING ABOUT IT?
LET'S GO, HUN--
OOOOH A LONG LOOPING RIGHT GETS PAST ALI'S GUARD AND CONNECTS!

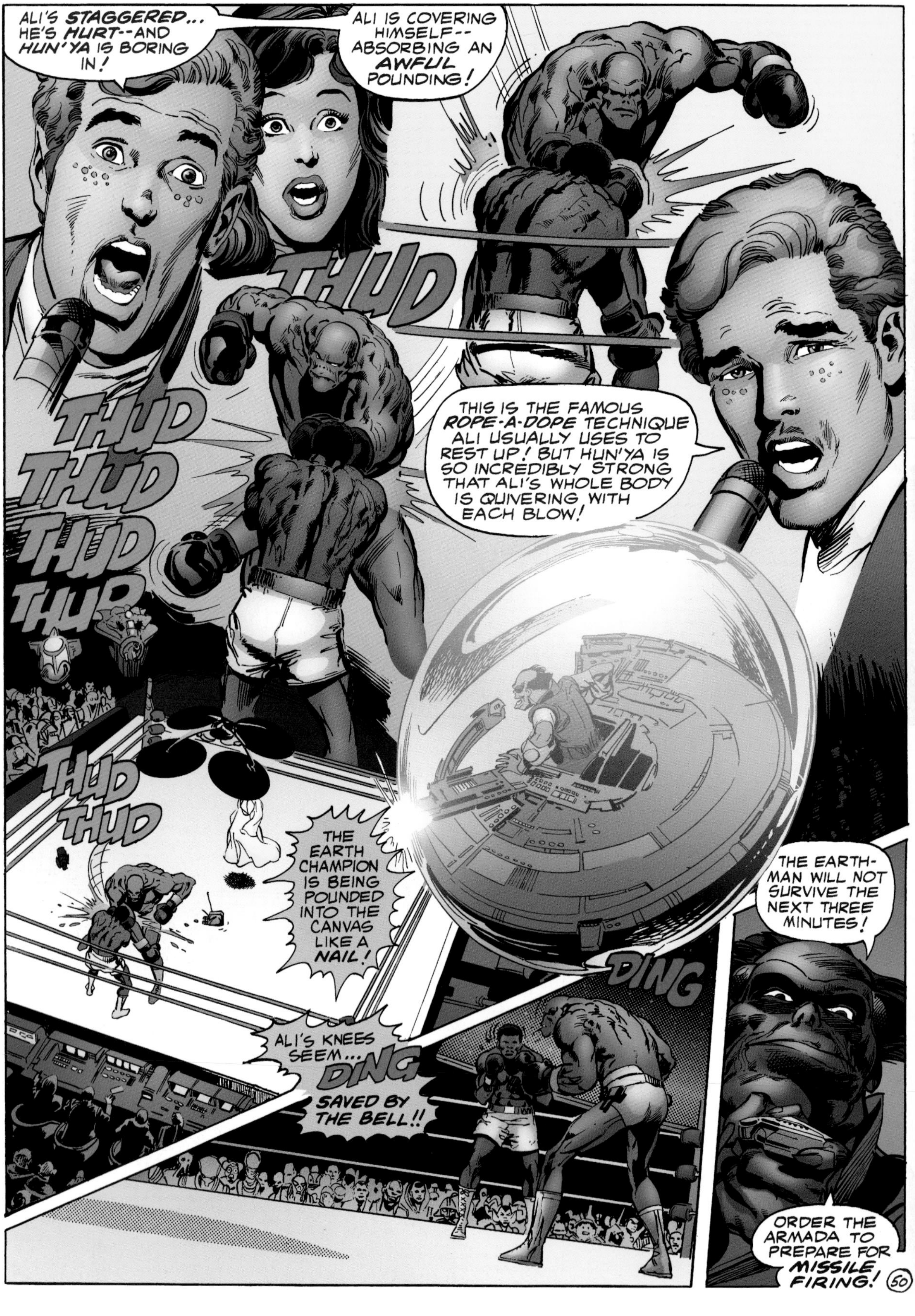
ALI'S STAGGERED... HE'S HURT--AND HUN'YA IS BORING IN!
ALI IS COVERING HIMSELF--ABSORBING AN AWFUL POUNDING!
THUD
THIS IS THE FAMOUS ROPE-A-DOPE TECHNIQUE ALI USUALLY USES TO REST UP! BUT HUN'YA IS SO INCREDIBLY STRONG THAT ALI'S WHOLE BODY IS QUIVERING WITH EACH BLOW!
THUD THUD THUD THUD
THUD THUD
THE EARTH CHAMPION IS BEING POUNDED INTO THE CANVAS LIKE A NAIL!
THE EARTH-MAN WILL NOT SURVIVE THE NEXT THREE MINUTES!
DING
ALI'S KNEES SEEM... DING SAVED BY THE BELL!!
ORDER THE ARMADA TO PREPARE FOR MISSILE FIRING!

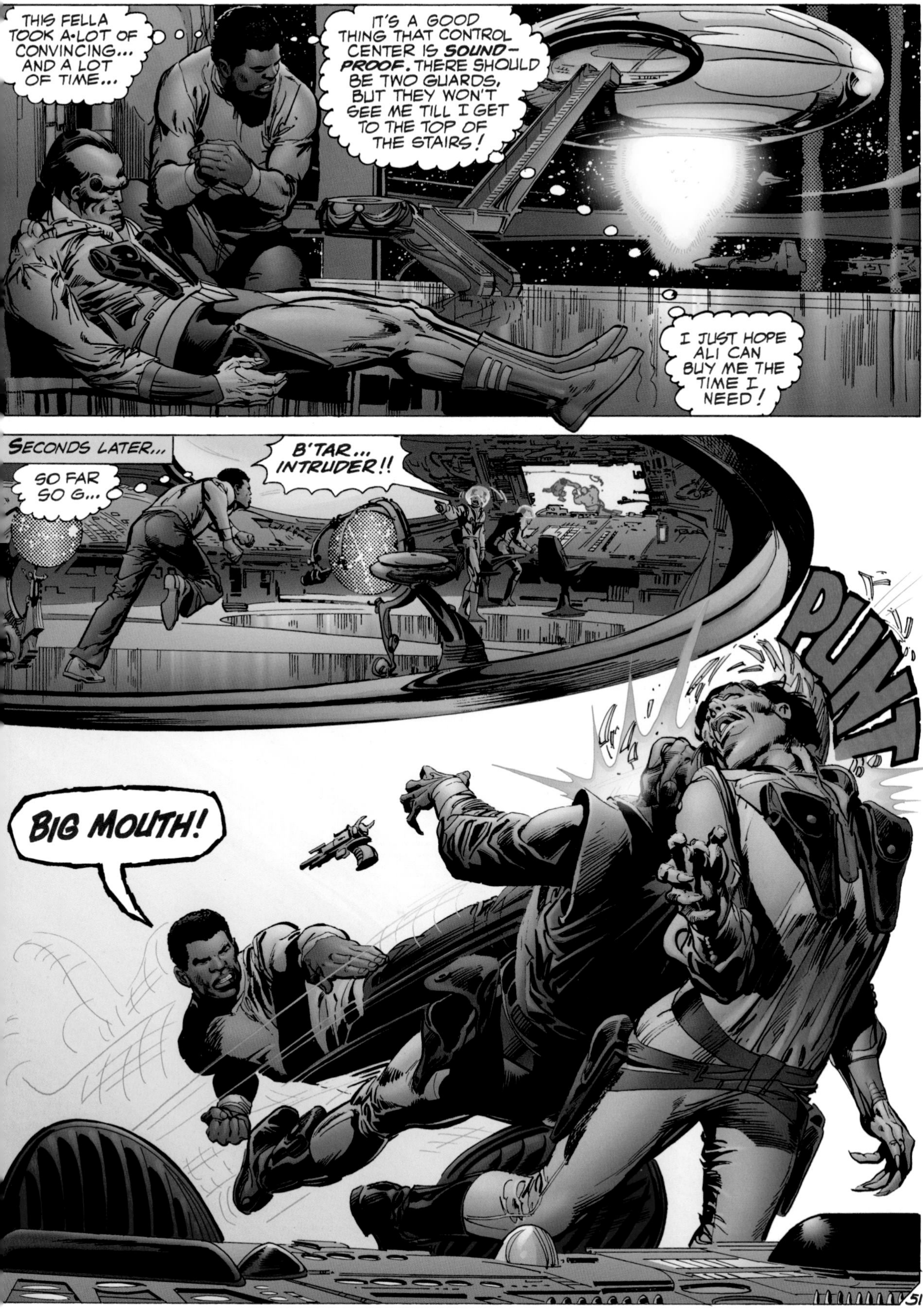
THIS FELLA TOOK A•LOT OF CONVINCING... AND A LOT OF TIME...
IT'S A GOOD THING THAT CONTROL CENTER IS SOUND-PROOF. THERE SHOULD BE TWO GUARDS, BUT THEY WON'T SEE ME TILL I GET TO THE TOP OF THE STAIRS!
I JUST HOPE ALI CAN BUY ME THE TIME I NEED!
SECONDS LATER...
SO FAR SO G...
B'TAR... INTRUDER!!
PUNT
BIG MOUTH!
51

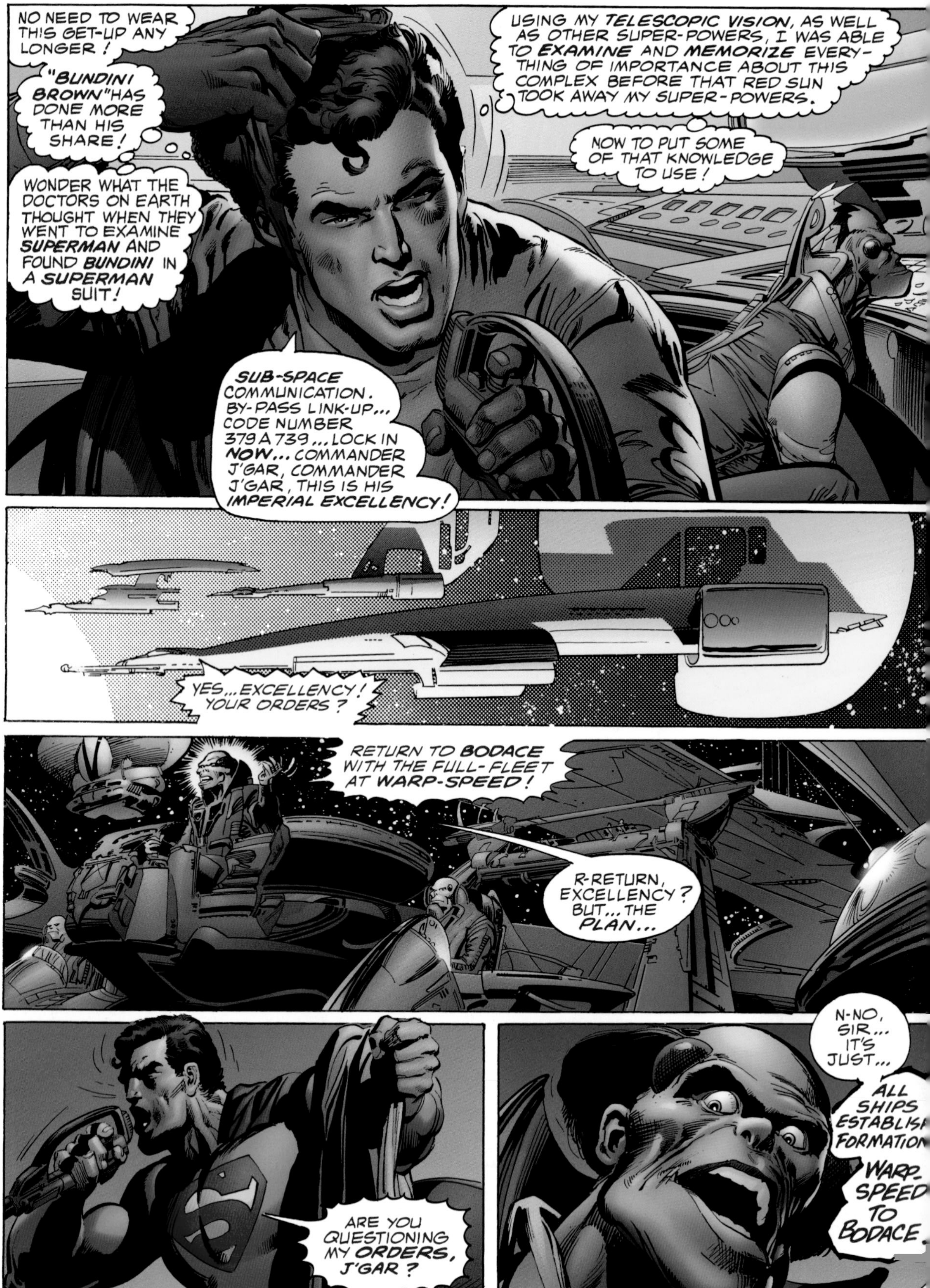
NO NEED TO WEAR THIS GET-UP ANY LONGER!
"BUNDINI BROWN" HAS DONE MORE THAN HIS SHARE!
WONDER WHAT THE DOCTORS ON EARTH THOUGHT WHEN THEY WENT TO EXAMINE SUPERMAN AND FOUND BUNDINI IN A SUPERMAN SUIT!
USING MY TELESCOPIC VISION, AS WELL AS OTHER SUPER-POWERS, I WAS ABLE TO EXAMINE AND MEMORIZE EVERYTHING OF IMPORTANCE ABOUT THIS COMPLEX BEFORE THAT RED SUN TOOK AWAY MY SUPER-POWERS.
NOW TO PUT SOME OF THAT KNOWLEDGE TO USE!
SUB-SPACE COMMUNICATION. BY-PASS LINK-UP... CODE NUMBER 379A739... LOCK IN NOW... COMMANDER J'GAR, COMMANDER J'GAR, THIS IS HIS IMPERIAL EXCELLENCY!
YES... EXCELLENCY! YOUR ORDERS?
RETURN TO BODACE WITH THE FULL-FLEET AT WARP-SPEED!
R-RETURN, EXCELLENCY? BUT... THE PLAN...
ARE YOU QUESTIONING MY ORDERS, J'GAR?
N-NO, SIR... IT'S JUST...
ALL SHIPS ESTABLISH FORMATION
WARP-SPEED TO BODACE

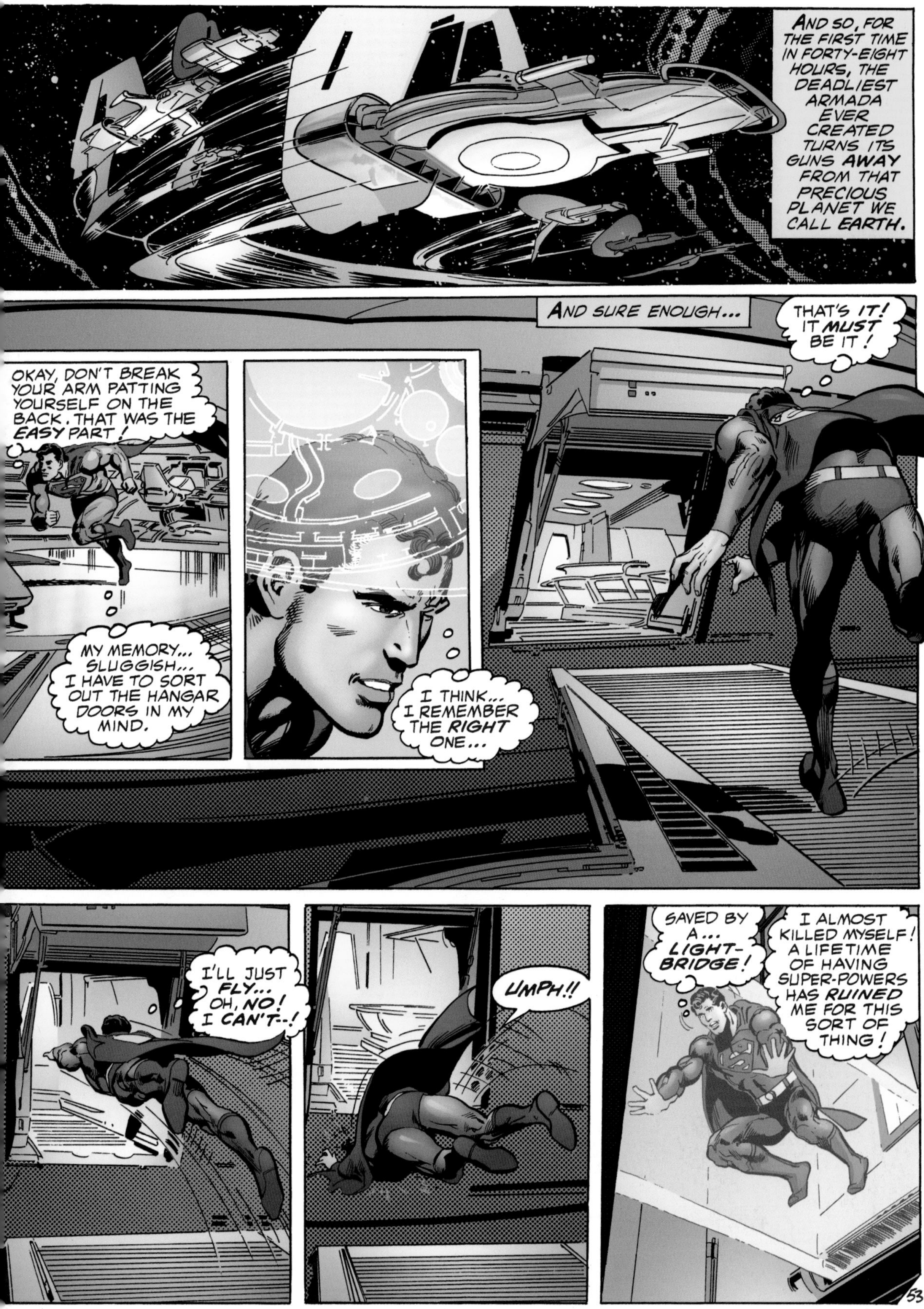
AND SO, FOR THE FIRST TIME IN FORTY-EIGHT HOURS, THE DEADLIEST ARMADA EVER CREATED TURNS ITS GUNS AWAY FROM THAT PRECIOUS PLANET WE CALL EARTH.
AND SURE ENOUGH...
OKAY, DON'T BREAK YOUR ARM PATTING YOURSELF ON THE BACK. THAT WAS THE EASY PART!
MY MEMORY... SLUGGISH... I HAVE TO SORT OUT THE HANGAR DOORS IN MY MIND.
I THINK... I REMEMBER THE RIGHT ONE...
THAT'S IT! IT MUST BE IT!
I'LL JUST FLY... OH, NO! I CAN'T--!
UMPH!!
SAVED BY A... LIGHT-BRIDGE!
I ALMOST KILLED MYSELF! A LIFETIME OF HAVING SUPER-POWERS HAS RUINED ME FOR THIS SORT OF THING!

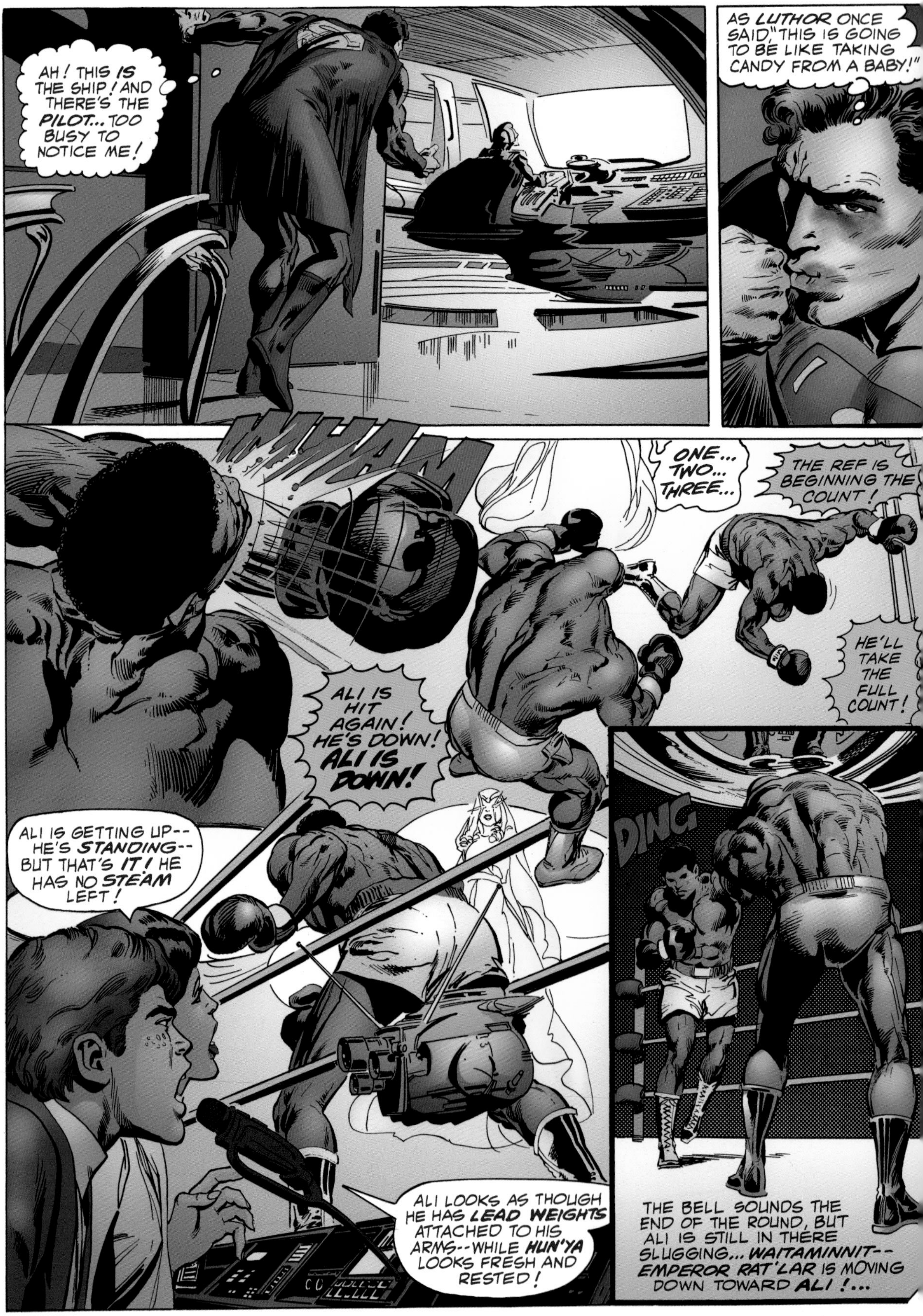

AH! THIS IS THE SHIP! AND THERE'S THE PILOT... TOO BUSY TO NOTICE ME!
AS LUTHOR ONCE SAID, "THIS IS GOING TO BE LIKE TAKING CANDY FROM A BABY!"
WHAM
ONE... TWO... THREE...
THE REF IS BEGINNING THE COUNT!
HE'LL TAKE THE FULL COUNT!
ALI IS HIT AGAIN! HE'S DOWN! ALI IS DOWN!
ALI IS GETTING UP-- HE'S STANDING-- BUT THAT'S IT! HE HAS NO STEAM LEFT!
ALI LOOKS AS THOUGH HE HAS LEAD WEIGHTS ATTACHED TO HIS ARMS--WHILE HUN'YA LOOKS FRESH AND RESTED!
DING
THE BELL SOUNDS THE END OF THE ROUND, BUT ALI IS STILL IN THERE SLUGGING... WAITAMINNIT-- EMPEROR RAT'LAR IS MOVING DOWN TOWARD ALI!...

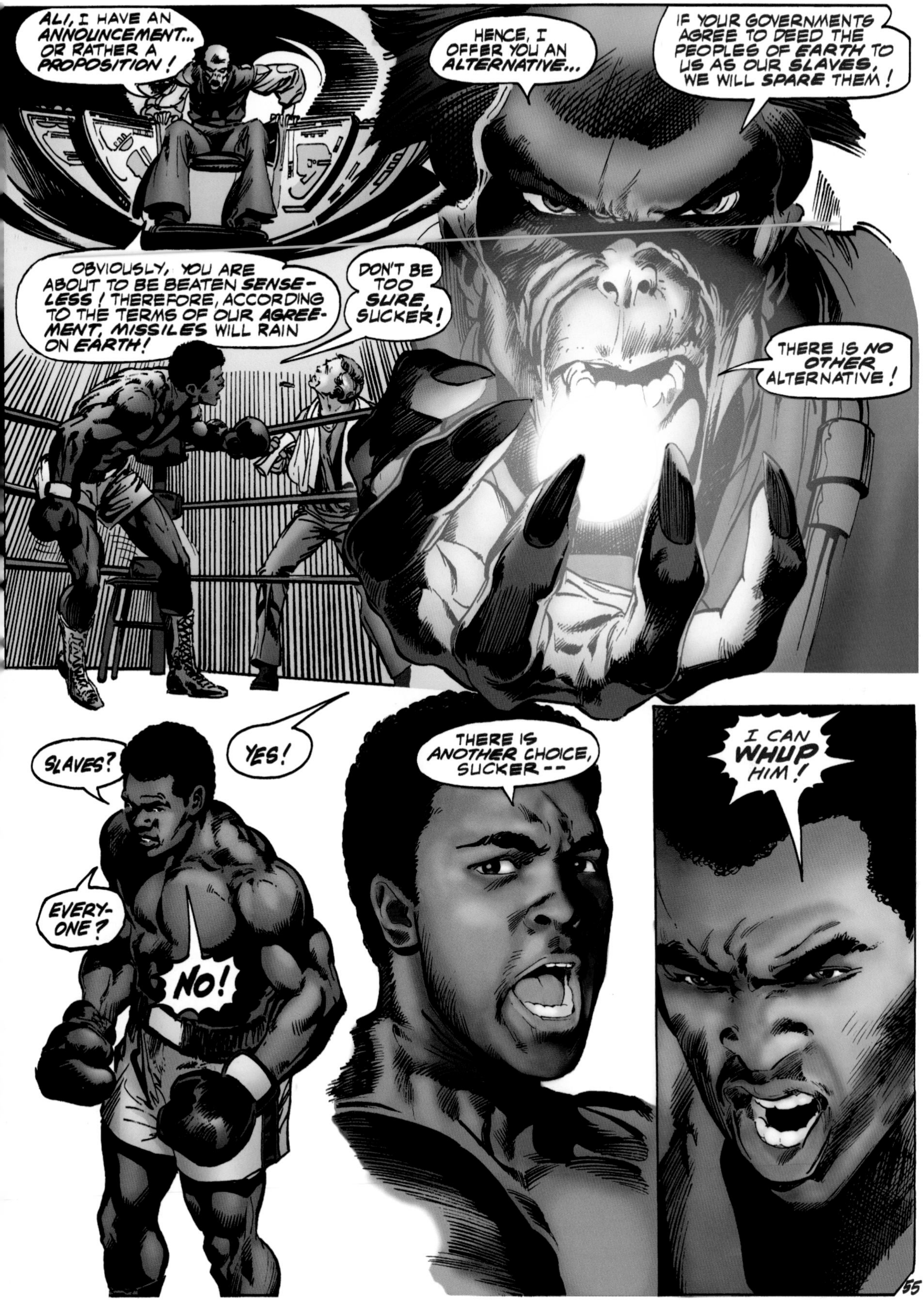
ALI, I HAVE AN ANNOUNCEMENT... OR RATHER A PROPOSITION!
HENCE, I OFFER YOU AN ALTERNATIVE...
IF YOUR GOVERNMENTS AGREE TO DEED THE PEOPLES OF EARTH TO US AS OUR SLAVES, WE WILL SPARE THEM!
OBVIOUSLY, YOU ARE ABOUT TO BE BEATEN SENSE-LESS! THEREFORE, ACCORDING TO THE TERMS OF OUR AGREE-MENT, MISSILES WILL RAIN ON EARTH!
DON'T BE TOO SURE, SUCKER!
THERE IS NO OTHER ALTERNATIVE!
SLAVES?
YES!
EVERY-ONE?
NO!
THERE IS ANOTHER CHOICE, SUCKER--
I CAN WHUP HIM!

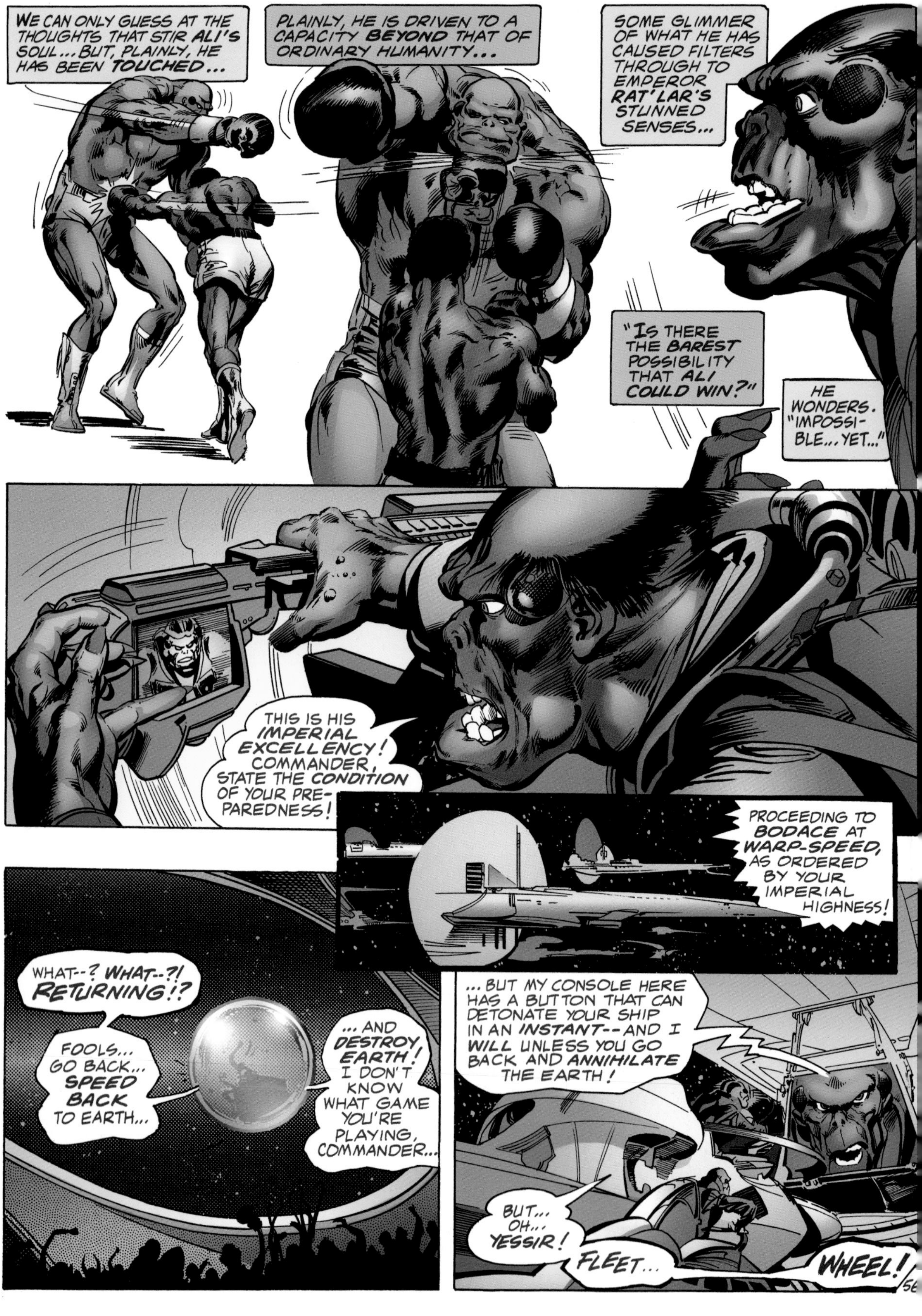

WE CAN ONLY GUESS AT THE THOUGHTS THAT STIR ALI'S SOUL... BUT, PLAINLY, HE HAS BEEN TOUCHED...
PLAINLY, HE IS DRIVEN TO A CAPACITY BEYOND THAT OF ORDINARY HUMANITY...
SOME GLIMMER OF WHAT HE HAS CAUSED FILTERS THROUGH TO EMPEROR RAT'LAR'S STUNNED SENSES...
"IS THERE THE BAREST POSSIBILITY THAT ALI COULD WIN?"
HE WONDERS. "IMPOSSI-BLE... YET..."
THIS IS HIS IMPERIAL EXCELLENCY! COMMANDER, STATE THE CONDITION OF YOUR PRE-PAREDNESS!
PROCEEDING TO BODACE AT WARP-SPEED, AS ORDERED BY YOUR IMPERIAL HIGHNESS!
WHAT--? WHAT--?! RETURNING!?
FOOLS... GO BACK... SPEED BACK TO EARTH...
...AND DESTROY EARTH! I DON'T KNOW WHAT GAME YOU'RE PLAYING, COMMANDER...
...BUT MY CONSOLE HERE HAS A BUTTON THAT CAN DETONATE YOUR SHIP IN AN INSTANT--AND I WILL UNLESS YOU GO BACK AND ANNIHILATE THE EARTH!
BUT... OH... YESSIR!
FLEET...
WHEEL!

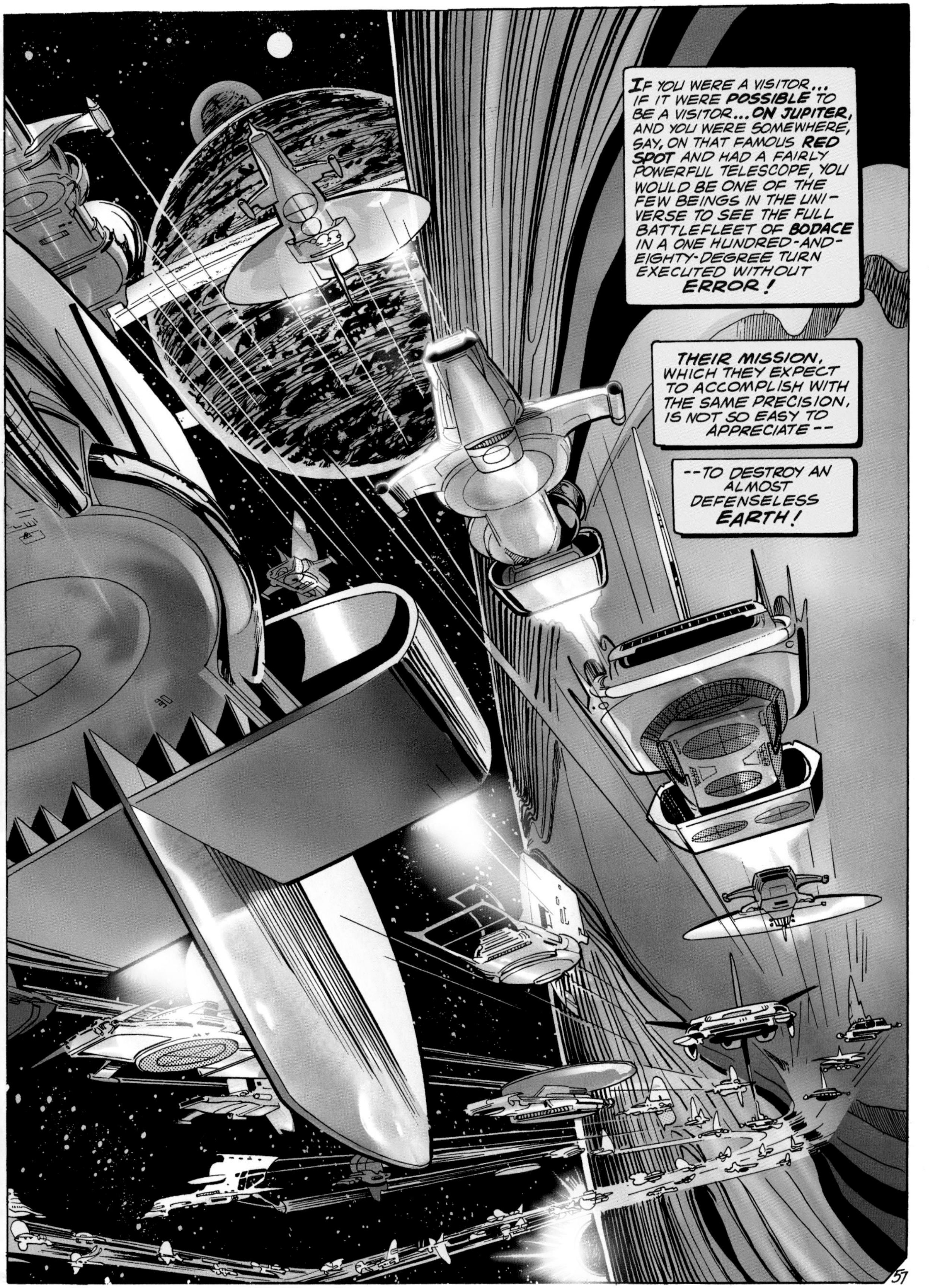
IF YOU WERE A VISITOR... IF IT WERE POSSIBLE TO BE A VISITOR... ON JUPITER, AND YOU WERE SOMEWHERE, SAY, ON THAT FAMOUS RED SPOT AND HAD A FAIRLY POWERFUL TELESCOPE, YOU WOULD BE ONE OF THE FEW BEINGS IN THE UNI-VERSE TO SEE THE FULL BATTLEFLEET OF BODACE IN A ONE HUNDRED-AND-EIGHTY-DEGREE TURN EXECUTED WITHOUT ERROR!
THEIR MISSION, WHICH THEY EXPECT TO ACCOMPLISH WITH THE SAME PRECISION, IS NOT SO EASY TO APPRECIATE--
--TO DESTROY AN ALMOST DEFENSELESS EARTH!

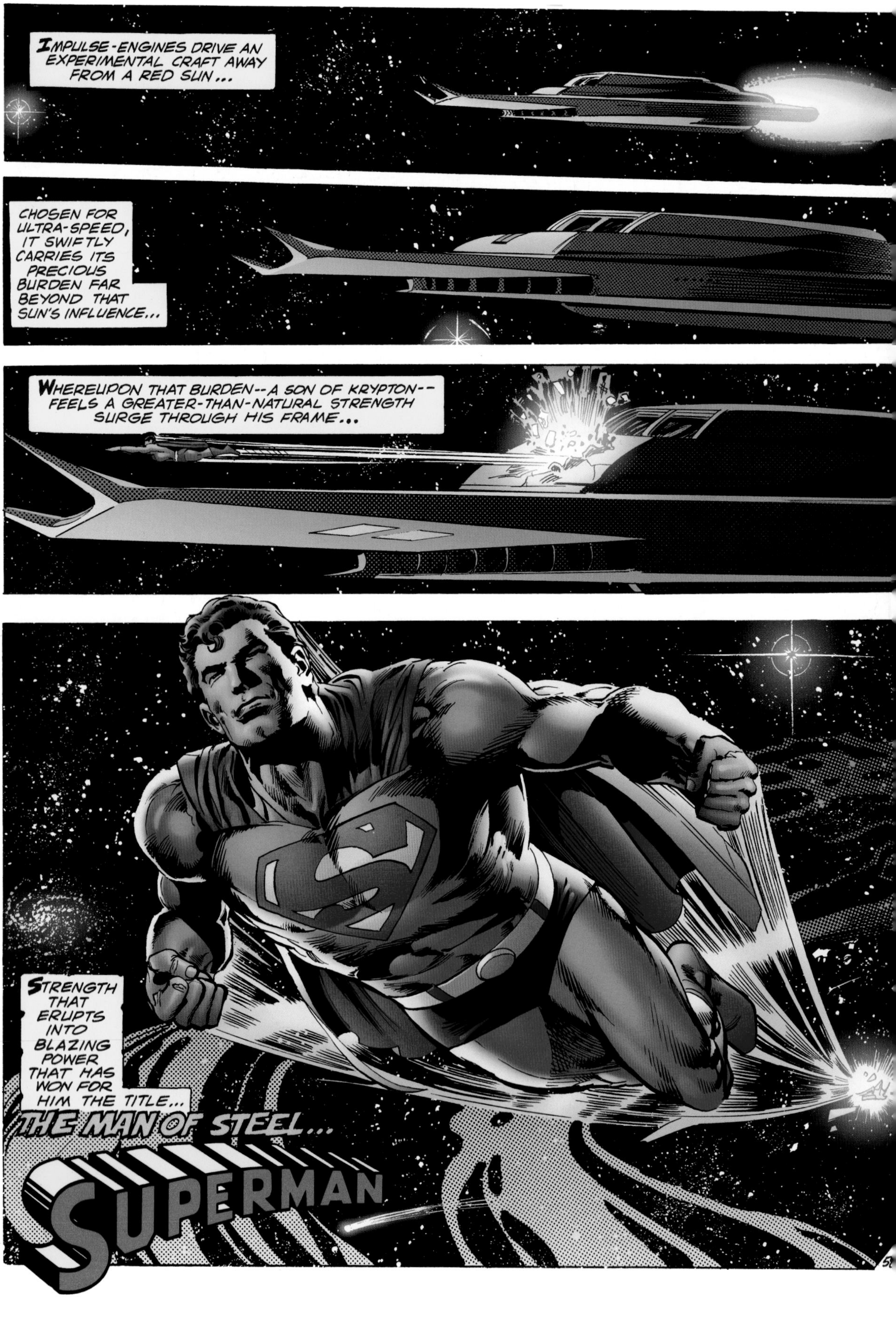
IMPULSE-ENGINES DRIVE AN EXPERIMENTAL CRAFT AWAY FROM A RED SUN...
CHOSEN FOR ULTRA-SPEED, IT SWIFTLY CARRIES ITS PRECIOUS BURDEN FAR BEYOND THAT SUN'S INFLUENCE...
WHEREUPON THAT BURDEN--A SON OF KRYPTON--FEELS A GREATER-THAN-NATURAL STRENGTH SURGE THROUGH HIS FRAME...
STRENGTH THAT ERUPTS INTO BLAZING POWER THAT HAS WON FOR HIM THE TITLE...
THE MAN OF STEEL...
SUPERMAN

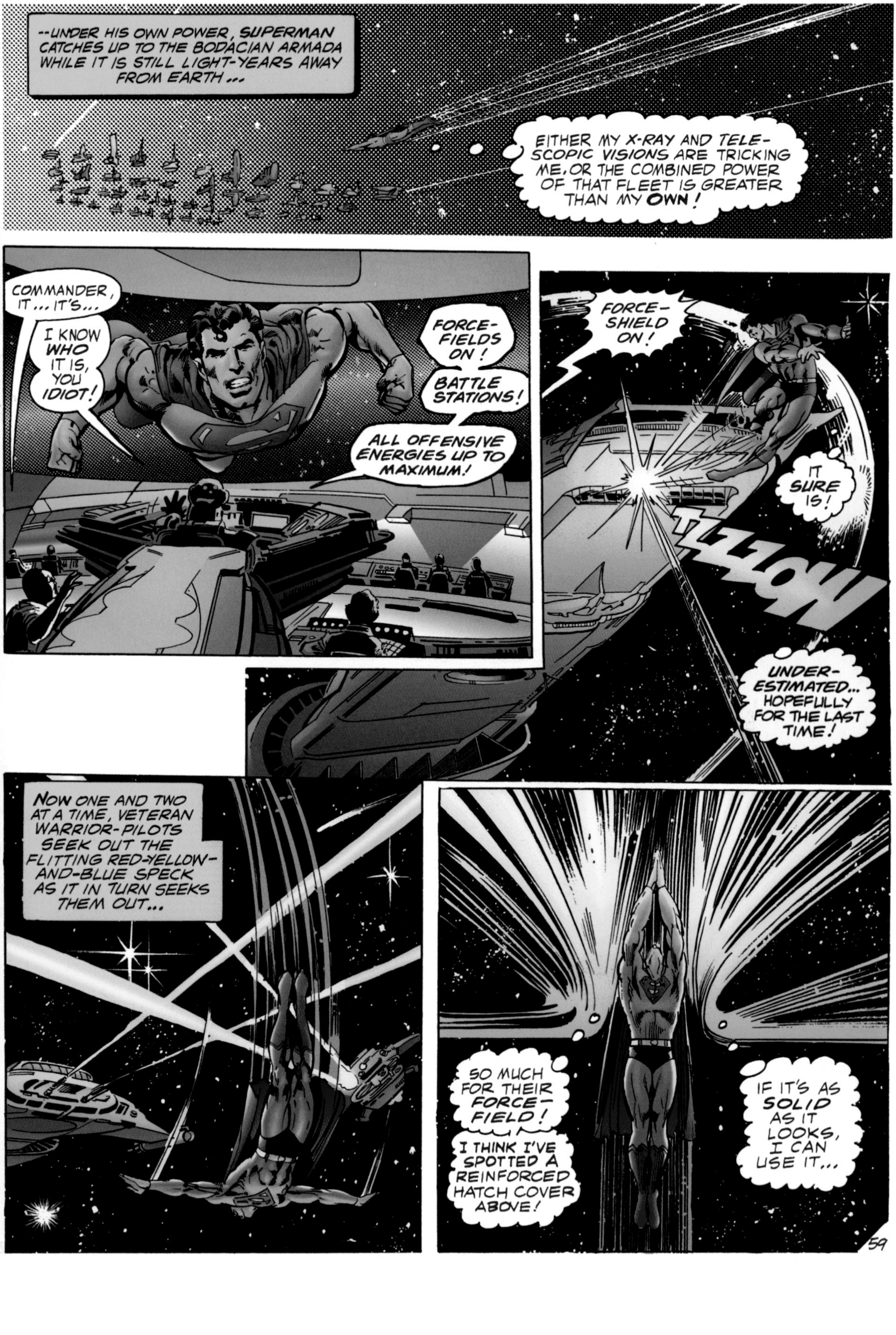
--UNDER HIS OWN POWER, SUPERMAN CATCHES UP TO THE BODACIAN ARMADA WHILE IT IS STILL LIGHT-YEARS AWAY FROM EARTH...
EITHER MY X-RAY AND TELESCOPIC VISIONS ARE TRICKING ME, OR THE COMBINED POWER OF THAT FLEET IS GREATER THAN MY OWN!
COMMANDER, IT... IT'S...
I KNOW WHO IT IS, YOU IDIOT!
FORCE-FIELDS ON!
BATTLE STATIONS!
ALL OFFENSIVE ENERGIES UP TO MAXIMUM!
FORCE-SHIELD ON!
IT SURE IS!
TZZOW
UNDER-ESTIMATED... HOPEFULLY FOR THE LAST TIME!
NOW ONE AND TWO AT A TIME, VETERAN WARRIOR-PILOTS SEEK OUT THE FLITTING RED-YELLOW-AND-BLUE SPECK AS IT IN TURN SEEKS THEM OUT...
SO MUCH FOR THEIR FORCE-FIELD!
I THINK I'VE SPOTTED A REINFORCED HATCH COVER ABOVE!
IF IT'S AS SOLID AS IT LOOKS, I CAN USE IT...

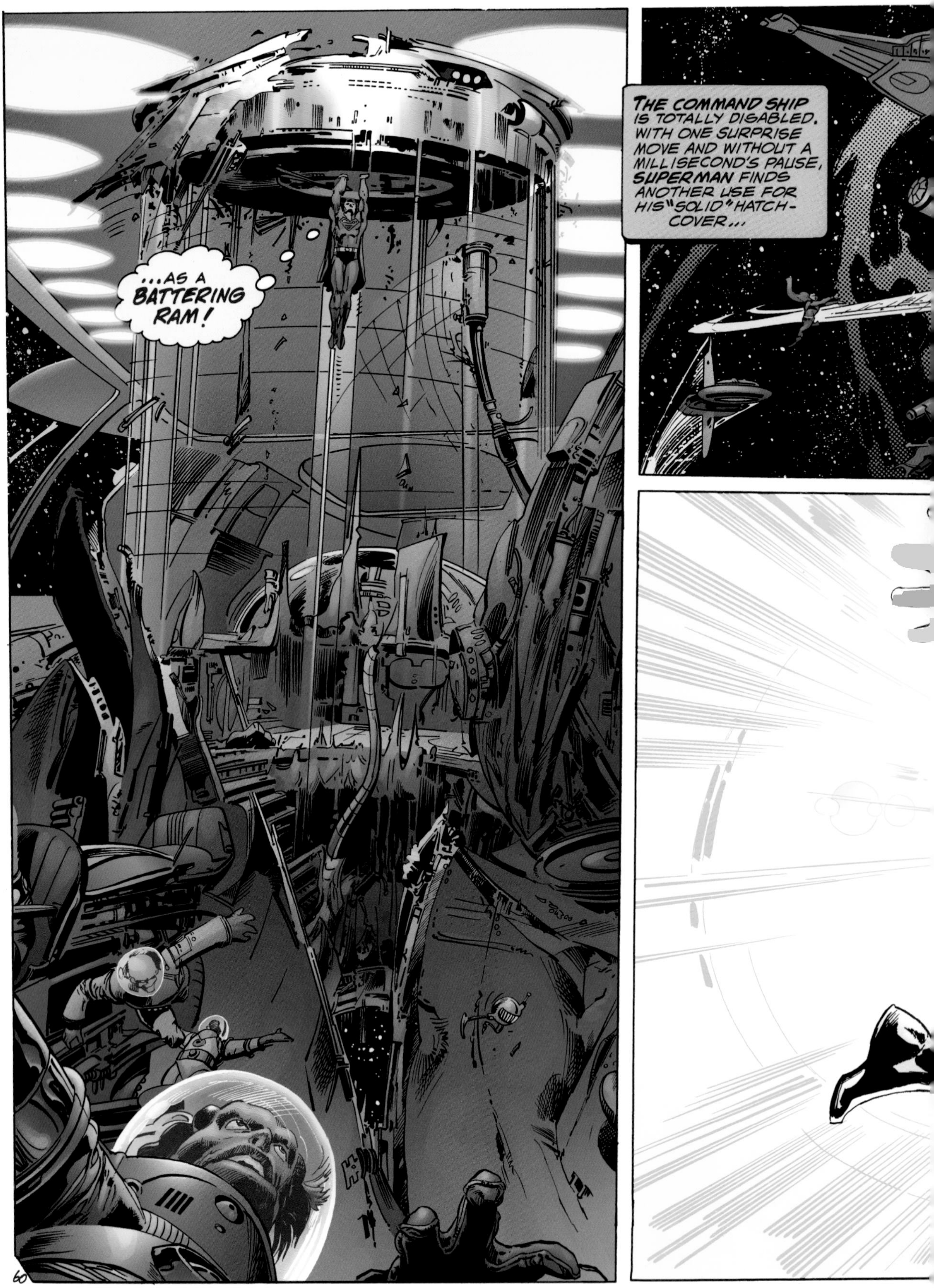
...AS A BATTERING RAM!
THE COMMAND SHIP IS TOTALLY DISABLED. WITH ONE SURPRISE MOVE AND WITHOUT A MILLISECOND'S PAUSE, SUPERMAN FINDS ANOTHER USE FOR HIS "SOLID" HATCH-COVER...

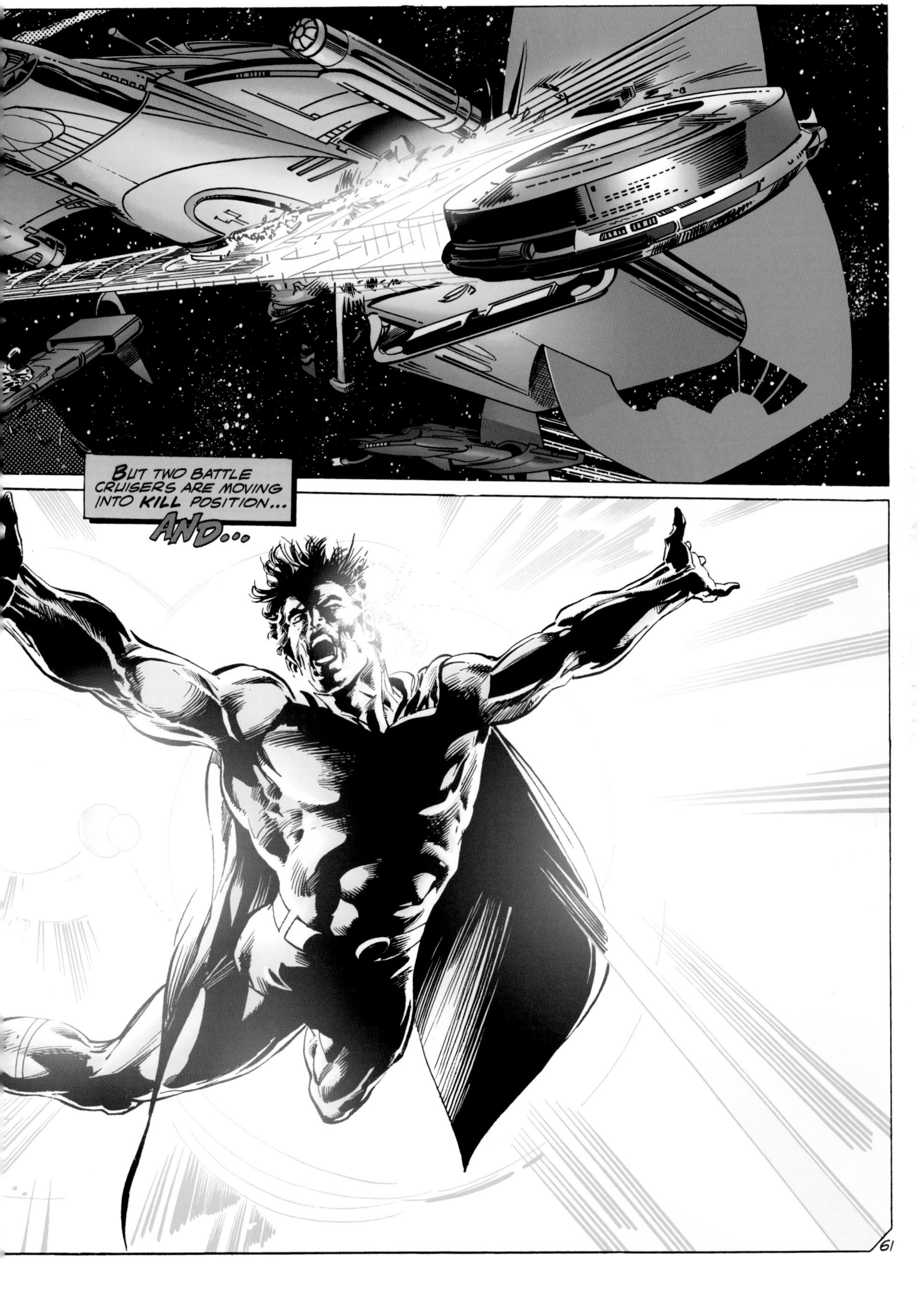
BUT TWO BATTLE CRUISERS ARE MOVING INTO KILL POSITION...
AND...

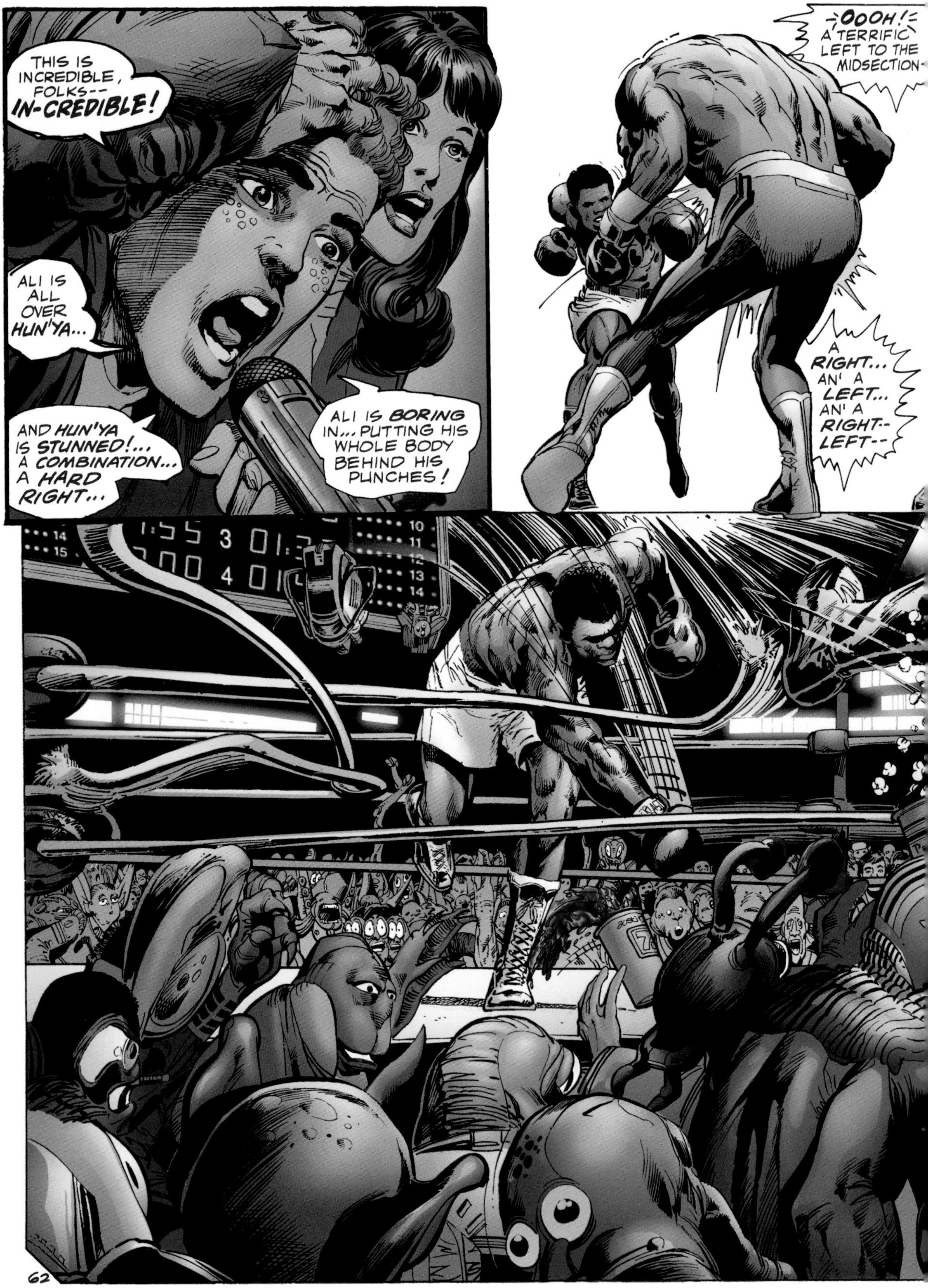

THIS IS INCREDIBLE, FOLKS-- IN-CREDIBLE!
ALI IS ALL OVER HUN'YA...
AND HUN'YA IS STUNNED!... A COMBINATION... A HARD RIGHT...
ALI IS BORING IN... PUTTING HIS WHOLE BODY BEHIND HIS PUNCHES!
-OOOH!- A TERRIFIC LEFT TO THE MIDSECTION-
A RIGHT... AN' A LEFT... AN' A RIGHT-- LEFT--

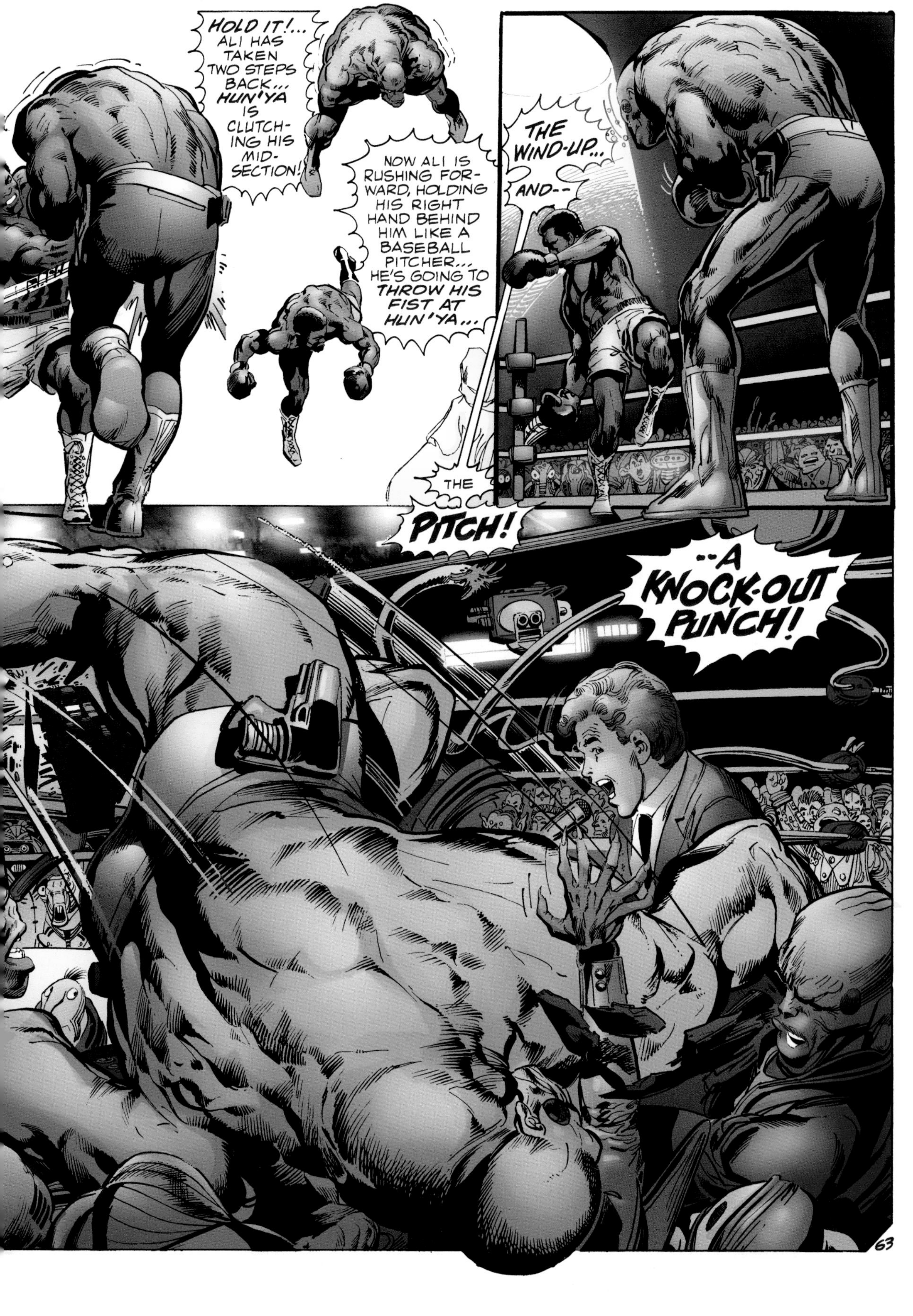
HOLD IT!... ALI HAS TAKEN TWO STEPS BACK... HUN'YA IS CLUTCHING HIS MID-SECTION!
NOW ALI IS RUSHING FORWARD, HOLDING HIS RIGHT HAND BEHIND HIM LIKE A BASEBALL PITCHER... HE'S GOING TO THROW HIS FIST AT HUN'YA...
THE WIND-UP...
AND--
THE
PITCH!
--A KNOCK-OUT PUNCH!

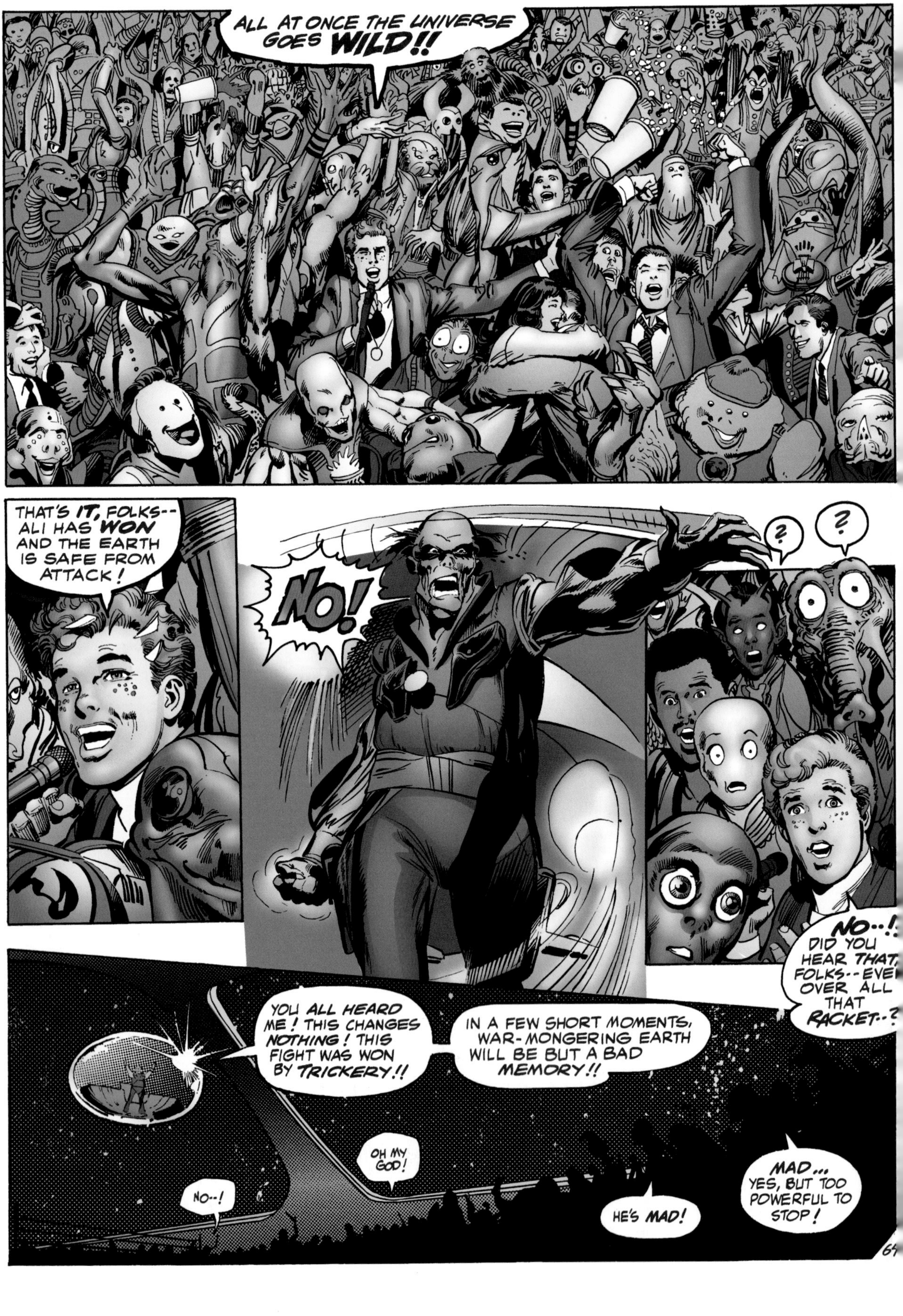

ALL AT ONCE THE UNIVERSE GOES WILD!!
THAT'S IT, FOLKS-- ALI HAS WON AND THE EARTH IS SAFE FROM ATTACK!
NO!
?
?
NO..! DID YOU HEAR THAT, FOLKS--EVE OVER ALL THAT RACKET..?
YOU ALL HEARD ME! THIS CHANGES NOTHING! THIS FIGHT WAS WON BY TRICKERY!!
IN A FEW SHORT MOMENTS, WAR-MONGERING EARTH WILL BE BUT A BAD MEMORY!!
NO--!
OH MY GOD!
HE'S MAD!
MAD... YES, BUT TOO POWERFUL TO STOP!

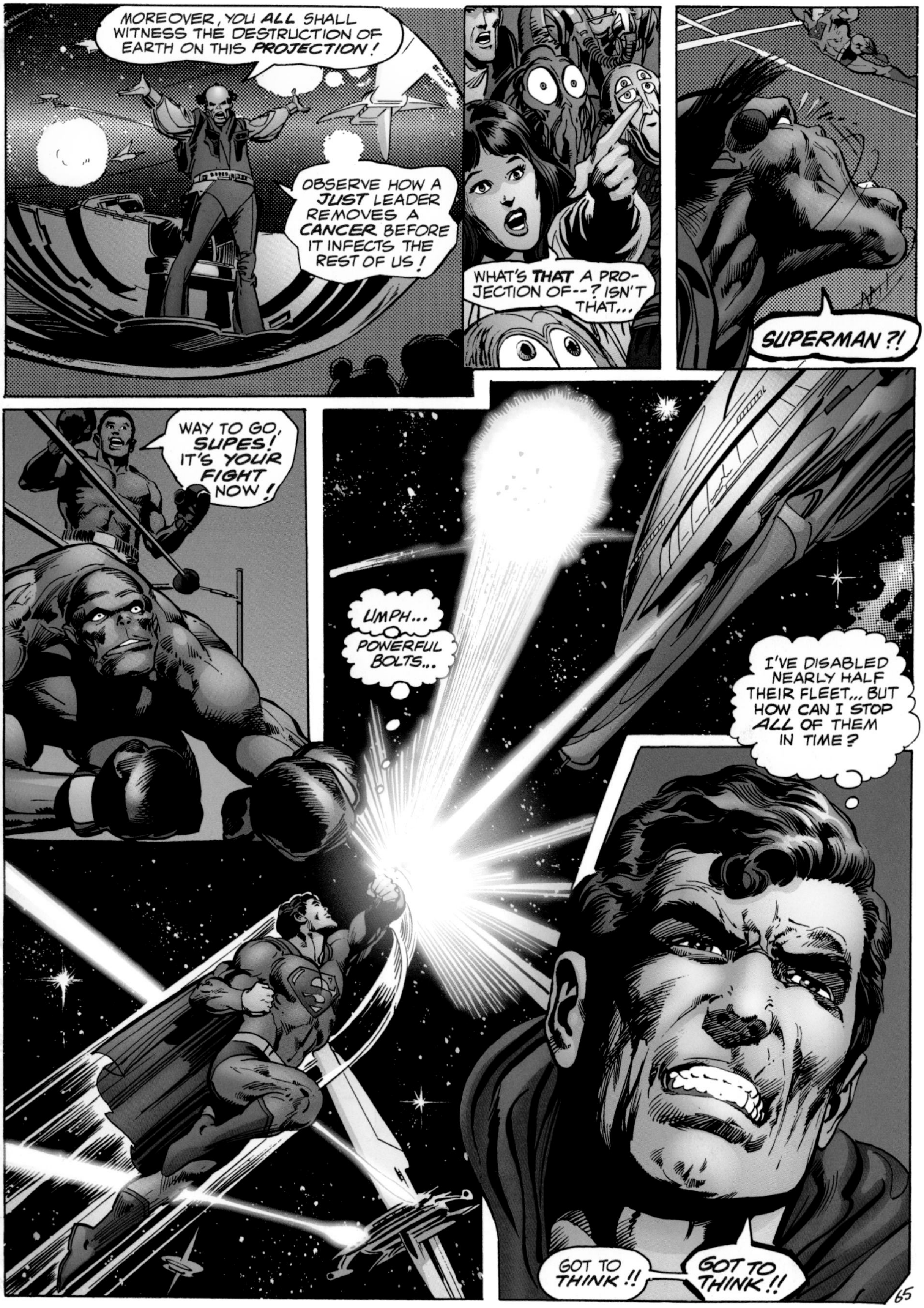
MOREOVER, YOU ALL SHALL WITNESS THE DESTRUCTION OF EARTH ON THIS PROJECTION!
OBSERVE HOW A JUST LEADER REMOVES A CANCER BEFORE IT INFECTS THE REST OF US!
WHAT'S THAT A PROJECTION OF--? ISN'T THAT...
SUPERMAN?!
WAY TO GO, SUPES! IT'S YOUR FIGHT NOW!
UMPH...
POWERFUL BOLTS...
I'VE DISABLED NEARLY HALF THEIR FLEET... BUT HOW CAN I STOP ALL OF THEM IN TIME?
GOT TO THINK!!
GOT TO THINK!!

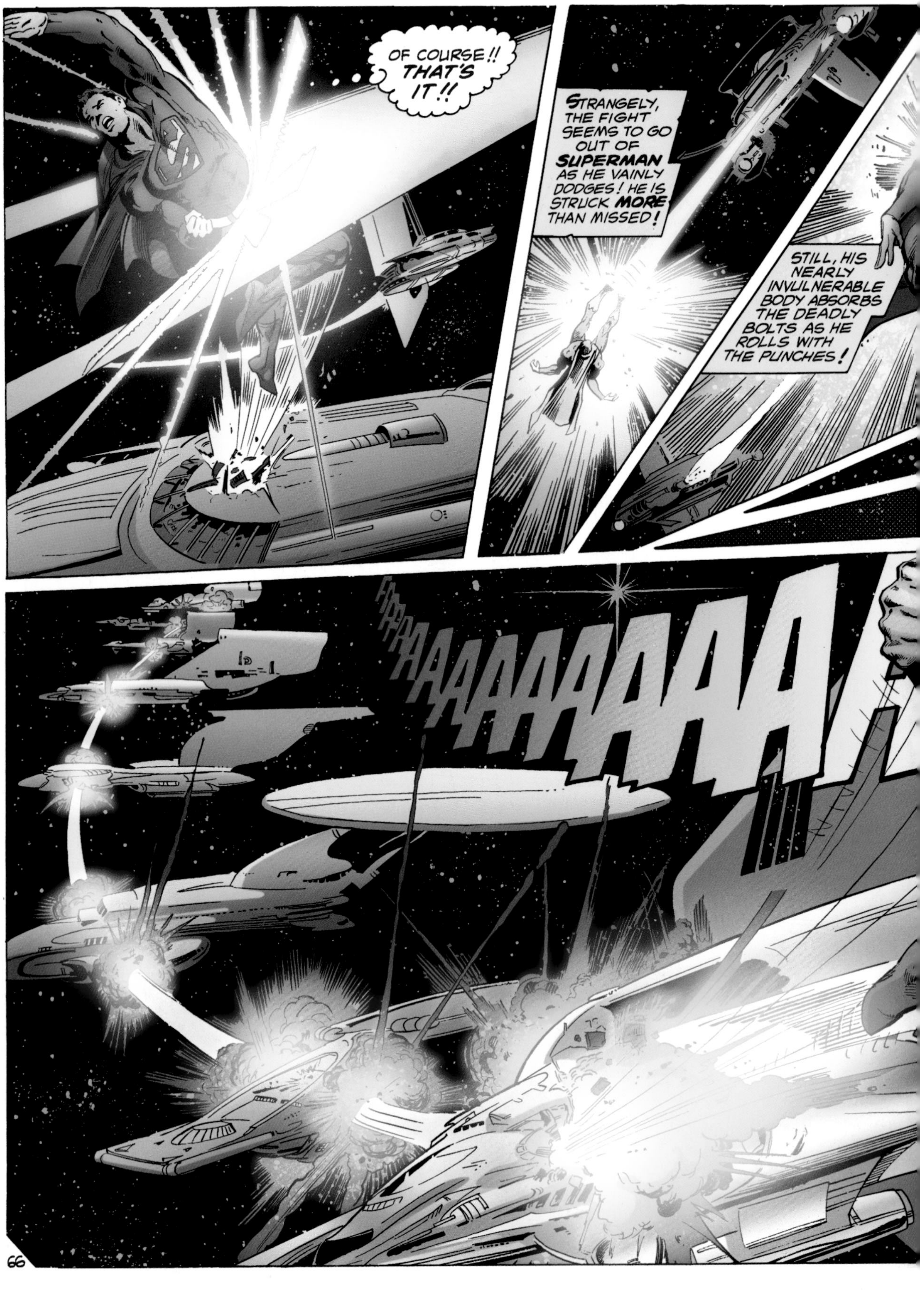

OF COURSE!! THAT'S IT!!
STRANGELY, THE FIGHT SEEMS TO GO OUT OF SUPERMAN AS HE VAINLY DODGES! HE IS STRUCK MORE THAN MISSED!
STILL, HIS NEARLY INVULNERABLE BODY ABSORBS THE DEADLY BOLTS AS HE ROLLS WITH THE PUNCHES!

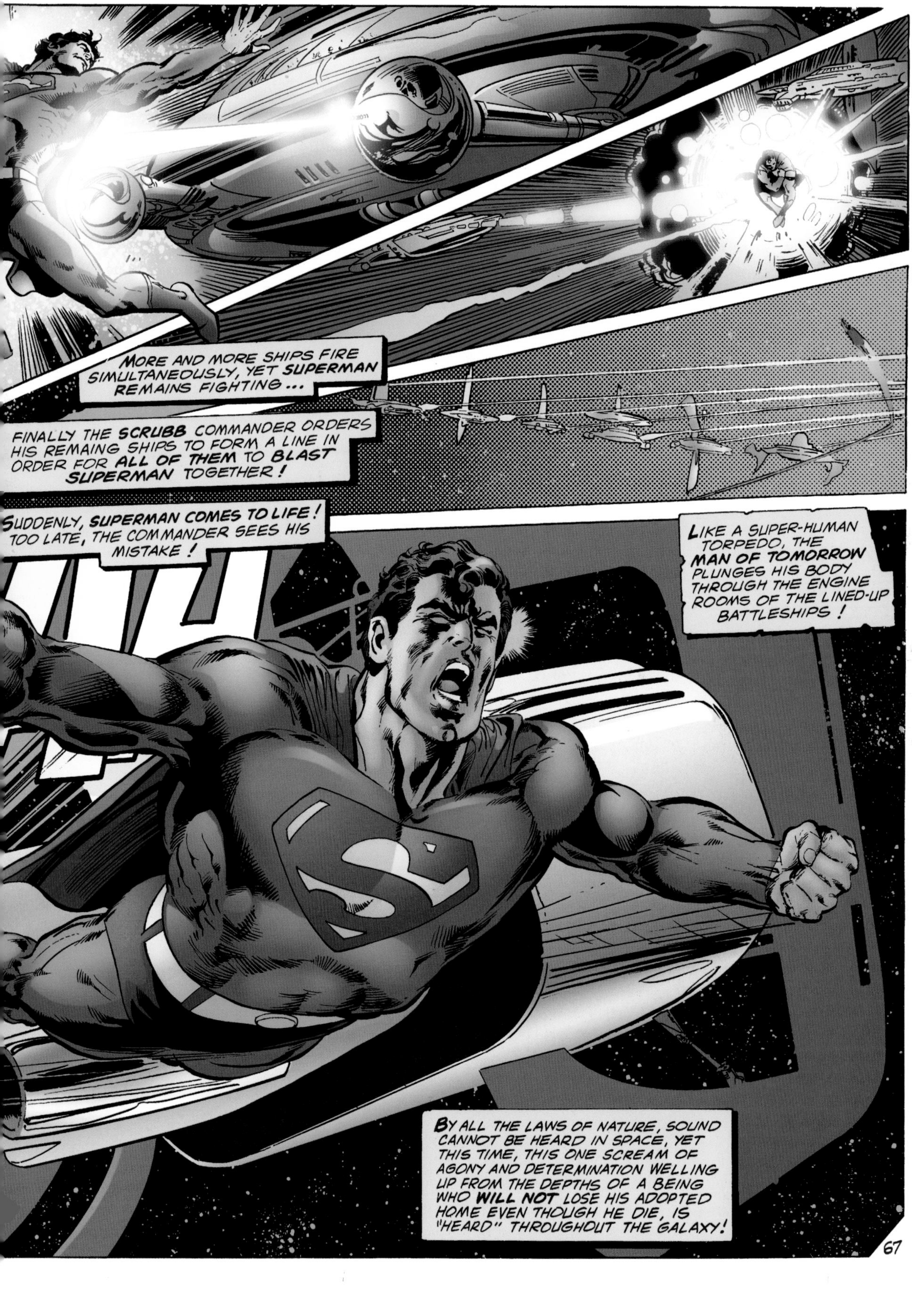
MORE AND MORE SHIPS FIRE SIMULTANEOUSLY, YET SUPERMAN REMAINS FIGHTING...
FINALLY THE SCRUBB COMMANDER ORDERS HIS REMAING SHIPS TO FORM A LINE IN ORDER FOR ALL OF THEM TO BLAST SUPERMAN TOGETHER!
SUDDENLY, SUPERMAN COMES TO LIFE! TOO LATE, THE COMMANDER SEES HIS MISTAKE!
LIKE A SUPER-HUMAN TORPEDO, THE MAN OF TOMORROW PLUNGES HIS BODY THROUGH THE ENGINE ROOMS OF THE LINED-UP BATTLESHIPS!
BY ALL THE LAWS OF NATURE, SOUND CANNOT BE HEARD IN SPACE, YET THIS TIME, THIS ONE SCREAM OF AGONY AND DETERMINATION WELLING UP FROM THE DEPTHS OF A BEING WHO WILL NOT LOSE HIS ADOPTED HOME EVEN THOUGH HE DIE, IS "HEARD" THROUGHOUT THE GALAXY!

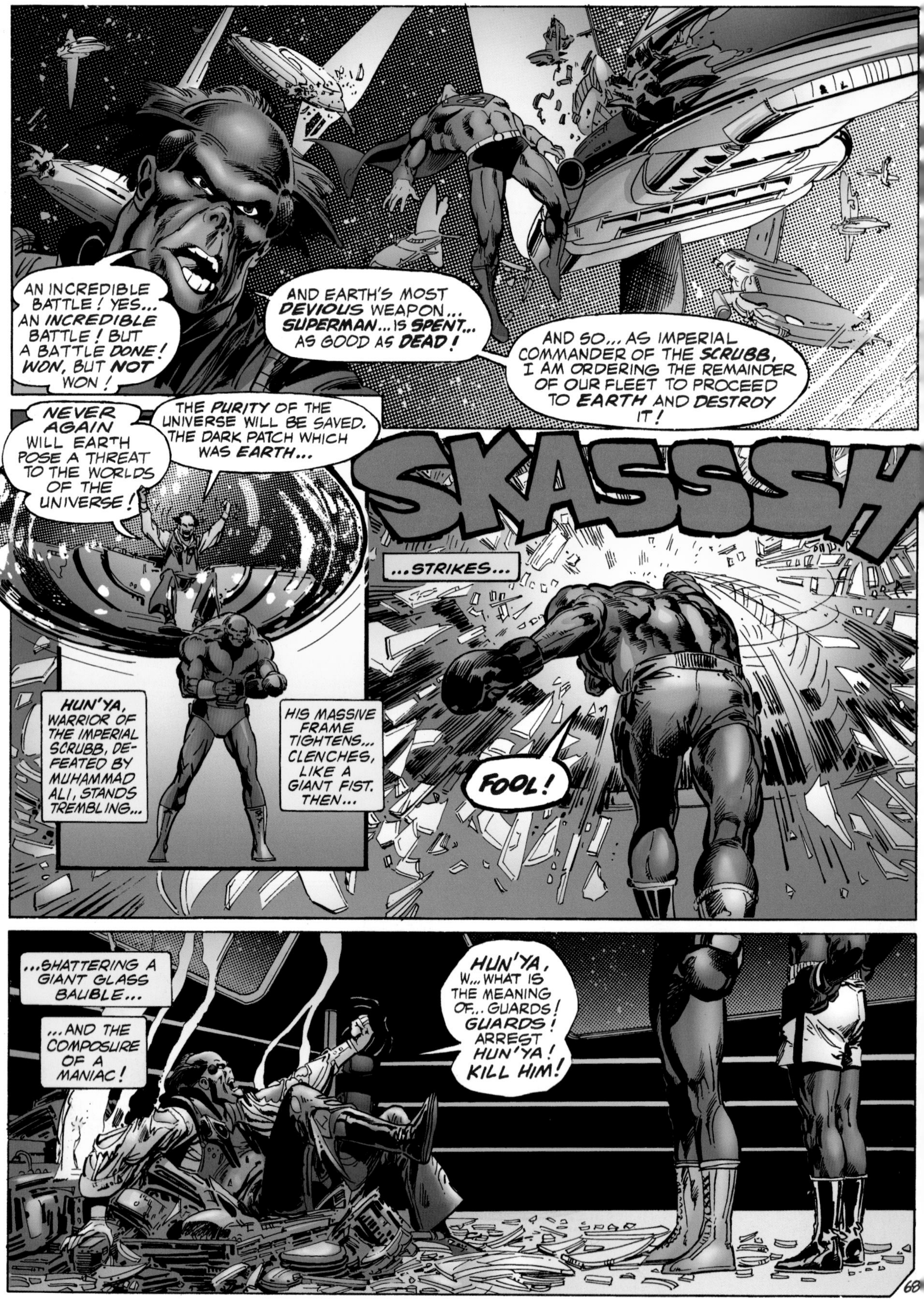
AN INCREDIBLE BATTLE! YES... AN INCREDIBLE BATTLE! BUT A BATTLE DONE! WON, BUT NOT WON!
AND EARTH'S MOST DEVIOUS WEAPON... SUPERMAN... IS SPENT... AS GOOD AS DEAD!
AND SO... AS IMPERIAL COMMANDER OF THE SCRUBB, I AM ORDERING THE REMAINDER OF OUR FLEET TO PROCEED TO EARTH AND DESTROY IT!
NEVER AGAIN WILL EARTH POSE A THREAT TO THE WORLDS OF THE UNIVERSE!
THE PURITY OF THE UNIVERSE WILL BE SAVED. THE DARK PATCH WHICH WAS EARTH...
HUN'YA, WARRIOR OF THE IMPERIAL SCRUBB, DEFEATED BY MUHAMMAD ALI, STANDS TREMBLING...
HIS MASSIVE FRAME TIGHTENS... CLENCHES, LIKE A GIANT FIST. THEN...
SKASSSH
...STRIKES...
FOOL!
...SHATTERING A GIANT GLASS BAUBLE...
...AND THE COMPOSURE OF A MANIAC!
HUN'YA, W... WHAT IS THE MEANING OF... GUARDS! GUARDS! ARREST HUN'YA! KILL HIM!

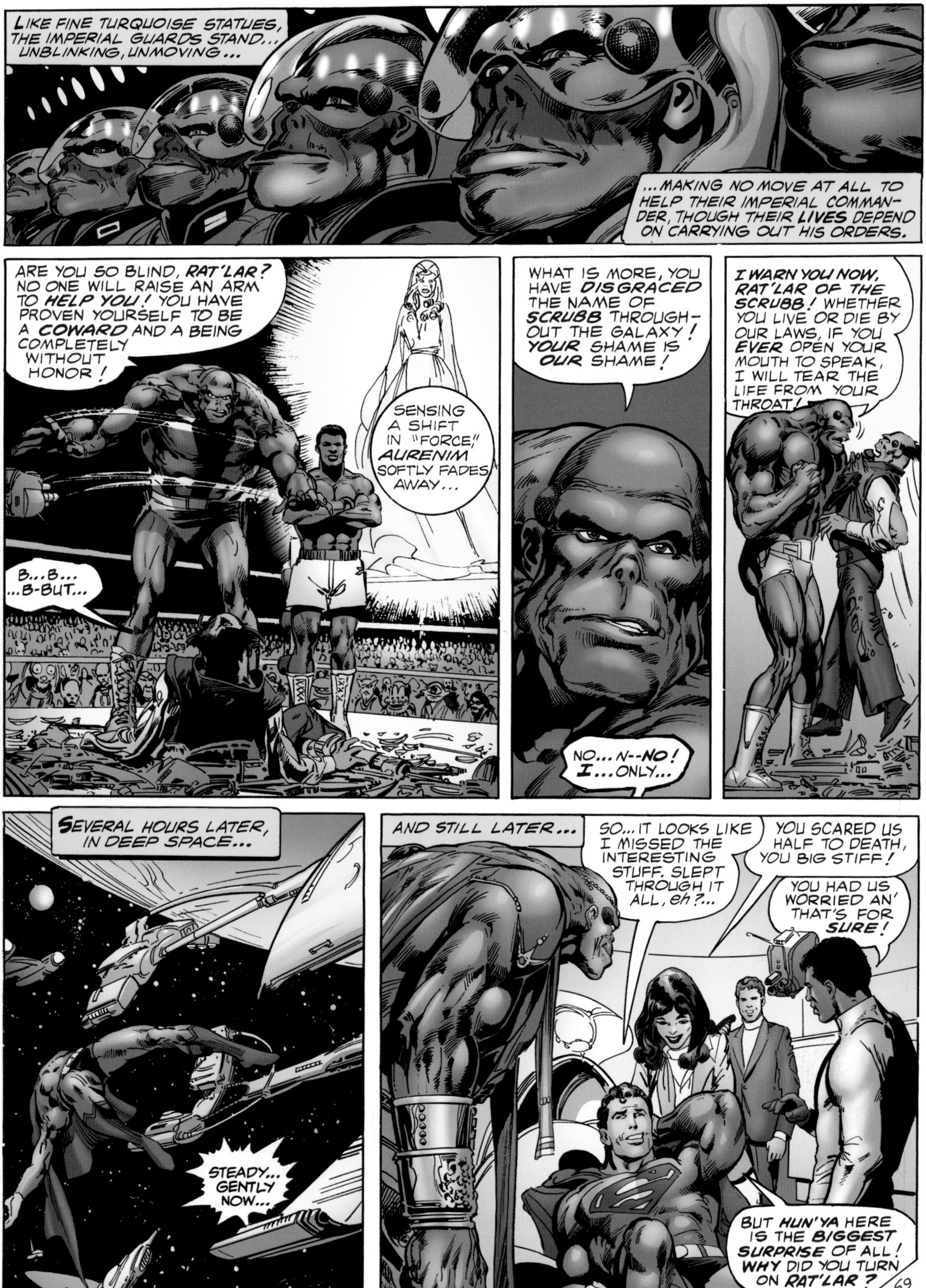

LIKE FINE TURQUOISE STATUES, THE IMPERIAL GUARDS STAND... UNBLINKING, UNMOVING...
...MAKING NO MOVE AT ALL TO HELP THEIR IMPERIAL COMMANDER, THOUGH THEIR LIVES DEPEND ON CARRYING OUT HIS ORDERS.
ARE YOU SO BLIND, RAT'LAR? NO ONE WILL RAISE AN ARM TO HELP YOU! YOU HAVE PROVEN YOURSELF TO BE A COWARD AND A BEING COMPLETELY WITHOUT HONOR!
SENSING A SHIFT IN "FORCE," AURENIM SOFTLY FADES AWAY...
B...B... ...B-BUT...
WHAT IS MORE, YOU HAVE DISGRACED THE NAME OF SCRUBB THROUGHOUT THE GALAXY! YOUR SHAME IS OUR SHAME!
NO... N--NO! I...ONLY...
I WARN YOU NOW, RAT'LAR OF THE SCRUBB! WHETHER YOU LIVE OR DIE BY OUR LAWS, IF YOU EVER OPEN YOUR MOUTH TO SPEAK, I WILL TEAR THE LIFE FROM YOUR THROAT!
SEVERAL HOURS LATER, IN DEEP SPACE...
STEADY... GENTLY NOW...
AND STILL LATER...
SO... IT LOOKS LIKE I MISSED THE INTERESTING STUFF. SLEPT THROUGH IT ALL, eh?...
YOU SCARED US HALF TO DEATH, YOU BIG STIFF!
YOU HAD US WORRIED AN' THAT'S FOR SURE!
BUT HUN'YA HERE IS THE BIGGEST SURPRISE OF ALL! WHY DID YOU TURN ON RAT'LAR?

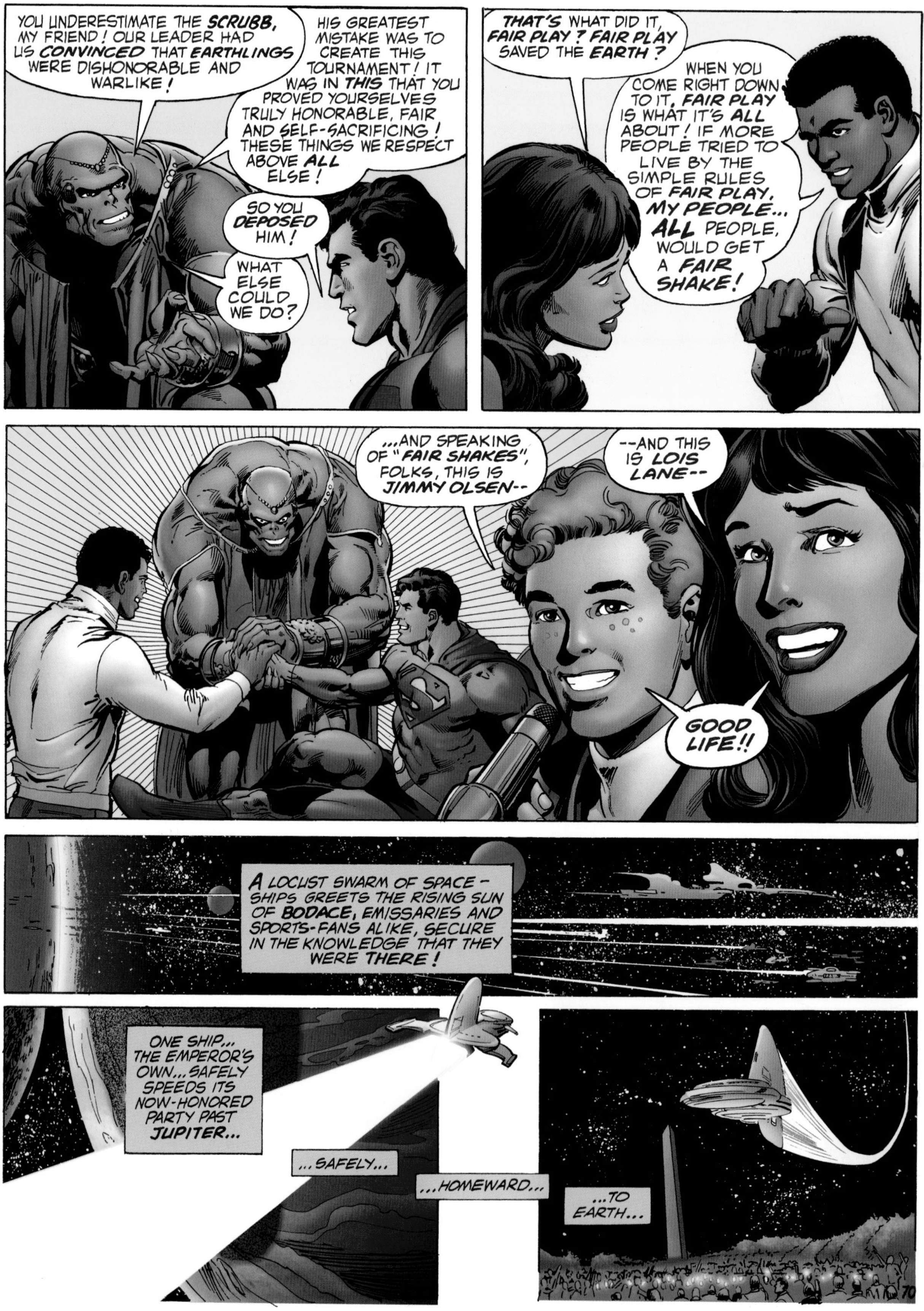
YOU UNDERESTIMATE THE SCRUBB, MY FRIEND! OUR LEADER HAD US CONVINCED THAT EARTHLINGS WERE DISHONORABLE AND WARLIKE!
HIS GREATEST MISTAKE WAS TO CREATE THIS TOURNAMENT! IT WAS IN THIS THAT YOU PROVED YOURSELVES TRULY HONORABLE, FAIR AND SELF-SACRIFICING! THESE THINGS WE RESPECT ABOVE ALL ELSE!
SO YOU DEPOSED HIM!
WHAT ELSE COULD WE DO?
THAT'S WHAT DID IT, FAIR PLAY? FAIR PLAY SAVED THE EARTH?
WHEN YOU COME RIGHT DOWN TO IT, FAIR PLAY IS WHAT IT'S ALL ABOUT! IF MORE PEOPLE TRIED TO LIVE BY THE SIMPLE RULES OF FAIR PLAY, MY PEOPLE... ALL PEOPLE, WOULD GET A FAIR SHAKE!
...AND SPEAKING OF "FAIR SHAKES", FOLKS, THIS IS JIMMY OLSEN--
--AND THIS IS LOIS LANE--
GOOD LIFE!!
A LOCUST SWARM OF SPACE-SHIPS GREETS THE RISING SUN OF BODACE, EMISSARIES AND SPORTS-FANS ALIKE, SECURE IN THE KNOWLEDGE THAT THEY WERE THERE!
ONE SHIP... THE EMPEROR'S OWN... SAFELY SPEEDS ITS NOW-HONORED PARTY PAST JUPITER...
...SAFELY...
...HOMEWARD...
...TO EARTH...

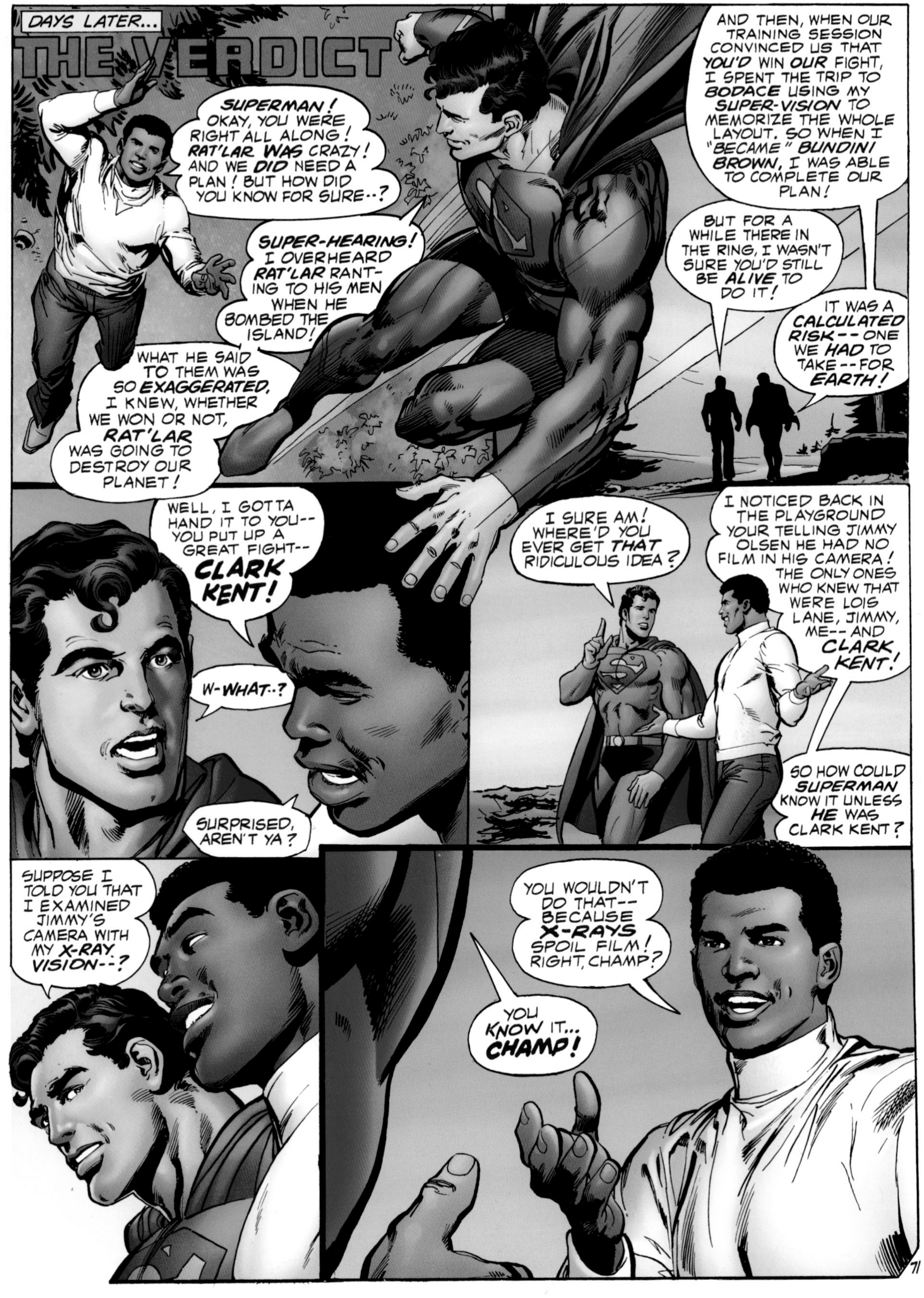

DAYS LATER...
THE VERDICT
SUPERMAN! OKAY, YOU WERE RIGHT ALL ALONG! RAT'LAR WAS CRAZY! AND WE DID NEED A PLAN! BUT HOW DID YOU KNOW FOR SURE..?
SUPER-HEARING! I OVERHEARD RAT'LAR RANTING TO HIS MEN WHEN HE BOMBED THE ISLAND!
WHAT HE SAID TO THEM WAS SO EXAGGERATED, I KNEW, WHETHER WE WON OR NOT, RAT'LAR WAS GOING TO DESTROY OUR PLANET!
AND THEN, WHEN OUR TRAINING SESSION CONVINCED US THAT YOU'D WIN OUR FIGHT, I SPENT THE TRIP TO BODACE USING MY SUPER-VISION TO MEMORIZE THE WHOLE LAYOUT. SO WHEN I "BECAME" BUNDINI BROWN, I WAS ABLE TO COMPLETE OUR PLAN!
BUT FOR A WHILE THERE IN THE RING, I WASN'T SURE YOU'D STILL BE ALIVE TO DO IT!
IT WAS A CALCULATED RISK--ONE WE HAD TO TAKE--FOR EARTH!
WELL, I GOTTA HAND IT TO YOU--YOU PUT UP A GREAT FIGHT--CLARK KENT!
W-WHAT..?
SURPRISED, AREN'T YA?
I SURE AM! WHERE'D YOU EVER GET THAT RIDICULOUS IDEA?
I NOTICED BACK IN THE PLAYGROUND YOUR TELLING JIMMY OLSEN HE HAD NO FILM IN HIS CAMERA! THE ONLY ONES WHO KNEW THAT WERE LOIS LANE, JIMMY, ME--AND CLARK KENT!
SO HOW COULD SUPERMAN KNOW IT UNLESS HE WAS CLARK KENT?
SUPPOSE I TOLD YOU THAT I EXAMINED JIMMY'S CAMERA WITH MY X-RAY VISION--?
YOU WOULDN'T DO THAT--BECAUSE X-RAYS SPOIL FILM! RIGHT, CHAMP?
YOU KNOW IT... CHAMP!

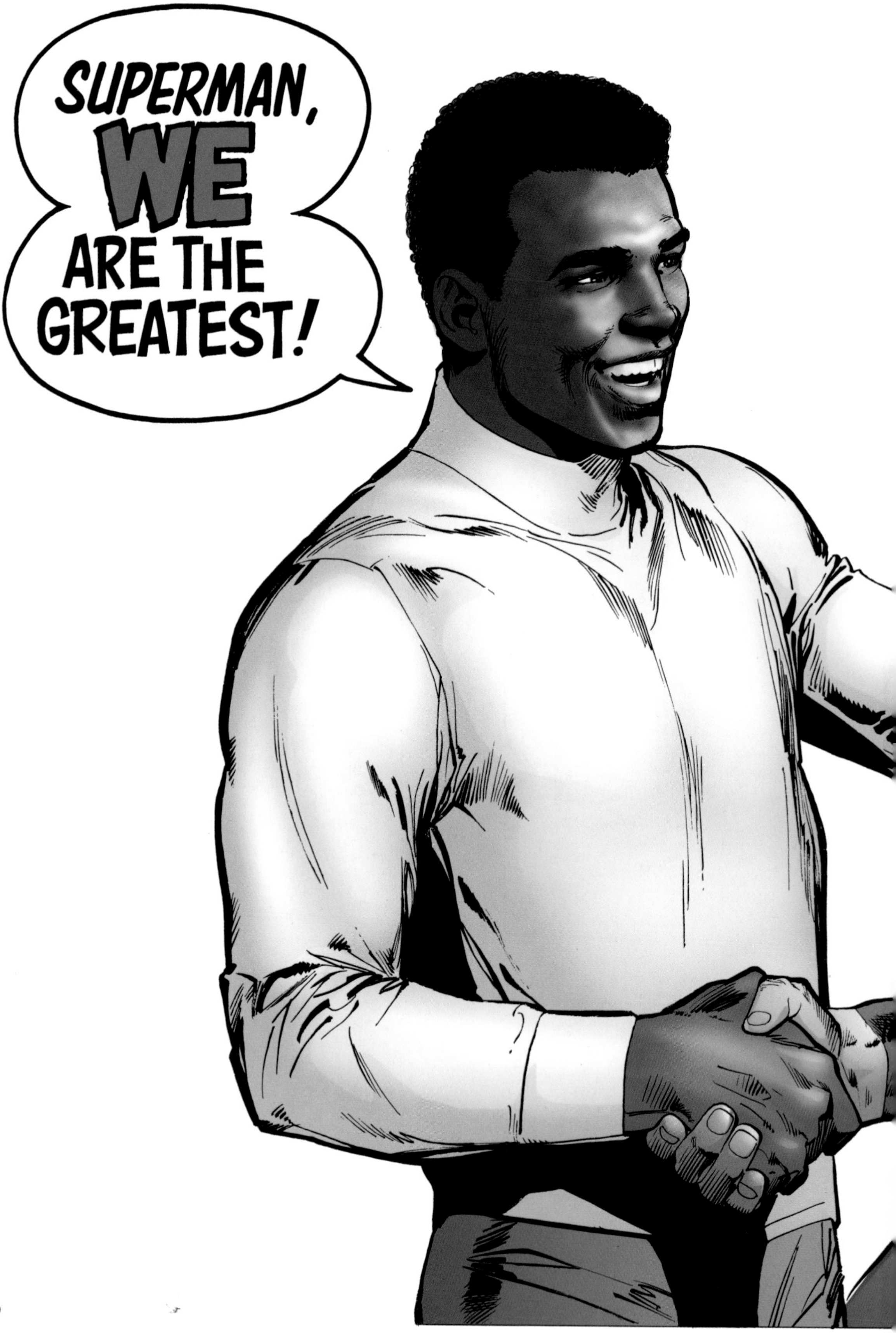
SUPERMAN, WE ARE THE GREATEST!

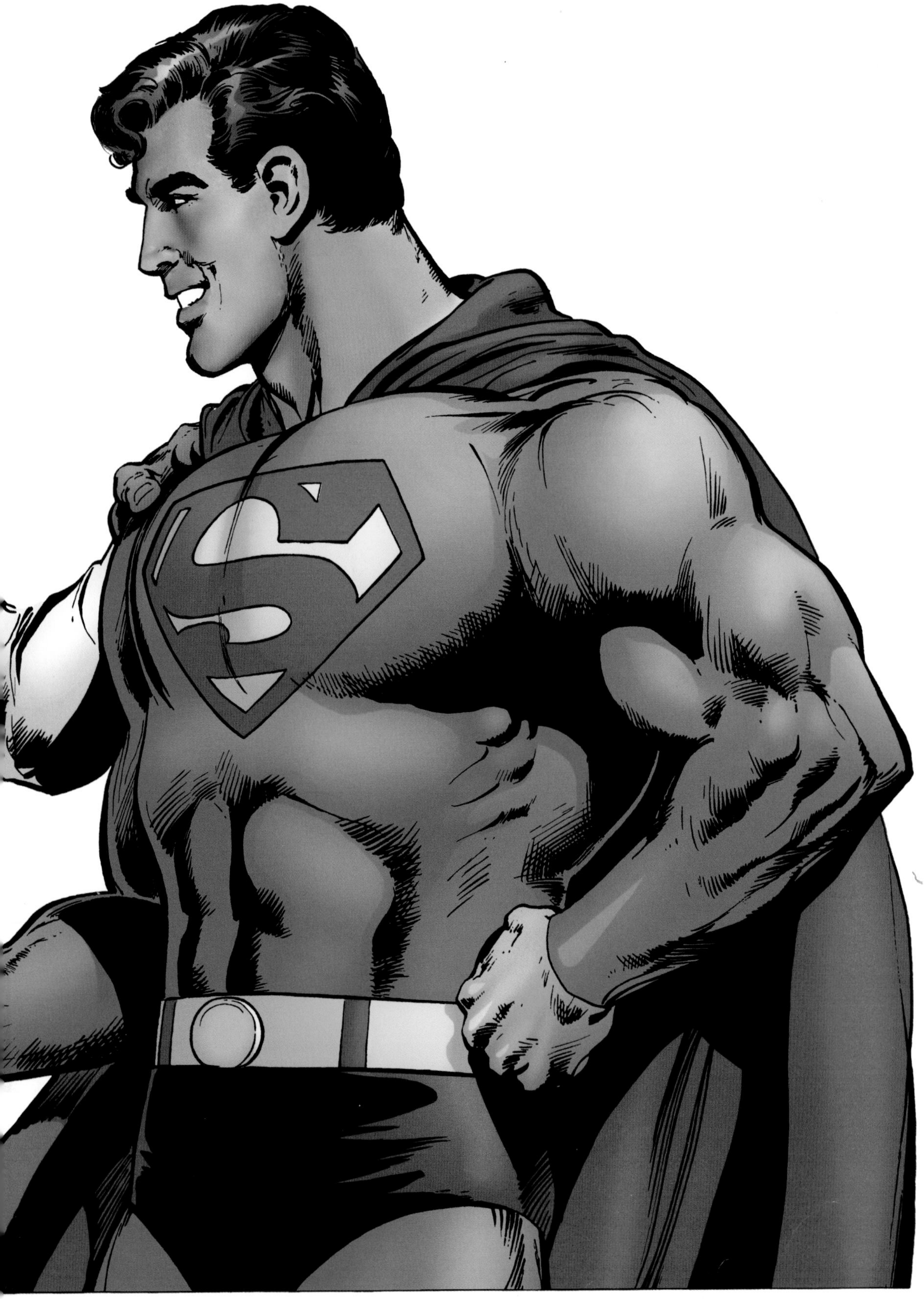

The original *Superman* vs. *Muhammad Ali* wraparound cover, featuring DC Comics characters, staff and the biggest celebrities of the late 1970s.

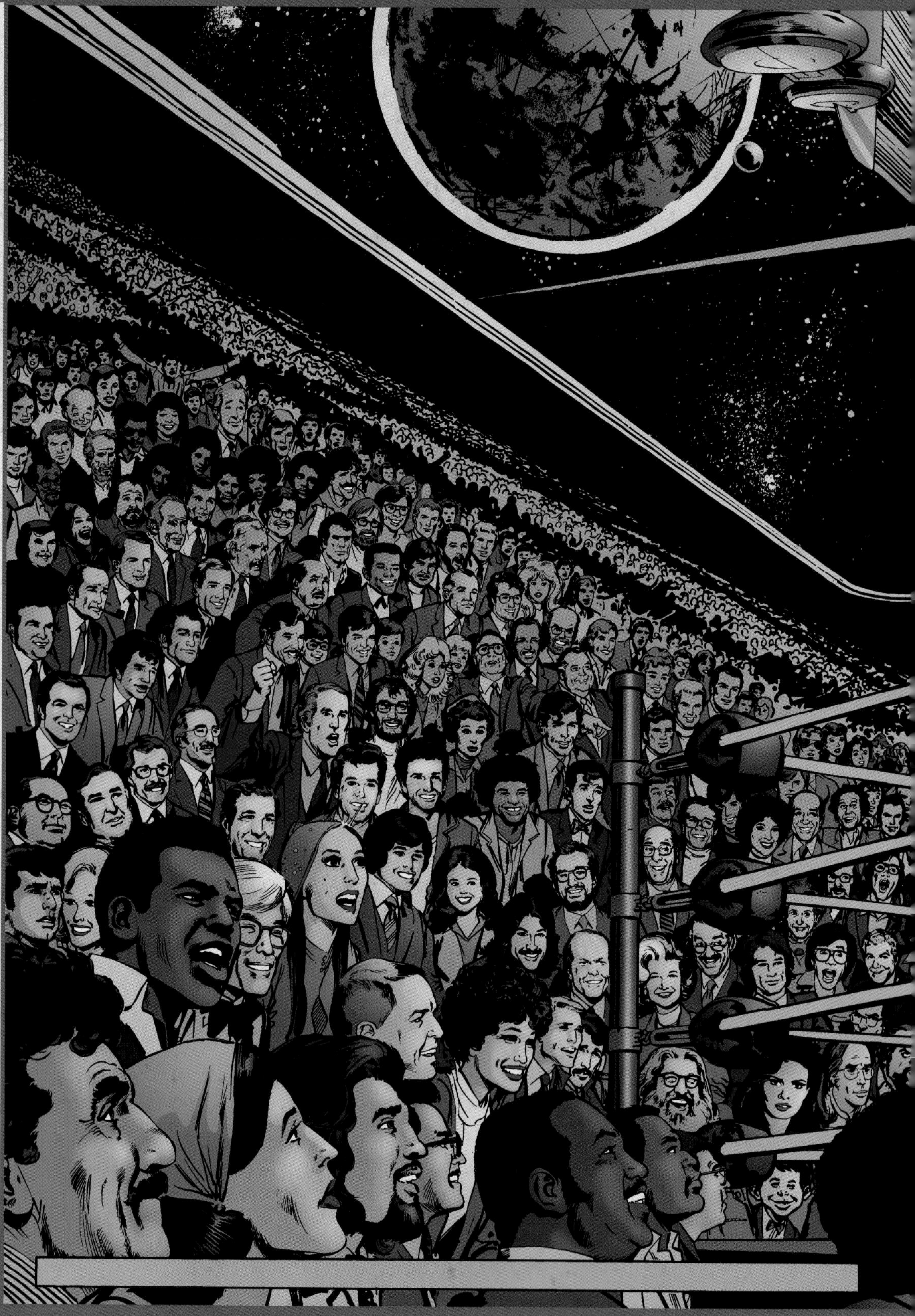

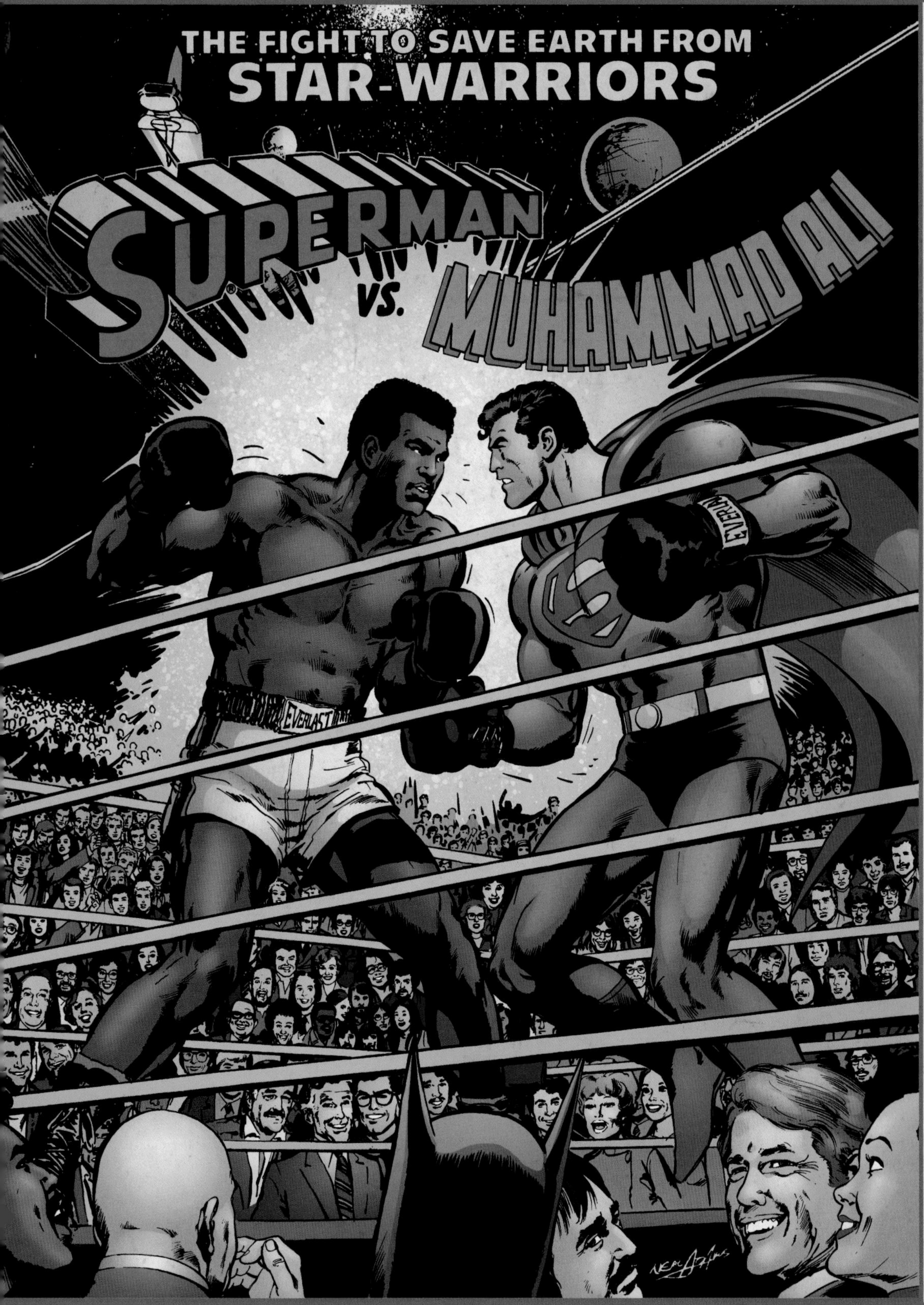
THE FIGHT TO SAVE EARTH FROM
STAR-WARRIORS
SUPERMAN
VS.
MUHAMMAD ALI
EVERLAST
EVERLAST

★ Cover Key

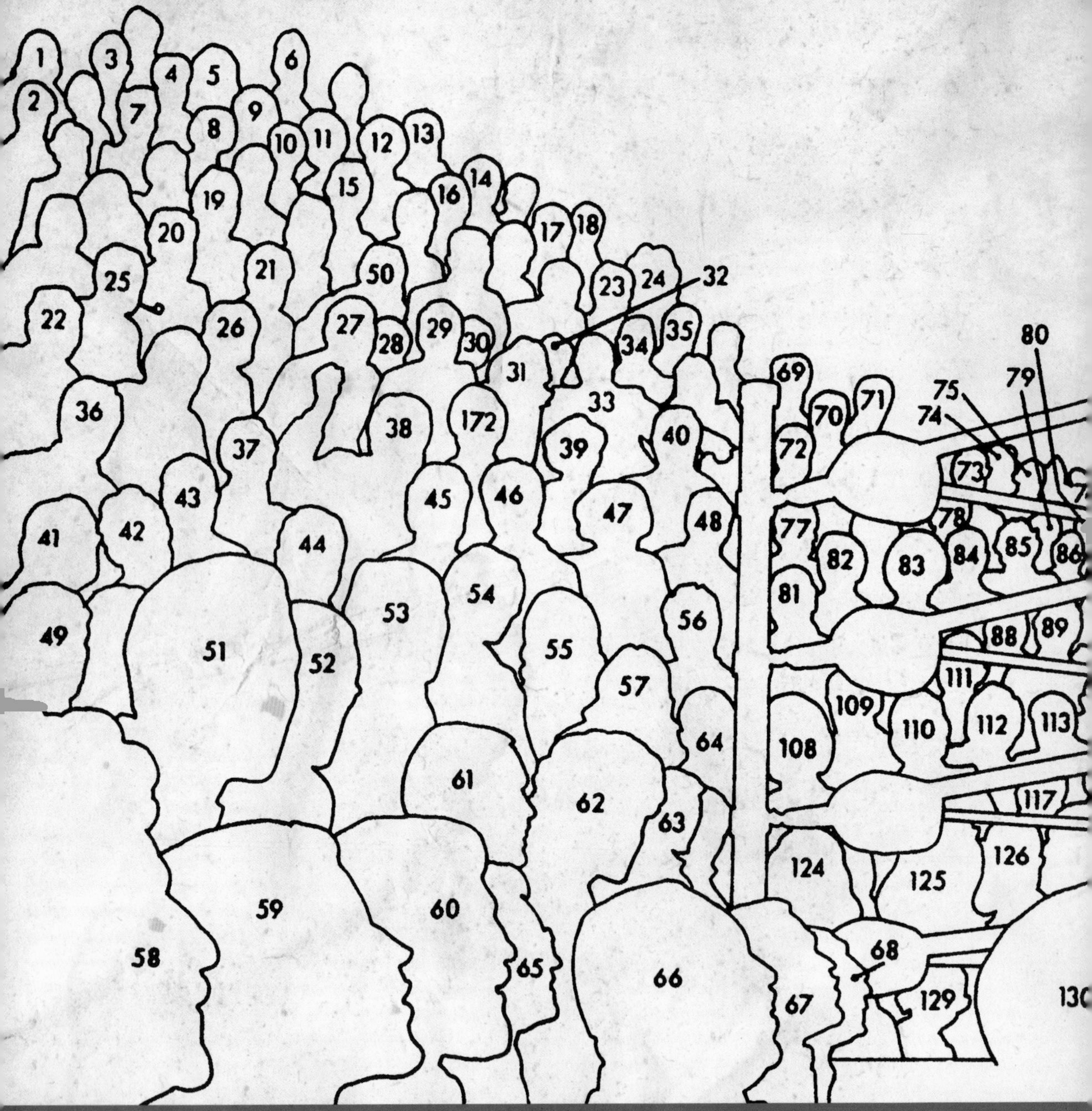

1
3
6
4
5
2
7
9
8
10
11
12
13
14
16
15
19
17
18
20
21
50
25
24
32
23
22
26
27
28
29
30
34
35
31
80
69
36
33
172
38
70
71
75
79
74
40
37
39
72
73
78
43
45
46
47
48
77
41
42
44
85
86
82
83
84
54
53
56
81
88
89
49
51
52
55
57
111
109
113
112
110
64
108
61
62
63
117
126
124
125
59
60
58
68
65
66
67
129

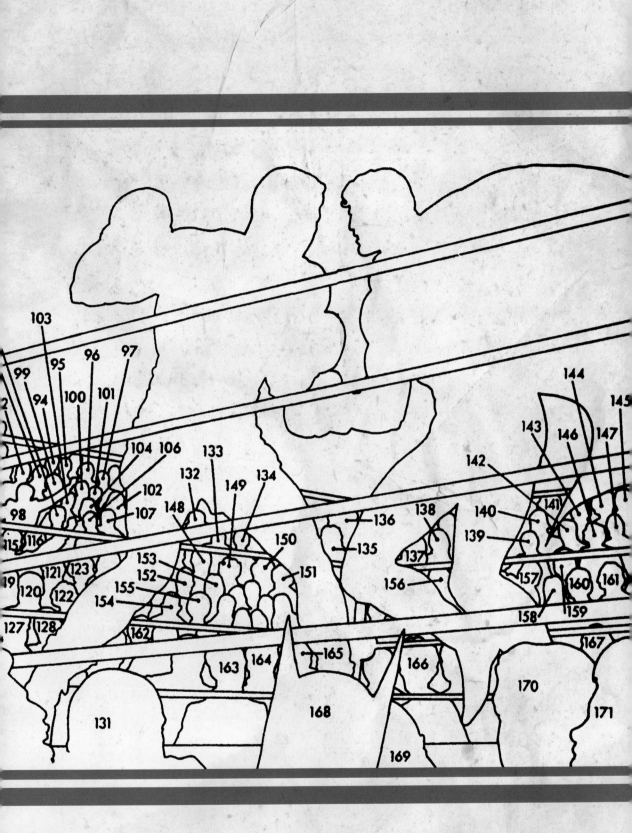

Cover Code

★ ★ ★ ★ ★ ★ ★

A. SHOW-BIZ PERSONALITIES

B. CELEBRITIES: B1. POLITICS, B2. SPORTS, B3. LITERATURE AND THE ARTS

C. DC STAFFERS

D. WARNER COMMUNICATIONS EXECUTIVES

E. NEAL ADAMS' CONTINUITY ASSOCIATES

F. MUHAMMAD ALI CORNERMEN

G. EDITORS/WRITERS/ARTISTS

H. DC CHARACTERS

1. Berni Wrightson - G	63. Ron Howard - A	117. Paul Kirchner - G
2. Boston (Deadman) Brand - H	64. Gerald R. Ford - B1	118. Jack C. Harris - C
3. Wallace Wood - G	65. Charles Lomax - F	119. Murray Boltinoff - C
4. Ed Davis - G	66. Herbert Muhammad - F	120. Sol Harrison - C, D
5. Flo Steinberg - G	67. Bundini Brown - F	121. Bob Rozakis - C
6. Gil Kane - G	68. Angelo Dundee - F	122. Mrs. Sol Harrison
7. Tex Blaisdell - G	69. Red Ryan - H	123. Midge Bregman - C
8-12. The Jacksons - A	70. Ace Morgan - H	124. William M. (MAD) Gaines - B3
13. Sergio Aragones - G	71. Prof. Haley - H	125. Raquel Welch - A
14. Howard Chaykin - G	72. Rocky Davis - H	126. Vince Alcazar - G
15. Archie Goodwin - G	73. Plastic Man - H	127. Wayne Rogers - A
16. Walt Simonson - G	74. Mary (Mary Marvel) Batson - H	128. Joe Letterese - C
17. Alan Weiss - G	75. Freddy (Capt. Marvel, Jr.)	129. Alfred E. Neuman - B3
18. Rac Shade - H	Freeman - H	130. Don King - F
19. Sol Himmelman - D	76. Doc Magnus	131. Lex Luthor - H
20. Caesar Kimmel - D	& the Metal Men - H	132. Barbara (Batgirl) Gordon - H
21. Joseph P. Grant - D	77. Bob Le Rose - C	133. Steve Trevor - H
22. Bert Wasserman - D	78. Bob Layton - G	134. Diana (Wonder Woman)
23. Byron Preiss - G	79. Billy (Capt. Marvel) Batson - H	Prince - H
24. Ms. Mystic - H	80. J'onn (Martian Manhunter)	135. Pat Rooney - G
25. Frank Herrera - D	J'onzz - H	136. Pat Bastienne - G
26. Albert Sarnoff - D	81. Julius Schwartz - C	137. Ralph Reese - G
27. Dick Giordano - G	82. Denny O'Neil - G	138. Larry Hama - C
28. Joel Adams	83. Carol Fein - C	139. Trevor Von Eeden - E, G
29. Neal Adams - E, G	84. Dan Goldstein - D	140. Mark Alexander - E
30. Jason Adams	85. Morris Waldinger - C	141. Joe DiEsposito - E, G
31. Kristine Adams	86. Carter (Hawkman) Hall - H	142. Jack Abel - E, G
32. Zeea Adams	87. Shiera (Hawkgirl) Hall - H	143. Joe Rubinstein - G
33. Joe Orlando - C	88. Paul Kupperberg - G	144. Joe Barney - E, G
34. Arthur Gutowitz - C	89. Anthony Tollin - C	145. Marshall Rogers - E, G
35. Allen Milgrom - C	90. Milton Snapinn - C	146. Bob Wiacek - E, G
36. Jay Emmett - D	91. Carol Ferris - H	147. John Fuller - E, G
37. David Horowitz - D	92. Hal (Green Lantern) Jordan - H	148. Liberace - A
38. Steven J. Ross - D	93. Oliver (Green Arrow) Queen - H	149. Frieda Sacco - C
39. Noel Neill - A	94. Ray (Atom) Palmer - H	150. Bruce Patterson - G
40. Kirk Alyn - A	95. Alfred (Wayne Butler)	151. Frank Cirocco - G
41. Joe Shuster - G	Pennyworth - H	152. Cary Burkett - G
42. Jerry Siegel - G	96. Arthur (Aquaman) Curry - H	153. Bill Morse - C
43. Emanuel Gerard - D	97. Morgan Edge - H	154. E. Nelson Bridwell - C
44. William Sarnoff - D	98. Dick (Robin) Grayson - H	155. Shelley Eiber - C
45. Kenneth S. Rosen - D	99. Dinah (Black Canary) Lance - H	156. Bob McLeod - G
46. Ron Palillo - A	100. Perry White - H	157. Mike Nasser - E, G
47. Robert Heyges - A	101. Jimmy Olsen - H	158. Joe Brozowsky - E, G
48. Jack Larson - A	102. Lois Lane - H	159. Carl Potts - E, G
49. Joe Namath - B2	103. Barry (Flash) Allen - H	160. Terry Austin - G
50. William Conrad - A	104. Iris Allen - H	161. Cary Bates - E, G
51. Pelé - B2	105. Roy (Speedy) Harper - H	162. Tom Sciacca - G
52. Andy Warhol - B3	106. Garth (Aqualad) - H	163. Johnny Carson - A
53. Cher - A	107. Wally (Kid Flash) West - H	164. Christopher Reeve - A
54. Donny Osmond - A	108. Betty Ford - B1	165. Greg Theakston - G
55. Marie Osmond - A	109. Jack Adler - C	166. Lucille Ball - A
56. Joe Kubert - C	110. Jim Bouton - B2	167. Rick Bryant - G
57. Tony Orlando - A	111. Lillian Mandel - C	168. The Batman - H
58. Kurt Vonnegut, Jr. - B3	112. Steve Mitchell - C	169. Sonny Bono - A
59. Jill Krementz - B3	113. Vince Colletta - C	170. Jimmy Carter - B1
60. Wolfman Jack - A	114. Paul Levitz - C	171. Rosalynn Carter - B1
61. Frank Sinatra - A	115. John Workman - C	172. Mike Gold - C
62. Jenette Kahn - C, D	116. Donna (Wonder Girl) Troy - H	

afterword

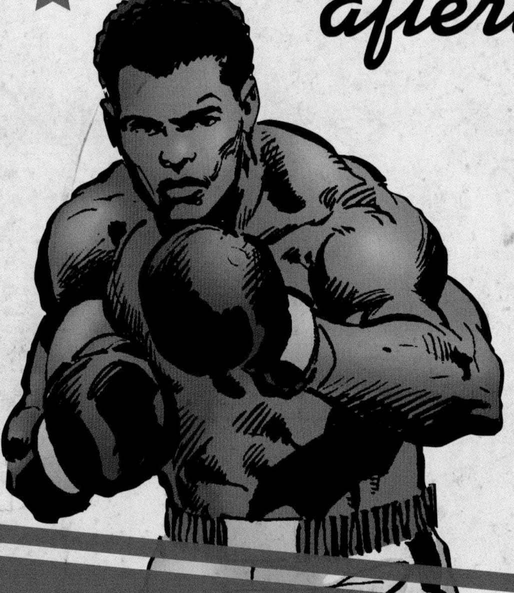

SUPERMAN *vs.* MUHAMMAD ALI

It started with Don King. A flamboyant boxing promoter called the "Electric Hairdo," although not directly to his face, it looked as though he'd shoved his fingers in a socket with the resulting shock of hair adding another six inches to his over-six-foot frame.

A survivor of the rough reaches of Cleveland, King had a hustler's heart and a visionary's imagination. He'd managed to snag the hem of Muhammad Ali's boxing robe and ride it to fisticuffs fame as promoter of the 1974 "Rumble in the Jungle," a 10-million-dollar-purse bout between Ali and George Foreman in the capital of Zaire.

King followed one year later with another incendiary international event. Dubbed by King "The Thrilla in Manila," it pitted Ali against heavyweight champ and bitter rival Joe Frazier. By late 1976, when King sauntered into the DC offices at 75 Rockefeller Plaza, he had cemented his relationship with Muhammad Ali.

1976 had already seen an unprecedented matchup, although not in boxing but in comics. Huge rivals themselves, and with their loyalist fans fueling the frenzy, DC and Marvel had agreed to have their flagship characters oppose one another in an oversized comic book titled *Superman vs. The Amazing Spider-Man: The Battle of the Century*. Comics back then seldom got press, but this was a media event of enormous proportions. Don King took note.

I had arrived at DC in February of that same year as the company's new publisher. The division of labor between me and Sol Harrison, DC's president, had still to be mapped, but happily, editorial was considered my bailiwick, and Don King's scheme fell smack within my turf.

What he proposed was that Superman take on a new contender – none other, of course, than Muhammad Ali. Other real-life figures had appeared in Superman comic books, but none had received equal billing or been an equal partner in the action. But in a year of outsized comics and outsized ambitions, this new matchup was particularly appealing.

By 1976, Ali was a folk hero of iconic proportions. He'd sacrificed nearly four of his best boxing years in defiance of the draft and the Vietnam War, and for all his brashness and bravado, he was considered a man of principle and an outspoken symbol of the struggle of black Americans. A Superman/Ali matchup would have to take into account who Muhammad Ali was as much outside the ring as in it.

What better team to go to than Denny O'Neil, Neal Adams and editor Julie Schwartz? They'd already made history with their socially conscious Green Lantern/Green Arrow series. A Superman/Ali comic book had to be not only an epic entertainment, but also an exploration of the ideals and actions that had made Superman and Ali heroes around the globe. Denny, Neal, and Julie were expert at both.

Once Denny had framed the story, I flew to Chicago with some early pencils of Neal's to meet with Herbert Muhammad, Ali's manager, and his attorney, Charles Lomax. What struck me most about that encounter was Herbert Muhammad's reaction to Neal's drawings. Pulling a finger across a page, he said, "Ali's calf is too narrow. It's fuller than that. Make sure you change it." It was the kind of exacting comment we would have made to an outsider intent on rendering any of our leading characters.

Finally, I met with Ali himself in the family room of his Chicago home. He was playful and relaxed and eager to have me regale him with the story. When he'd mulled the tale to his satisfaction and checked out the art, he dubbed me "the Superman Lady," and in the years that followed, that's who I always was to him.

Now that we had the approval of Ali and his camp, I returned to New York where Neal had taken over the writing duties from Denny. But he was still pressing hard on the art, and the pencils, richly limned by Dick Giordano's inks, couldn't have looked better. It was those pencils that led me to my folly.

As I said, it was a year of outsized comic books and outsized ambitions. We'd already decided that the double cover would feature Superman and Ali duking it out with a swarm of spectators cheering them on. Who would be ringside at such a spectacular event? Movie stars, athletes,

entertainers, heads of state — the world's glitterati. I thought of how real Ali looked in page after page of art, and knew if anyone could portray this luminous crowd, it was Neal.

And so we began filling the arena with well known people of the day--President and Mrs. Jimmy Carter, President Gerald Ford and his wife Betty, Raquel Welch, Sonny, Cher, Joe Namath, Andy Warhol, Frank Sinatra, Johnny Carson, Lucille Ball, The Jackson Five. But there was a catch. Apparently, we needed permission from everyone whose likeness we were using. Oops.

It's a good thing Neal had an eraser by his side. So many stars loved the idea of the fight and happily signed on to bear witness, but others unequivocally said no. George C. Scott's profile was already holding sway over the lower left corner of the back cover when he issued a firm refusal. Was there anyone with a similar physiognomy with whom we could replace him?

The cavalry arrived in the person of Kurt Vonnegut, whose crumpled nose was a near-match for Scott's. Neal quickly drew the writer where the actor had been and added his wife Jill Krementz.

Absolutely not, said Carroll O'Connor, whose bowling ball-shaped head had loomed right above Andy Warhol's. Luckily, the great soccer star Pelé was playing for the New York Cosmos, a team funded by DC's parent Warner Communications, and he readily agreed to have his round visage substitute for the man best known as Archie Bunker.

The securing of permissions and the re-drawing of the crowd added to delays that had already dogged the book. What was scheduled for 1977 wasn't released until the following year, but it was well worth the wait. *Superman vs. Muhammad Ali*, with its pairing of black and white, its challenge to oppression, and its themes of courage, justice, and sacrifice, was a book for the ages. Freedom for all was the message, and it rang loud and clear long after the story was told.

Jenette
KAHN

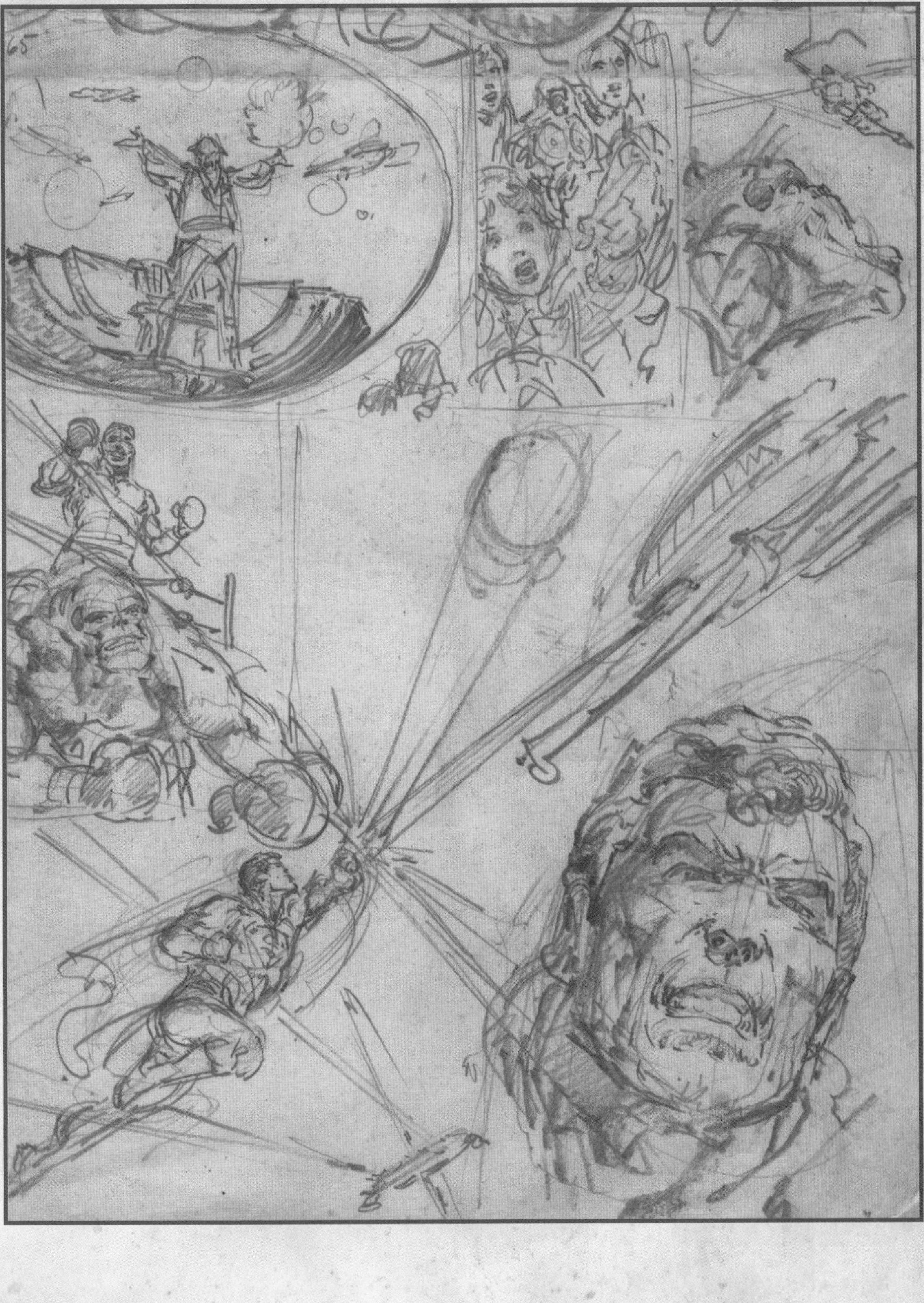

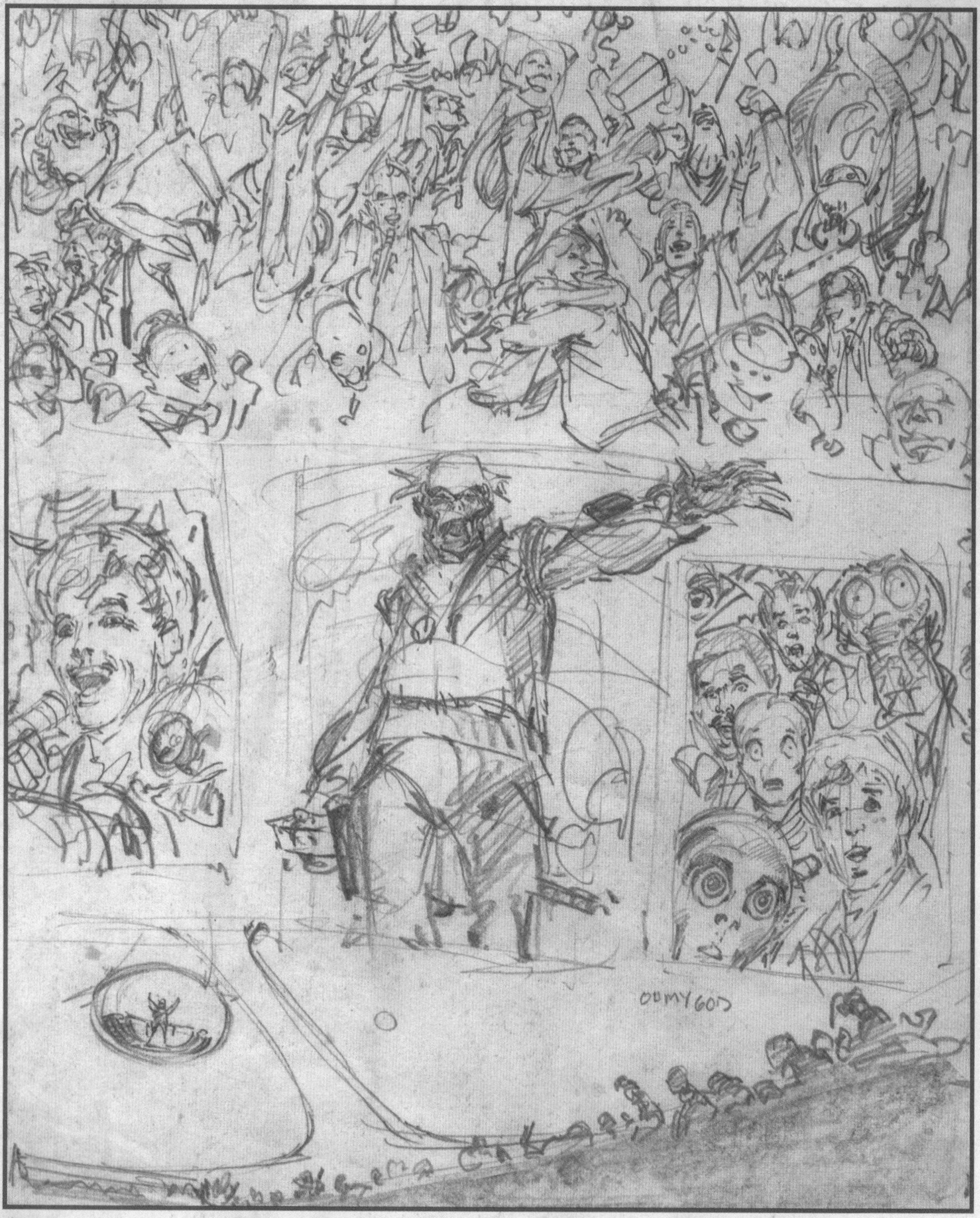
OOMYGOD

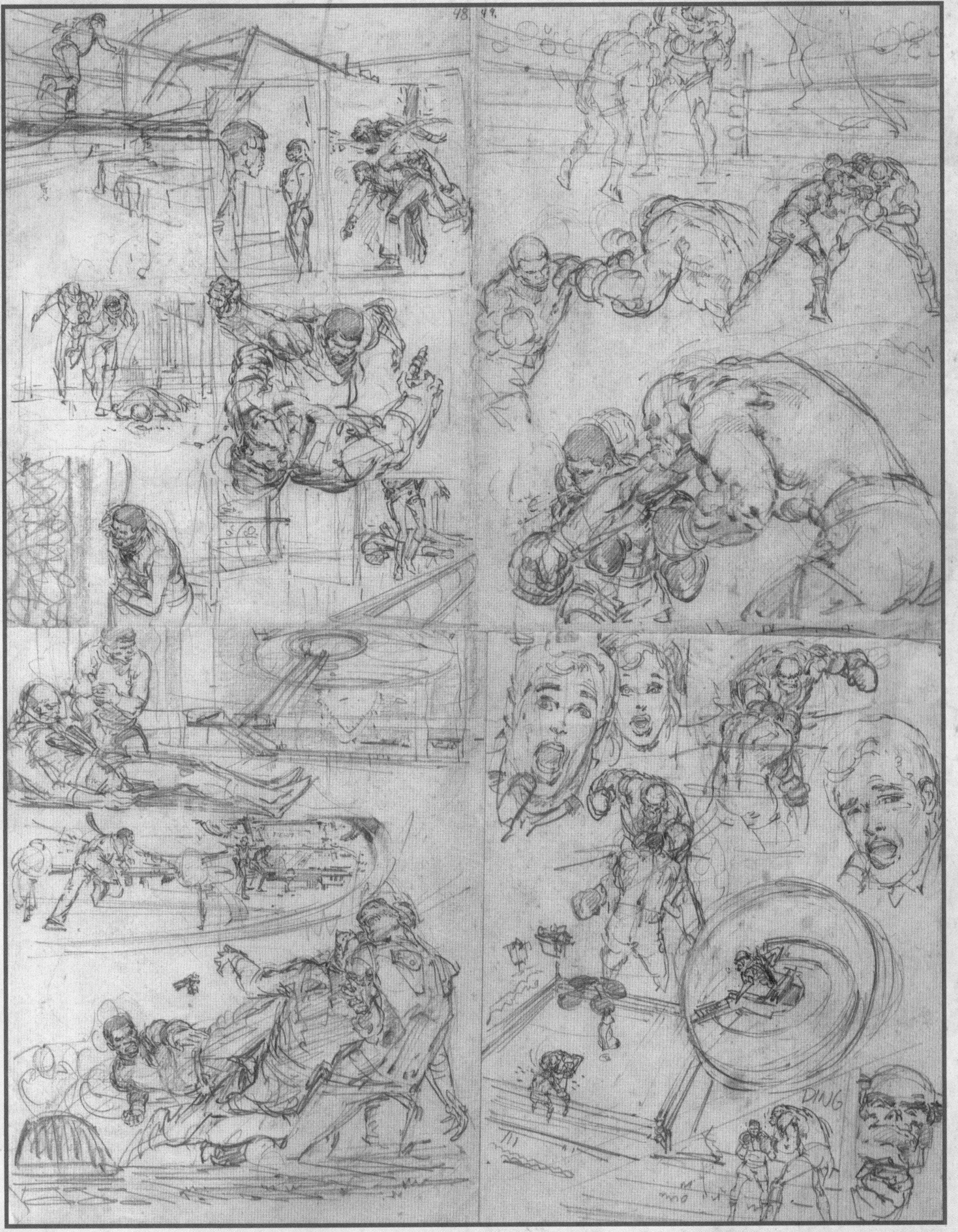
DING

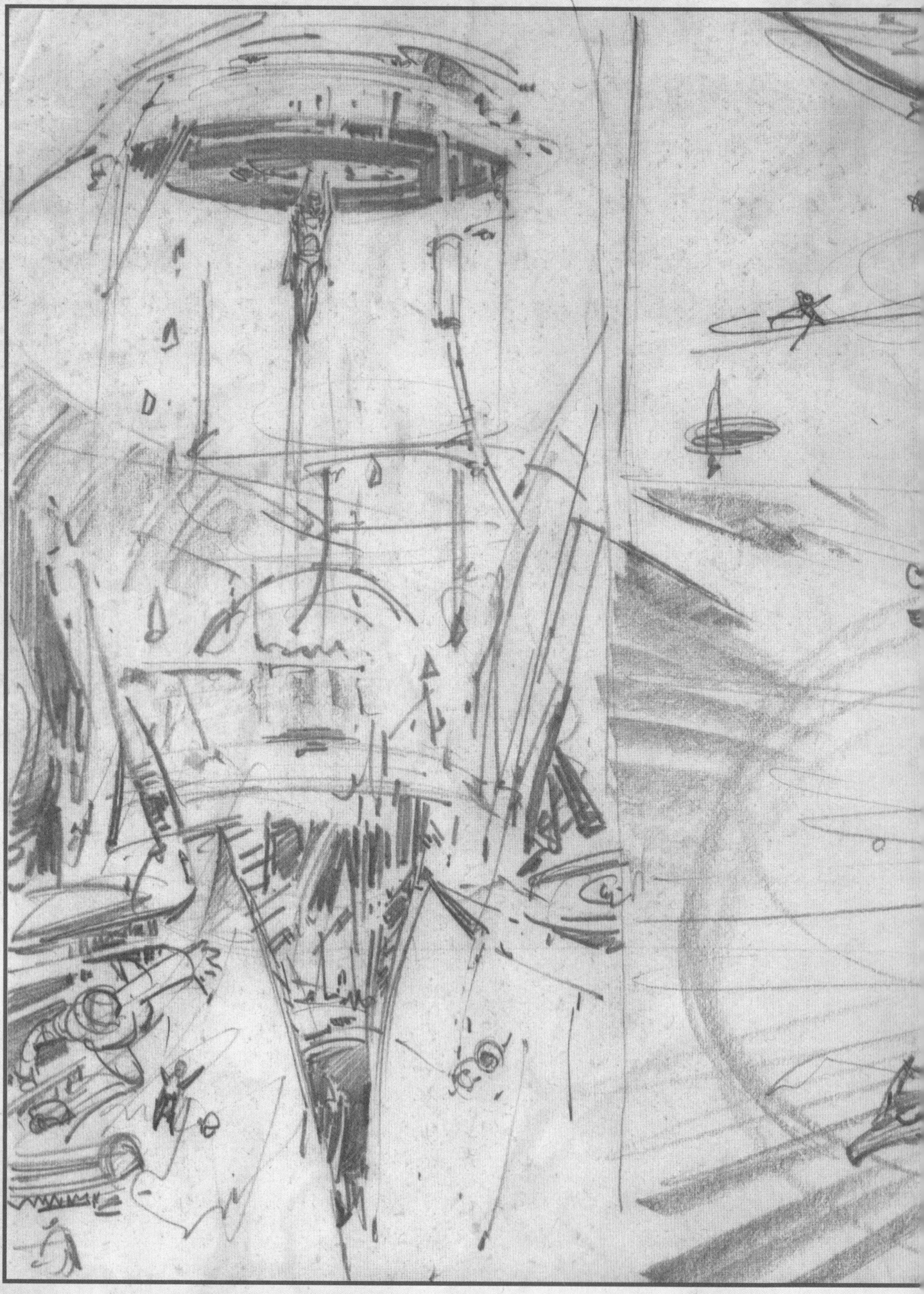

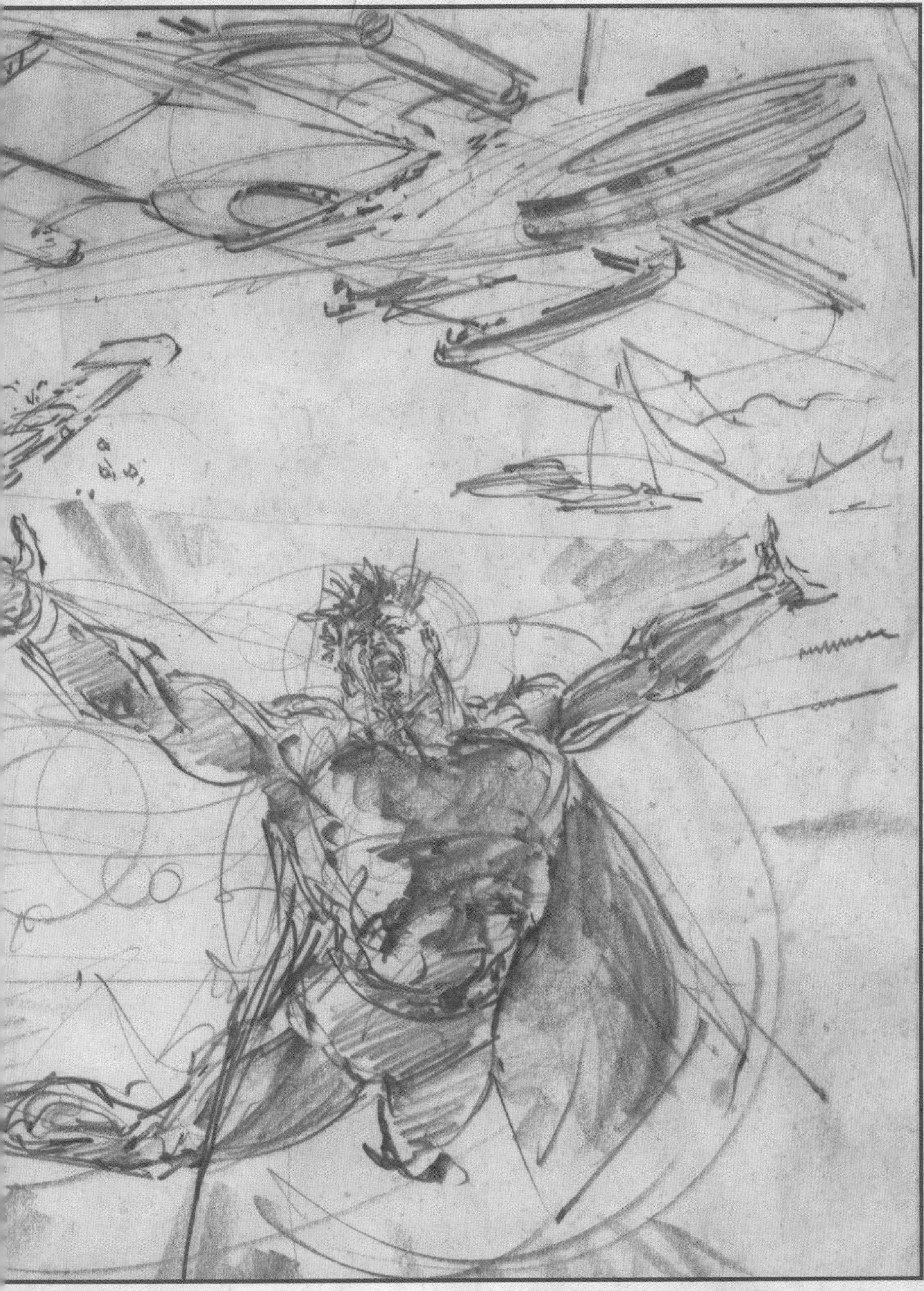

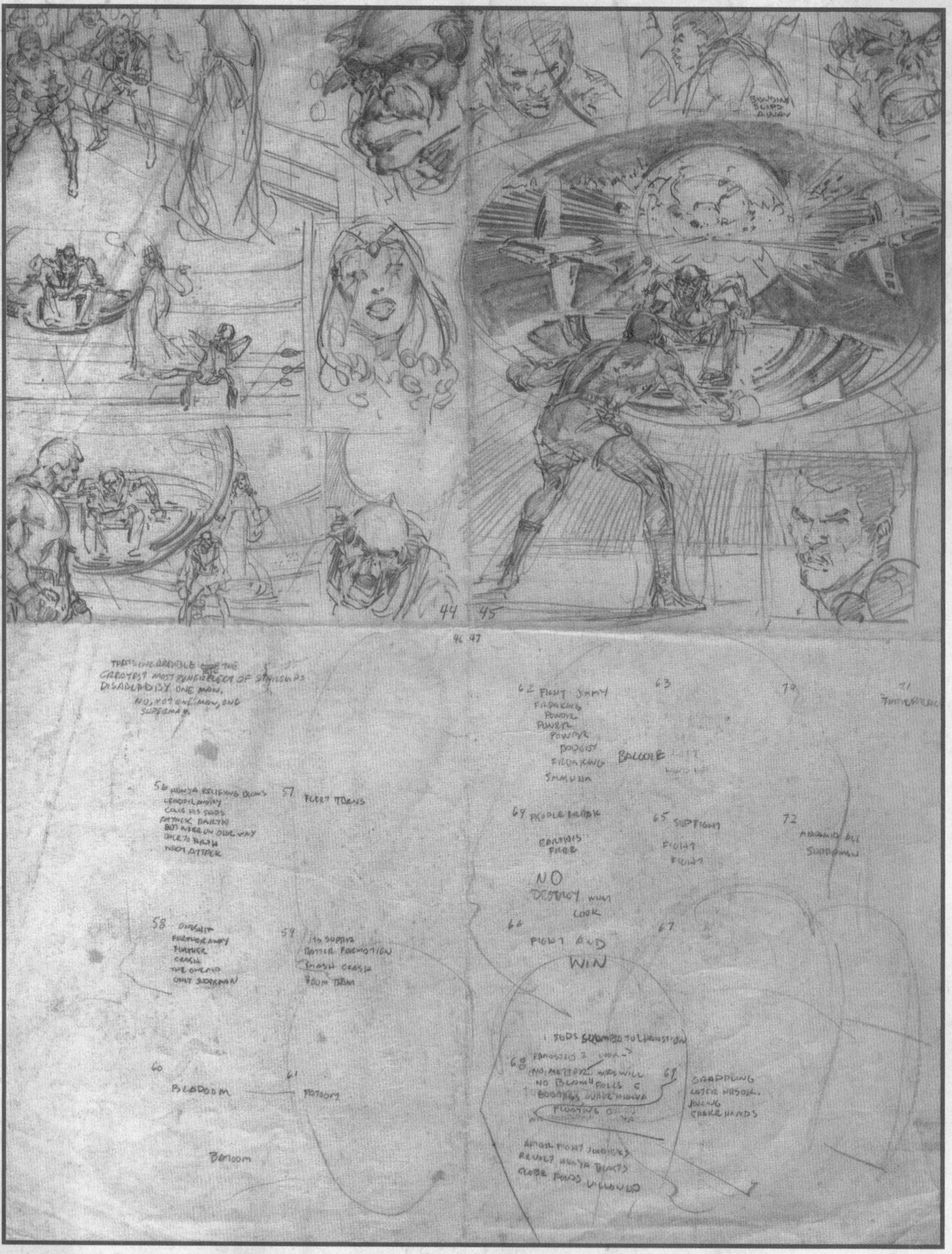

44
45
THAT'S INCREDIBLE
DISABLED BY ONE MAN.
NO, NOT ONE MAN, ONE SUPERMAN.
57 FLEET TURNS
58
59
FURTHER
CRASH
BETTER FORMATION
SMASH CRASH
60
61
62 FIGHT JIMMY
63
64 PEOPLE
65 SUP FIGHT
FIGHT
FIGHT
66
67
NO
LOOK
FIGHT AND WIN
68
69
GRAPPLING
70
71
72
BOOM

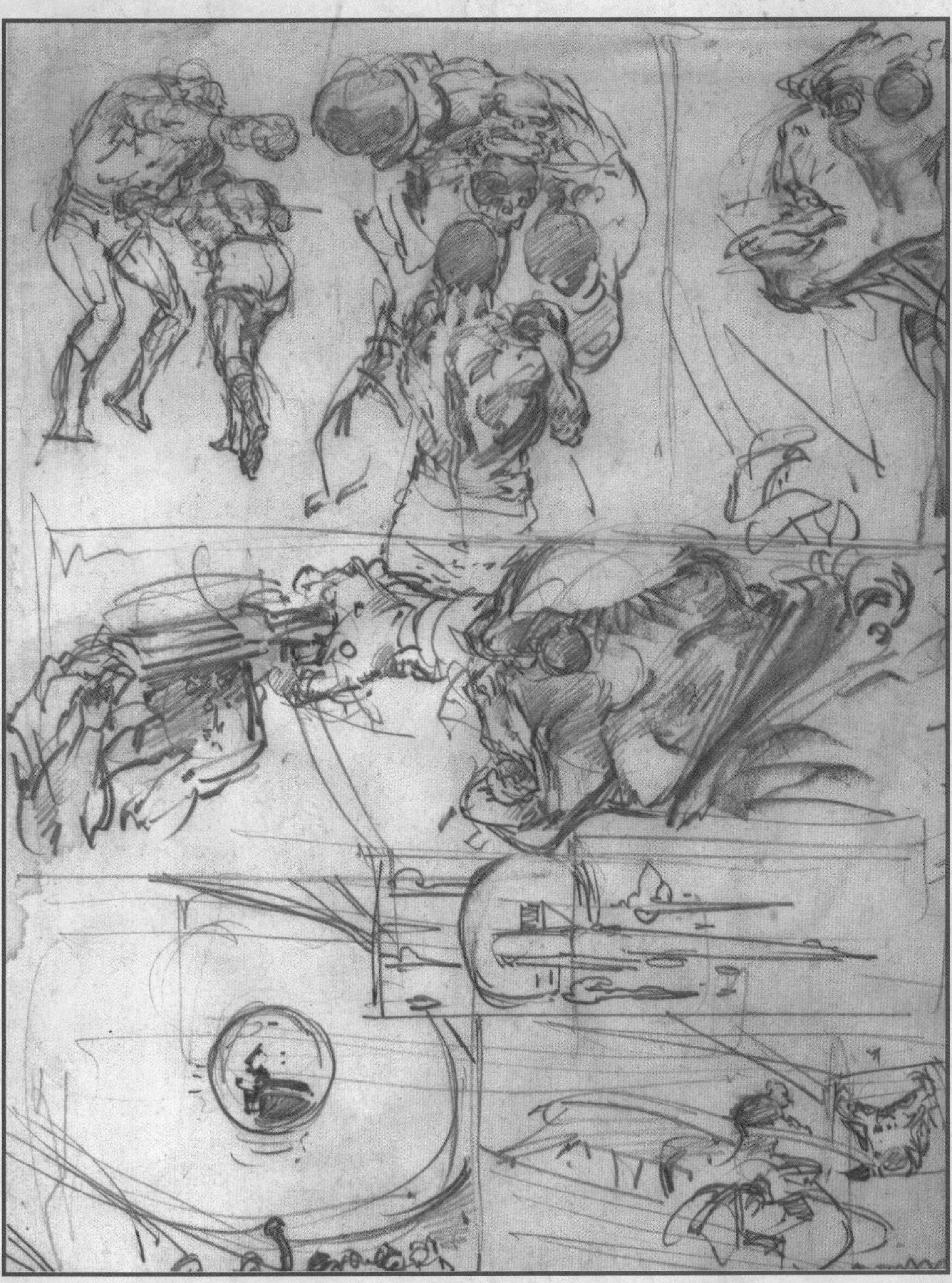

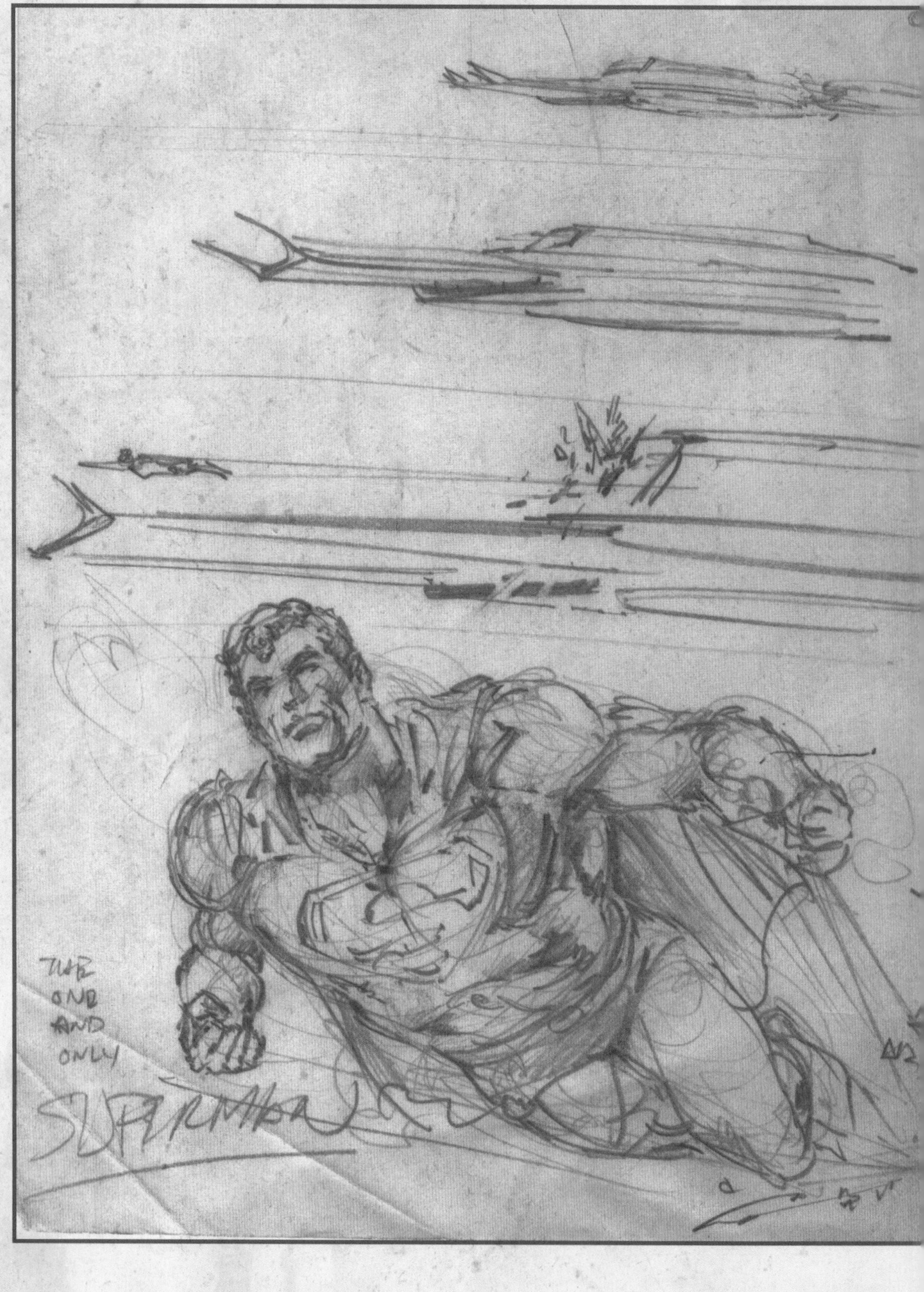
THE ONE AND ONLY
SUPERMAN

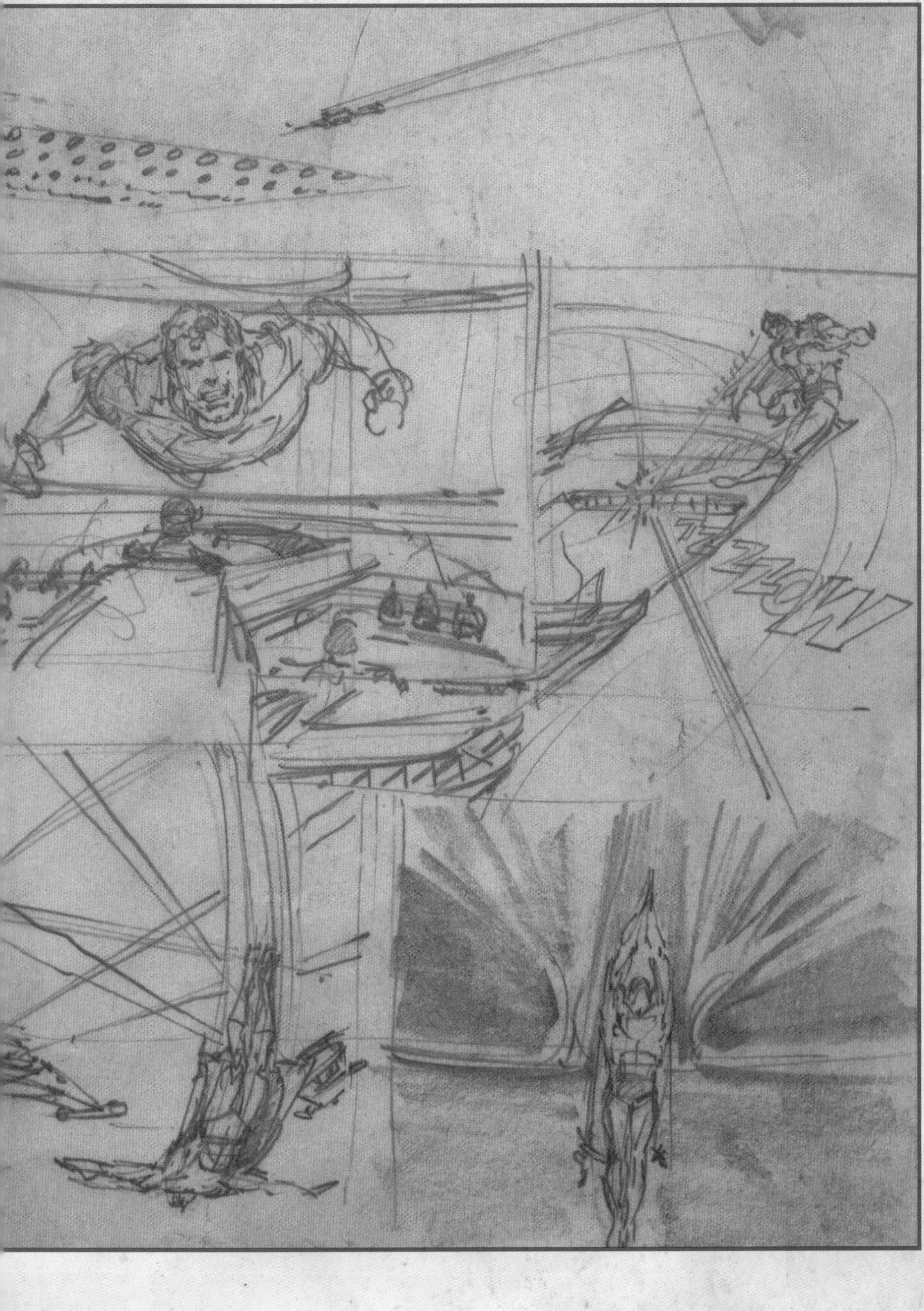
ZZZOW

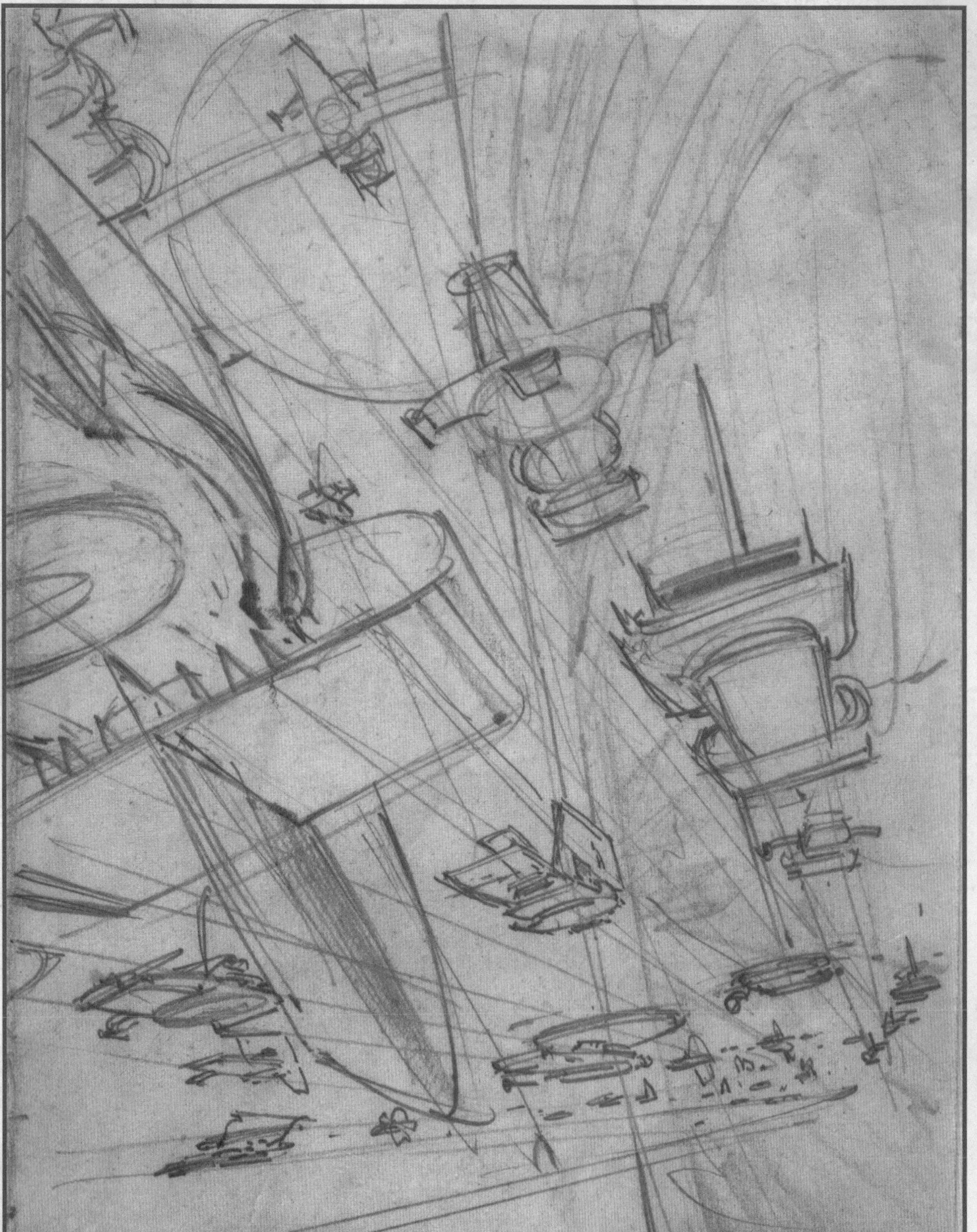

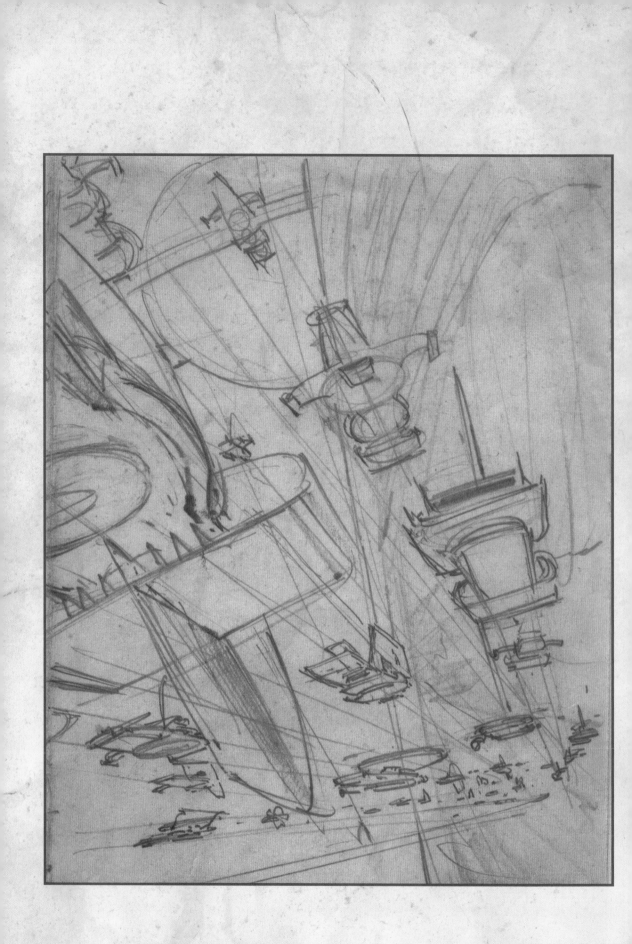

...ANOTHER TWO PAGE-SPREAD, BUT A VERY COMPLICATED ONE. WE'LL TRY TO

GET IT DESCRIBED.

IN CENTER, THE PLANET BODACE, AS SEEN IN EARLIER FLASHBACK. ~~CCCNVCRGIGN~~

CONVERGING ON IT, MANY, MANY SCRUBB SPACECRAFT--A VANISHING POINT

SHOT. NOW, AROUND THE SHIPS, OVALS WITH SHOTS OF ALIENS--A LOT OF

WHOM YOU'LL HAVE TO CREATE, BUT I SUGGEST WE GET THE GUARDIANS OF OA;

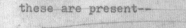 MARTIANS, THE BIRD ~~PEOPLE~~ -LIKE GREEN LANTERN, TOMAR-RE; ~~SSSS~~

J'ONN J'ONNZ'

ADAM STRANGE IN FULL REGALIA; BRAINIAC; BIZARRO.

CAPTION I: --the most MASSIVE migration in the history of the universe...

CAPTION II: ...intelligent beings from a THOUSAND worlds, sped to

Bodace by the Scrubb...

CAPTION III: ...any people whose past or present has ever been tainted

by STRIFE ...

CAPTION IV.: ...any people fascinated by SPORT...

CAPTION V: ...any people able to APPRECIATE the coming SPECTACLE--

these are present--

Neal ADAMS

was born June 6, 1941 in New York, and along with Jim Shooter, formed the vanguard of the coming "youthquake" that would shake up the ultraconservative DC Comics during the late 1960s and early 1970s. A maverick whose wildly experimental art style was nurtured and encouraged by then-publisher Carmine Infantino, Adams became an overnight sensation by infusing a new visual vitality into longtime characters who were in danger of becoming stodgy. Working closely with Infantino, Adams quickly became DC's preeminent cover artist during this period, contributing radical and dynamic illustrations to virtually the company's entire line. Adams went on to become one of the most talked-about creator/writer/artist/publishers in the medium, and continues to influence, directly and indirectly, today's young comics artists.

began his career as a comic book writer in 1965 at Charlton, where then-editor Dick Giordano assigned him to several features. When Giordano moved to DC, O'Neil soon followed. At DC, O'Neil scripted several series for Giordano and Julius Schwartz, quickly becoming one of the most respected writers in comics. O'Neil earned a reputation for being able to "revamp" such characters as Superman, Green Lantern, Captain Marvel — and The Batman, whom O'Neil (with the help of Neal Adams and Giordano) brought back to his roots as a dark, mysterious gothic avenger. Besides being the most important Batman writer of the 1970s, O'Neil served as an editor at both Marvel and DC. After a long tenure as Group Editor of the Batman line of titles, Denny retired to write full-time. O'Neil, fittingly, wrote a Green Lantern novel for Pocket Books, published in 2005.

Superman vs. Muhammad Ali

4-11

ad

33500011367737   Inn